**This book is to be returned on or before
the last date stamped below.**

the complete

A-Z
LEISURE,
TRAVEL &
TOURISM

h a n d b o o k

Ray Youell.

Hodder & Stoughton

A MEMBER OF THE HODDER HEADLINE GROUP

Order queries: Please contact Bookpoint Ltd, 130 Milton Park, Abingdon, Oxon OX14 4SB. Telephone: (44) 01235 827720. Fax: (44) 01235 400454. Lines are open from 9 am – 6 pm Monday to Saturday, with a 24 hour message answering service. Email address: orders@bookpoint.co.uk

British Library Cataloguing in Publication Data

Youell, Ray
    Complete A–Z Leisure and Tourism Handbook
    I. Title
    338.4791

ISBN 0–340–64789–2

First published 1996
Impression number   12 11 10 9 8 7 6
Year   2004 2003 2002

Typeset by GreenGate Publishing Services, Tonbridge, Kent.
Printed in Great Britain for Hodder & Stoughton Educational,
a division of Hodder Headline Plc, 338 Euston Road, London NW1 3BH
by The Bath Press, Bath.

HOW TO USE THIS BOOK

The *A–Z Leisure, Travel and Tourism Handbook* is an alphabetical textbook designed to be used easily by students and people working in the leisure, travel and tourism industries. Each entry contains a clear definition, with further explanation and examples where necessary. This will help the user to add precision and depth to essays, reports, tests and case studies.

Entries are developed in line with the relative importance of the topic covered. The more important the term or organisation, the more detailed the entry. *Carnet*, for example, is covered in just a few lines, whereas *tourism* receives more in-depth analysis. The latter would provide sufficient material to enrich an essay or to clarify a point that the reader has not understood. Numerate topics are developed with the help of worked examples.

The study of leisure, travel and tourism can be developed further by making use of the cross-referenced entries. For example, the entry for the *National Coaching Foundation* (NCF) refers the reader to the *Sports Council*. All cross-referenced entries are in italics. The author has limited the use of cross-referencing to important, linked concepts. Essay and report writing should, therefore, be enhanced by following the logical pathways indicated by italicised entries.

Students of leisure, travel and tourism sometimes have difficulty with the language and 'jargon' of these subjects. This stems from several factors:

- the diverse nature of the industries, with many different sectors
- students come from a variety of backgrounds
- the dynamic nature of the industries, with new concepts being constantly introduced and others going out of date
- some textbooks use different terms for the same subject (such as 'green' tourism and responsible tourism)

The *A–Z Leisure, Travel and Tourism Handbook* provides a single, comprehensive and up-to-date solution to these problems. In addition, the entries have sufficient detail to make it a valuable reference and revision companion.

To help students studying for the Advanced GNVQ external tests, lists of the top revision topics for each unit are included at the back of the book.

I hope that the *A–Z Leisure, Travel and Tourism Handbook* proves an invaluable resource, fully relevant from the first day of study and on into working life.

Ray Youell

ACKNOWLEDGEMENTS

I am indebted to the many organisations and individuals who supplied up-to-date information and examples for inclusion in the handbook. Their support is greatly appreciated.

Thanks are also due to Ian Marcousé, the series editor, and Tim Gregson-Williams and Julie Hill at Hodder Headline for suggestions and advice throughout the preparation of the book.

A big thank you to Sue, Megan and Owen, without whose support the book would never have materialised.

Ray Youell
Aberystwyth, 1996

AA: see *Automobile Association*

á la carte refers to a menu in a restaurant or *hotel* from which customers select from a range of items, each of which is priced separately and cooked to order. (See also *table d'hôte.*)

ABC Travel Guides are a series of regular reference books and timetables published by the Reed Travel Group, covering many forms of travel and *accommodation*. Titles include the Hotel and Travel Index, Official Hotel Guide, ABC Guide to International Travel, Air Travel Atlas, ABC Cruise and Ferry Guide, Air Cargo Guide and the ABC Rail Guide. ABC also provide access for travel agents to their air timetables and fares information electronically.

above-the-line promotion refers to *marketing* and promotional activity for which a *commission* is normally paid by the chosen media to an *advertising agency*, e.g. *advertising* by a leisure or tourism organisation on television, at the cinema, in newspapers and magazines or on commercial radio. (See also *below-the-line promotion.*)

ABSA: see *Association for Business Sponsorship of the Arts*

ABTA: see *Association of British Travel Agents*

ABTA bond: all *travel agent* and *tour operator* members of *ABTA* are required to provide a bond to protect their customers in the event of financial failure. The bond can take a number of forms, but is often an insurance policy for the amount required by ABTA or a bank guarantee. This financial protection offered by the bonding scheme enables ABTA, in the event of a member's failure, to arrange for clients whose *holidays* are in progress at the time of the failure to continue their holidays, as far as possible as originally planned, and in any event to make sure that customers abroad are returned to the UK. Alternatively, customers whose holidays have not started can be reimbursed the cost of their holidays or can ask ABTA to make suitable alternative arrangements.

ABTA National Training Board: see *Travel Training Company*

ABTAC stands for ABTA Travel Agents Certificate. It is an examination-based qualification for those working, or wishing to work, in the travel industry and was developed jointly by ABTA's Travel Agents Council and the *Travel Training Company*. Launched in September 1994, ABTAC replaces the former COTAC (Certificate of Travel Agency Competence) qualification, and is aligned to the new *National Vocational Qualifications (NVQs)*. Available by distance learning and in a number of regional centres, ABTAC counts towards the staff qualifications requirement for membership of ABTA.

Abtech: a technology advisory service offered by *ABTA* to its members, which aims to give unbiased advice on all matters relating to the use of computer systems in travel agencies and tour operations.

ACAC: see *Activity Centre Advisory Committee*

ACAS: see *Advisory Conciliation and Arbitration Service*

ACC: see *Association of County Councils*

access in *leisure, travel and tourism* is an all-embracing term covering both physical access to buildings and facilities, as well as the opportunity for all people to participate in a range of activities regardless of their gender, race, age, social status, income level or personal mobility. Bodies such as the *Sports Council* have done much to widen participation in sport and recreation, through promotional campaigns such as *Sport for All.* Organisations such as the *Council for the Protection of Rural England* and the *Ramblers' Association* campaign strongly for the right of access to the countryside.

accommodation is one of the three major components of the *travel and tourism industry*, along with *transportation* and *attractions/entertainment.* It employs around 20 per cent of the total UK tourism workforce and is a significant revenue earner; the *British Tourist Authority (BTA)* estimates that more than one-third of all expenditure by *overseas visitors* to Britain and by UK residents is for accommodation. The accommodation sector comprises a wide range of establishments, including city-centre hotels, motels, cottages, caravans, lodges, farm guesthouses and country house hotels, to name but a few. Accommodation can be classified in a number of ways, for example:

- commercial or non-commercial
- serviced or self-catering
- urban or rural
- static or mobile

Perhaps the most useful classification is into *serviced* or *self-catering*, the former including hotels and guesthouses, the latter cottages and chalets. In the UK, figures show that self-catering is more popular than serviced accommodation, although the single most popular type of accommodation is hotels, acccounting for approximately 25 per cent of all accommodation used. *Visiting friends and relatives (VFR)* is also an important category of accommodation.

accommodation grading schemes: initiatives that aim to ensure consistency in the quality of service and facilities at establishments offering accommodation for business and leisure travellers. Schemes may be either compulsory, as is the case in many European countries, or voluntary, the position in the UK. The three best-known schemes in the UK are the *Crown Classification Scheme*, administered by the *National* and *Regional Tourist Boards*, and the 'star' systems operated by the *Automobile Association (AA)* and RAC (Royal Automobile Club). Tour operators sometimes devise their own classification schemes to supplement those offered by the tourist boards, e.g. the *Thomson* 'T' scheme. The use of a number of different schemes with varying criteria can be confusing for customers, and many in the industry are calling for a simplified scheme applicable to all establishments.

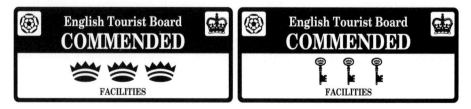

The Crown and Key schemes operated by the English Tourist board

Accor group is the biggest of the European hotel companies, operating under several brand names, including Novotel, Sofitel, Mercure, Ibis, Formule 1, Altea and Urbis. With headquarters in France, Accor has a stock of more than 100 000 rooms in its hotels, mainly found in France, Belgium, UK, Germany, Italy and Spain. The bulk of Accor's expansion in the 1990s has taken place in the budget hotels sector of the market.

account: a written record in which details of an organisation's financial transactions are entered. These may relate to an individual supplier, a type of expense or receipt, or a particular *asset* or *liability*. In *advertising* and sales, an 'account' is the name given to an individual organisation to whom services are provided, e.g. a travel agent that handles all the business of J Smith Engineering Company will refer to it as the Smith account.

accountability: the extent to which an individual is held responsible for his or her actions. In the workplace, managers have to accept ultimate *responsibility* for the control of their resources, including staff, plant and machinery, finance and facilities, and they are judged on the results they achieve. (See also *delegation, authority.*) In the public sector, local authority employees are accountable to their *Council Tax* payers through their elected representatives (councillors).

account executive: an employee of an *advertising agency* who acts as the link between the clients, known as 'accounts', and all the other specialist staff within the agency who will be working on particular campaigns. Working under the direction of an account director, the account executive will meet face-to-face with clients and liaise with the agency's *media planners* and *buyers,* creative teams and *market research* staff to make sure that a campaign meets its objectives and that the clients are satisfied with the service they receive.

accountant's pricing: see *cost-plus pricing*

accounting is the process of recording an organisation's financial transactions in accordance with standard book-keeping practice. Accounting can be divided into *financial accounting,* which is concerned with the preparation of summary reports for the shareholders or owners of a business, and *management accounting,* which focuses on the provision of financial information to help with business decision making and planning. All organisations need accurate and reliable accounting systems, so that they can monitor their performance, control *costs* and meet any legal requirements for the presentation of figures.

accounting period: the period of time over which a business prepares its *profit and loss account* and at the end of which it draws up its *balance sheet.*

acculturation is the study of the reactions and impacts when people from different cultures come into contact with each other. This may be by direct contact, e.g. a group of UK *tourists* meeting the Masai people on a safari holiday to East Africa, or via the influence of the *mass media.*

ACE: see *Association for Conferences and Events*

acid-test ratio: see *liquidity ratio*

ACORN stands for 'a classification of residential neighbourhoods', a computer *database* developed to help organisations carry out effective *target marketing* and *direct mail* campaigns. ACORN uses the electoral register to classify individuals according to the type of residential area in which they live and can be programmed to produce names and addresses in particular postcode areas of the country for use in direct mail campaigns. The system can give names and addresses of people who are likely to buy particular types of *holidays* and follow certain leisure pursuits.

acquisition: the takeover of one company by another, e.g. in 1995 Whitbread PLC acquired a number of Marriott Hotels and the David Lloyd Leisure chain. The company making the acquisition is usually sufficiently large to be able to finance the takeover. Acquisitions that may not be in the public interest are sometimes referred to the *Monopolies and Mergers Commission.*

ACRE: see *Action with Communities in Rural England*

acronym: a word formed from the first letters of other words, e.g. *WTO = World Tourism Organisation, ABTA = Association of British Travel Agents* and *ACORN = a classification of residential neighbourhoods.*

action plan: a statement, usually in written form, giving a series of actions to be carried out within a certain period of time. The action plan may result from a review of the *management* of a department, an appraisal of an individual member of staff or perhaps an evaluation of a marketing campaign. Action plans, which may form part of a wider business plan, should indicate who is responsible for carrying out each of the tasks identified.

Action with Communities in Rural England (ACRE): a voluntary membership organisation that represents the interests of rural areas in England, and the social and economic welfare of those living and working in them. ACRE undertakes research on rural issues and provides information, training and support to rural communities, including advice on *rural tourism.*

activity: a term used in assessing company performance. It is a measure of how well an organisation is using its *assets*, determined by comparing *financial ratios* with previous years or comparing actual with forecast results.

Activity Centre Advisory Committee (ACAC): a group which includes representatives of the major professional, trade and statutory bodies with an interest in the UK outdoor activity industry. Members of ACAC developed a voluntary *code of practice* in 1994 covering the safety and welfare of those who use *outdoor activity centres.* ACAC proposed an accreditation scheme for participating centres that guarantee to adhere to the code of practice. Centres must also agree to submit themselves to independent inspection and accept a customer complaints procedure. Members of ACAC include the *English Tourist Board, CCPR, BAHA,* PGL Young Adventure and the *Sports Council.*

activity holidays have grown in popularity in the UK in recent years, due to an increased concern for health, exercise and fitness in the population generally. Activity holidays range from the very intensive, e.g. off-road mountain biking, orienteering and water-skiing, to the relatively leisurely, e.g. walking and golf. *Tour operators* and hoteliers have responded to the growth in healthy pursuits by offering activity and special interest holidays and short breaks, aimed at individuals, groups and families. Activity holidays are set to be one of the growth sectors of the *leisure* and *tourism* industries up to and beyond the year 2000.

ADAS: see *Agricultural Development and Advisory Service*

ADC: see *Association of District Councils*

additional voluntary contribution (AVC): an extra payment made by a person to top-up his or her personal or company *pension*, so as to provide extra income in retirement. Some companies subsidise the payment of AVCs for their employees or even meet the full cost of the extra payments on their behalf.

add-on: something extra provided for a customer for which an additional charge is normally levied, e.g. an excursion taken while on a *package holiday* abroad, a baby seat installed in a hire car or insurance for an activity holiday in a Lake District country house hotel.

ad-hoc team: a group of people set up at short notice to investigate a particular occurrence, e.g. a sudden rise in the number of complaints to a *tour operator* about a particular *hotel*.

administrative systems are found throughout the *leisure* and *tourism* industries providing support to managers in their decision-making roles and staff in their every-day tasks. Administrators carry out both routine and non-routine functions; routine functions include servicing committees, producing letters and *reports* and preparing financial data. Non-routine functions could include providing administrative sup-port to a one-off event or an unplanned visit by an inspector from the *Health and Safety Executive*. Leisure and tourism organisations need effective administrative sys-tems in order to be able to:

- record and monitor organisational performance
- support the operation of resources – human, financial and physical
- monitor the effectiveness and efficiency of the organisation
- comply with relevant *legislation*

Some of the most important areas in leisure and tourism that need administrative sys-tems are *stock control*, the handling and recording of cash, cleaning and maintenance, health and safety and booking systems. Nowadays, administrative systems invariably involve the use of *computers*.

advance purchase excursion (APEX): a travel ticket purchased in advance of a journey at a discount price. APEX fares are available for a number of modes of trav-el, including airlines, ferries, coaches and *British Rail*. As well as having to be purchased in advance, APEX tickets sometimes have other conditions attached to them, e.g. the requirement to stay for a minimum number of nights at a destination.

advantages statement: that part of the sales process in leisure and tourism, before the *customer* has made a decision whether or not to purchase, when a sales person indicates what the product or service can do in general for the customer, e.g. the fact that a departure time of 14.00 hrs for a ferry crossing means that a client will not have to make an early start to reach the ferry port. An advantages statement will often fol-low on from a *features statement*, which gives general information about a product or service. (See also *benefits statement*.)

adventure tourism: the term used to describe a particular type of tourist activity that focuses on exploration and discovery, rather than a passive experience. Trekking in the Himalayas, walking in the jungles of Borneo and white water canoeing in the

Rocky Mountains would all be classified as adventure tourism. Providing adventure tourism products is a form of *niche marketing*.

advertisement: a paid insertion in the *printed* or *broadcast media* that informs readers, viewers or listeners about products and services, in the hope of raising awareness and persuading them to buy. Advertisements are also found at the cinema, on billboards, at sports stadia and on many forms of transport, including buses, taxis and the London Underground. Advertisements in newspapers and magazines can be either *classified*, which are paid for by the word or line, or display/semi-display, which are larger and charged on a pro-rata basis for space used. Current prices for advertising in all types of media can be found in *BRAD*.

advertising is the most visible part of an organisation's *promotional mix*. It seeks to inform and persuade existing and potential purchasers or users of products and services. Advertising is carried out in a wide range of *media*, including *television*, commercial radio, newspapers, magazines, billboards and by transport providers. The charges for advertising vary in direct proportion to the number of people who will see or hear the particular advertisement. Television is the most powerful, and most expensive, advertising medium, since it attracts the biggest audience.

In leisure and tourism there is a distinction between trade and consumer advertising; trade advertising is carried out on a business-to-business basis, e.g. a tour operator advertising its holidays in the Travel Trade Gazette or a sports goods' distributor advertising in Leisure Management magazine. Consumer advertising is communication between an organisation and its customers, e.g. a local sports centre advertising its services on local radio or a company such as First Choice Holidays placing an advertisement in the Daily Mail. To be effective, all advertising should follow the *AIDA* principle.

advertising agency: a company that can offer a range of services to help a *leisure* or *tourism* organisation achieve maximum impact with its *advertising* budget. Large agencies employ a number of specialists, including:

- *account executives* – the link between the clients and all sections of the agency
- creative teams – the 'ideas people', chosen for their skill in producing effective slogans and text (copywriters), or their artistic ability (artists and graphic designers)
- media personnel – plan a media schedule and liaise with the appropriate media to book space or buy *airtime*
- *market research* staff – commission or carry out research into new products and markets

Agencies charge a fee for their services, depending on the nature of the work and the media used. Lists of advertising agencies are produced by the Institute of Practioners in Advertising and the Advertising Agency Register. (See also *advertising, above-the-line promotion, below-the-line promotion, media buyer, media planner, media.*)

advertising campaign: the planning, execution and analysis of a series of events aimed at informing and persuading people to buy particular products and services. An advertising campaign, which may be carried out 'in-house' or through the services of an *advertising agency*, will have specific objectives, e.g. raising awareness of a new product or publicising the opening of a new theme park. The campaign will often spread beyond purely advertising in various *media*, to include other promotional techniques such as *direct mail* and *public relations* work. It is essential that the results of any advertising campaign are closely monitored to ensure that its original *objectives* are being met.

Advertising Standards Authority (ASA) is a self-regulatory body responsible for ensuring that advertisers in the various *media* conform to the British Code of Advertising Practice. This Code requires that all advertisements should be legal, decent, honest and truthful. Any material found to be contravening the Code will be withdrawn from publication.

Advisory Conciliation and Arbitration Service (ACAS) was set up under the terms of the Employment Protection Act of 1975, to promote the improvement of *industrial relations* and to act as a catalyst between employers and *trade unions* in the resolution of industrial disputes. ACAS can supply conciliation officials, who listen to both parties' views and aim to mediate to bring a dispute to a speedy and acceptable conclusion. ACAS is also active in encouraging organisations to develop approved codes of practice governing, for example, the handling of disciplinary matters in the workplace. Although it is most often invited to mediate in a dispute, ACAS does have powers under the 1975 Act to intervene, where this is felt to be in the public interest.

after-sales service is the recognition that the *sales process* does not finish when a customer has parted with his or her money for a product or service. Any *leisure* or *tourism* organisation should expect to have to handle a number of queries and even complaints after a sales transaction has taken place. The more progressive organisations will follow up a proportion of their sales to establish that customers are happy with the service they received. A *travel agent*, for example, may telephone a client to enquire if her holiday went well. The attention to an efficient after-sales service is also a good public relations exercise.

age structure: a *demographic* factor that can have important effects on the *demand* for leisure and tourism products and services. As part of its wider *market research* activities, an organisation needs to know the current age structure of its target markets and how it is likely to change in the future. In general, Western countries are moving towards ageing populations, with people living longer and more active lives.

agency agreement: a formal arrangement entered into by an agent and a *principal*, giving details of the terms under which each will operate and the scale of *commission* payable to the agent. In the case of a travel agency, it is likely to have agreements with a number of principals, including *tour operators*, airlines, car hire companies and ferry operators.

agenda: a formal list of the items to be discussed at a meeting. It is helpful if the agenda is sent out before the meeting, in order to give those attending a chance to study its content, but it may be given out at the start of the meeting. A note requesting items for an agenda is sometimes sent out to all those due to attend a meeting, giving them the opportunity to have particular items discussed.

Agenda 21: see *Earth Summit*

**Bramthorpe District Council
Leisure Services Committee**

The next meeting of the above committee will take place on Monday 7th October 1996 at 7.20pm in room B12.

AGENDA
1. Apologies for absence
2. Minutes of the last meeting
3. Matters arising
4. Chair's report
5. Secretary's report
6. National Lottery funding
7. 1997/98 budget
8. Staff training
9. AOB
10. Date of next meeting

John Sargeant
Secretary
30th August 1996

An example of an agenda

agent: a company or individual who sells goods and services on behalf of another company (known as the *principal*) in return for a fixed payment or, more usually, a percentage of the value of the sales (known as *commission*). By using agents, a company, such as a tour operator or car hire firm, saves on the costs of setting up its own sales operation. It does, however, run the risk of its own products not getting sufficient exposure if the agent sells on behalf of a number of principals.

AGM: see *annual general meeting*

Agricultural Development and Advisory Service (ADAS) is an agency within the *Ministry of Agriculture, Fisheries and Food (MAFF)* responsible for offering a range of advisory, research and consultancy services to farmers and other landowners. This includes advice for farmers on *diversification* into *leisure* and *tourism* enterprises.

Agricultural Training Board (ATB): see *ATB Landbase*

AIDA stands for attention, interest, desire and action. It is a principle that should be followed when carrying out any promotional work involved with *marketing communications*. If we take the example of designing a newspaper *advertisement* for a newly opened tourist attraction, AIDA could be applied as follows:

- interest is generated by using colour, bold headlines and a picture of a famous personality
- attention is maintained by keeping the wording as brief as possible and including language and images that the reader can relate to easily
- a desire to visit the attraction is created by offering a discount voucher within the advertisement
- action is triggered by stating clearly the opening times, including a location map and printing the address and telephone number for enquiries

AIDA is equally applicable when writing a *direct mail* letter, designing an exhibition stand or selecting *sales promotion* materials.

AIM: see *Association of Independent Museums*

aims: see *objectives*

Air Miles: a promotional scheme operated by *British Airways* and linked to purchases of goods and services, and the use of *credit cards*. Prospective travellers accumulate Air Miles every time they buy certain products and trade them in for flights of differing values. The scheme has proved to be extremely popular and is a good way for the airline to fill unsold capacity on aircraft.

air traffic control is concerned with guiding aircraft into and out of airports, and keeping pilots informed of weather and landing conditions. In the UK, air traffic control is the responsibility of the *Civil Aviation Authority (CAA)*, which regulates military and civilian flight movements in a number of clearly defined flight zones.

air travel is the category of *transportation* that includes *scheduled air services* and *charter flights*. It has grown in popularity dramatically since the end of the Second World War, coupled with the growth in *package holidays* from cooler northern European countries to sunny Mediterranean destinations. Air travel is also an important aspect of *business tourism*, with the advantages of speed, range and status. Recent developments in aircraft technology have allowed greater flight distances between stops, opening up hitherto remote parts of the world, the so-called *long haul destinations*, such as the Caribbean, India, the Far East and countries in Africa. The use of air travel for domestic purposes has grown significantly in the UK in recent years, with Heathrow and Gatwick alone handling more than 100 000 domestic flights per year. Linked to the steady growth in air travel has been the demand for greater capacity at airports, with extra runways and the expansion of facilities.

Air Travel Organisers' Licence (ATOL): a licence issued by the *Civil Aviation Authority (CAA)* and required by an individual or company selling holidays or seats on charter flights. Applicants must show that they are fit to hold an ATOL, have adequate financial arrangements and must lodge a bond with the CAA. In the event of company failure, the bond money is used to repatriate clients who might otherwise be stranded overseas and to refund, as far as possible, passengers who have paid in advance but not yet travelled. Where the bond is insufficient to meet all claims, the *Air Travel Trust Fund*, managed by the CAA, meets the shortfall.

Air Travel Reserve Fund: see *Air Travel Trust Fund*

Air Travel Trust Fund (ATTF): a fund administered by the *Civil Aviation Authority (CAA)* and used when a bond lodged by the holder of an *Air Travel Organisers' Licence (ATOL)* is insufficient to meet all the claims against it. Previously known as the Air Travel Reserve Fund, in 1990 the reserves of the ATTF stood at more than £25 million, but subsequent holiday company failures have reduced this amount considerably.

airline codes are unique reference symbols assigned to the world's airlines by the *International Civil Aviation Organisation (ICAO)* to be used in ticketing, timetables and reservations. Examples include BA (*British Airways*), BD (British Midland) and QF (Qantas).

airline deregulation is the process of withdrawing complete state control of *air travel* operations, creating a free market environment within which companies can compete with each other for business. The benefits of more private sector involvement in air travel should be better services and cheaper fares, although some people fear reductions in standards of safety and the withdrawal of loss-making routes. The USA was the first country to deregulate its airlines in 1978, leading to a rise in the number of carriers and the development of the *hub and spoke system*, as a way of reducing costs. Airline deregulation in Europe has yet to be fully achieved, with pressure from countries with existing state airlines, including France and Italy, to delay deregulation indefinitely.

airtime: the name given to time bought on radio or television as part of an *advertising campaign*. Airtime rates will vary greatly, depending on the size of the audience and the region of the country used.

AITO: see *Association of Independent Tour Operators*

Albemarle Report: an influential report published in 1960 with the full title 'The Youth Service in England and Wales', which stressed the need for a greater range and distribution of better quality facilities for *sport* and indoor *recreation* for young people.

Alliance of Independent Travel Agents (ARTAC): a *consortium* of independent *travel agents* in the UK who have joined forces to offer a united voice on matters of concern to smaller travel businesses. ARTAC has a preferred suppliers' scheme covering *tour operators*, ferry companies and cruise operators, with which it has agreed preferential business terms.

allocation: a block of airline seats, hotel rooms or *self-catering accommodation* that is reserved for the exclusive use of a particular *tour operator* or *travel agent*, under the terms of an agreement. The operator or agent has first call on their allocation until a specified release date, after which the seats or accommodation may be sold freely to other companies or individuals.

allocentric: one of a number of types of tourist behaviour developed by Plog in 1977 as part of a research study for airline companies. Allocentrics were people who enjoyed travel and cultural exploration, were in above average income groups, independent in mind and body, and adventurous. (See also *psychocentric, mid-centric*.)

alternative tourism: see *'green' tourism*

Alton Towers is currently the UK's number one *tourist attraction* for which an entrance fee is charged. Owned by the Pearson Corporation, Alton Towers includes a number of *white knuckle rides* and catering outlets. Located close to the M6 motorway, it has a regional and even national *catchment area*.

ALVA: see *Association of Leading Visitor Attractions*

AMA: see *Association of Metropolitan Authorities*

Amadeus: a *computerised reservation system (CRS)* operated by a number of European airlines including Iberia, SAS, Lufthansa and Air France, set up in 1987 to compete directly with the US *Sabre* and *Apollo* systems.

American Express (Amex): a multinational corporation that, like *Thomas Cook*, was one of the founding companies in the worldwide *travel and tourism industry*. It initiated *traveller's cheques* in the late nineteenth century in the USA and became involved in travel operations early in the twentieth century. American Express has concentrated primarily on providing services for business travellers and in currency exchange. The company is also well known for its *charge card*, which is managed by a separate business unit within the corporation.

American Plan: an accommodation arrangement based on full board, with a room and three meals per day provided. (See also *Modified American Plan, Continental Plan, European Plan.*)

American Society of Travel Agents (ASTA) is a representative body for *travel agents* and *tour operators* based in the USA. ASTA undertakes a similar role in its own country to that taken by *ABTA* in Britain, but it has a wider geographical sphere of influence given the importance of the USA as a major tourist-generating country. ASTA has in the region of 20 000 members in 125 countries around the world.

Amex: see *American Express*

Amtrak is the official government-funded rail service operated in the USA.

animateur: see *animator*

animator: a person who takes on the role of an entertainer of *tourists*, by becoming directly involved in the experience they are enjoying, e.g. a costumed guide at a *heritage museum* such as Ironbridge Gorge or a person acting the role of a Victorian teacher at Wigan Pier. Derived from the French word animateur, they become part of the tourist experience and are sometimes used as visitor management tools, e.g. actors and jugglers entertaining people queuing to get into Jorvik Viking Centre in York.

annual general meeting (AGM): a gathering held every twelve months to which members of a *company*, society or similar organisation are invited, often to elect new *directors* or officials. It is a legal requirement for a limited company to hold an AGM, to which all shareholders are invited, in order to approve the accounts for the year, take part in the election of directors and ask questions of the chairman and other board members.

annual report: a document which looks back over the previous twelve-month period of a *limited company* or other organisation, highlighting successes and achievements. By law, limited companies must publish an annual report and accounts, which must be sent to every *shareholder*. It must contain a *balance sheet*, a *profit and loss account*, and a *cash-flow statement*. Large *leisure* and *tourism* companies, such as Forte, British Airways and First Leisure, produce glossy annual reports to contribute towards their image building. Public sector organisations, such as the *BTA, Sports Council* and *Countryside Commission*, also produce an annual report, to give interested parties details of their activities and achievements.

annual percentage rate (APR) is a figure that gives the true cost of a *loan*, in percentage terms, based on the amount of the loan outstanding. Under the terms of the *Consumer Credit Act 1974*, lenders are legally obliged to quote the APR on loans, rather than the often misleading flat interest rate figure, which can make a loan seem cheaper than it really is. By comparing one APR with another, a borrower can identify the cheapest loan that meets his or her needs.

Ansoff's matrix is a model that can be used by an organisation to develop the most profitable range of *products* and services it offers to its customers, sometimes referred to as its *product portfolio*. It is a type of *portfolio analysis* that allows an organisation to examine what it can do to its products and the markets they are sold in, so as to expand its operation.

The diagram shows that an organisation has four possible courses of action. It can focus on existing customers by either modifying an existing product (sector 1) or introducing new products to them (sector 2), or concentrate on attracting new markets, with either new products (sector 3) or by repositioning an existing product (sector 4). All four courses of action have a degree of risk attached to them, although launching a new product to a new market is likely to be the highest-risk scenario of them all.

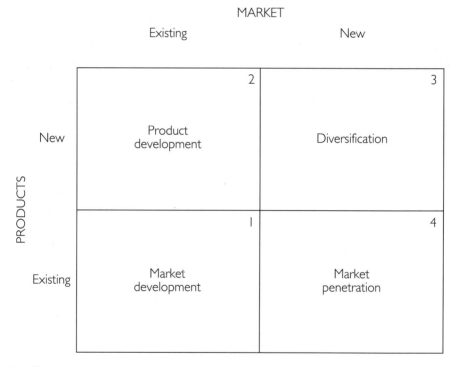

Ansoff's matrix

ANTOR: see *Association of National Tourist Office Representatives in Great Britain*

AONB: see *Area of Outstanding Natural Beauty*

apartotel: a term used to describe a type of *accommodation* which is a mixture of an apartment and a *hotel*, e.g. providing furnished accommodation plus optional services such as a restaurant or maid service.

APEX: see *advance purchase excursion*

Apollo: a *computerised reservation system (CRS)* developed by United Airlines in the USA and made available to agents in Europe from 1987. (See also *Galileo*.)

appraisal: see *staff appraisal*

appropriate tourism: see *'green' tourism*

APR: see *annual percentage rate*

arbitration is the practice of resolving a dispute by inviting an independent person to listen to both sides of an argument and make a judgement as to a fair resolution of the problem. Disputes in the workplace, perhaps concerning working conditions or pay, are often resolved through arbitration, sometimes involving experts from the *Advisory Conciliation and Arbitration Service (ACAS)*. Arbitration is sometimes known as conciliation or mediation.

Area of Outstanding Natural Beauty (AONB): set up under the 1949 National Parks and Access to the Countryside Act, there are currently 39 AONBs in England and Wales, given protected status on account of their scenic beauty. They range from the *green belt* countryside of the Surrey Hills to the open moorlands of the North Pennines. Many AONBs are popular destinations for *leisure* and *tourism*, although, unlike *National Parks*, they are not designated for their recreational value.

arena: a large, purpose-built indoor facility with the flexibility to be used for a variety of purposes, including *sports* events, exhibitions, concerts and circuses. Most large UK cities have at least one arena, e.g. NYNEX in Manchester, Sheffield Arena, Birmingham Arena at the *NEC* and Wembley Arena.

arithmetic average: see *mean*

ARR: see *average room rate*

ARTAC: see *Alliance of Independent Travel Agents*

Articles of Association: one of the two documents that *limited companies* must produce under the terms of the *Companies Act* 1985, the other being the *Memorandum of Association*. The Articles of Association is akin to the company's set of rules, outlining details regarding the frequency of meetings, types of shares, voting procedures, the names of *directors* and their powers, and other company matters.

arts and entertainment: an important sector within the UK *leisure and recreation industry*, covering a wide range of activities, including:

- visiting art galleries
- going to music concerts
- visits to the cinema and theatre
- attending exhibitions
- playing computer games at home
- playing bingo at a social club
- watching sports events
- taking evening classes
- following hobbies in the home
- visiting a pub or wine bar

While *public* and *voluntary sector* organisations are responsible for providing a range of arts and cultural facilities in their local communities, e.g. art galleries, *museums*, theatres, etc., the majority of arts and entertainment facilities are important revenue-earners for the *private sector*, with companies such as Rank, First Leisure and Granada being major players in the sector.

Arts Council of Great Britain is the national body established to foster the arts throughout Britain. It was established in 1946 and operates under a Royal Charter, which defines its *objectives* as:

- developing and improving the knowledge, understanding and practice of the arts
- increasing the accessibility of the arts to the public throughout Britain
- advising and co-operating with departments of government, local authorities and other bodies

The Arts Council is funded by the *Department of National Heritage* and is the body given the responsibility of distributing *National Lottery* funds to deserving arts projects. In the year 1993/94, the Council received government funds of £225 million, of which £44 million was allocated to the *Regional Arts Boards* and £23 million and £13 million to the Scottish and Welsh Arts Councils respectively. For the future, the Arts Council sees its priorities as being enhancing quality in the arts generally, ensuring *access* for all to the arts, improving the quality of service to customers and overseeing a growth in the arts economy.

ASA: see *Advertising Standards Authority*

assertiveness training is concerned with developing a degree of self-confidence in an individual, so that he or she is able to put across a point of view without appearing to be unduly aggressive. In the work environment, it is important for staff to be able to control their emotions, particularly in circumstances where they are in regular contact with the general public.

asset: an item that is owned by an individual or organisation and which has a certain value. In *leisure* and *tourism* businesses, assets are normally divided into those intended for long-term use (*fixed assets*), e.g. buildings, land, equipment and machinery, and those readily convertible into cash (*current assets*), e.g. stock such as food and drink.

Association of British Travel Agents (ABTA) is the trade body that represents over 90 per cent of *travel agents* and *tour operators* in the UK. It was formed in 1950, when new aircraft technology and greater personal freedom were giving people the means to travel further afield. ABTA's principal aims are:

- to establish an organisation which is fully representative of travel agents and tour operators in the UK
- to promote and develop the general interests of all its members
- to establish and maintain codes of conduct between members and the general public, with the object that membership of ABTA will be recognised as a guarantee of integrity, competence and high standards of service
- to discourage unfair competition without interfering with initiative and enterprise based on fair trading
- to promote friendly relations with others in the travel industry
- to liaise with other bodies concerned with the development of travel in the UK and abroad

The Association is a self-regulatory body run by its membership, via a network of councils and committees, with members appointed by member travel agents and tour operators. Members of ABTA are required to adhere to strict rules governing their business practice. These are contained in ABTA's Codes of Conduct which regulate all aspects of tour operators' and travel agents' relationships with their customers and which have been drawn up in conjunction with the *Office of Fair Trading*. In addition to its Codes of Conduct, ABTA seeks to protect the interests of the travelling public through its conciliation and arbitration schemes, which provide opportunities for travellers who have reason to complain to have their problems investigated and appropriate action taken. (See also *Stabiliser*, *ABTA bond*, *Tour Operators' Code of Conduct* and *Travel Agents' Code of Conduct*.)

Association of County Councils (ACC): an independent organisation representing the 47 Shire *county councils* in England and Wales, on matters such as transport policies, European legislation and economic development. *Tourism* is seen by members of the ACC as an increasingly important contributor to economic development and employment creation.

Association of District Councils (ADC): an independent body representing the interests of the 333 non-metropolitan *district councils* in England and Wales, on matters ranging from environmental policy, *Uniform Business Rates (UBR)* to *compulsory competitive tendering (CCT)*. The ADC seeks to promote local government and works towards forging partnerships between local and central government. The ADC is also active in promoting the value of *leisure* services and *tourism* at local level, and has completed a study into the economic position of *seaside resorts* in England and Wales.

Association of Independent Museums (AIM) was established in 1977 to provide a forum for *museums* not directly administered by central or local government. AIM endeavours to further the cause of independent museums, continue to increase professional standards and promote self-help among its 800 members, and generally increase museum awareness. The Association is run on a voluntary basis by members, with subscription fees kept as low as possible.

Association of Independent Tour Operators (AITO) is an alliance of over 150 smaller, specialist tour-operating companies in the UK. Established in 1976, AITO's *objectives* include helping member companies to market more effectively, ensuring the public can book members' holidays with confidence, promoting *sustainable tourism*, keeping members up to date with the issues of the day and encouraging higher standards and greater professionalism among its members.

Association of Leading Visitor Attractions (ALVA): an independent membership organisation that was set up in 1990 to fill a perceived gap in the framework of national tourism bodies. ALVA's mission is 'to represent to government, the tourism industry, the *media* and the public, the views and achievements of the country's foremost visitor attractions in matters which concern the effectiveness of *UK tourism* and the interests of the Association, whilst promoting co-operation and high standards of visitor management among its members'. Current members of ALVA include Blackpool Tower, *English Heritage*, the *National Trust*, the British Museum and York Minster.

Association of Metropolitan Authorities (AMA): an independent body representing the 36 metropolitan districts in England, 32 London boroughs and the Corporation of the City of London. *Tourism* is increasingly being seen by AMA members as an important factor in economic development and *urban regeneration*.

Association of National Tourist Office Representatives in Great Britain (ANTOR) is a voluntary body representing more than 80 *National Tourist Offices (NTOs)* based in Britain. It acts as a forum for the exchange of ideas among its members and works with the *travel trade* to promote its member countries. ANTOR produces its own World Travel Guide annually.

Association of Tourism Teachers and Trainers (ATTT): established in 1975 as the Association of Teachers of Tourism, with the aim of helping its members to be more effective teachers of tourism subjects, the ATTT is a specialist section within the *Tourism Society*. ATTT provides a forum for discussion of matters relating to tourism education and training at all levels. It acts as a *pressure group* to promote high standards of professionalism in tourism education and training, as well as extending links between employers and tourism educators and trainers. The affairs of the ATTT are organised by a voluntary committee elected from the membership.

Association for Business Sponsorship of the Arts (ABSA) is an independent organisation established in 1976 to promote and encourage partnerships between the private sector and the arts. ABSA was set up by the business community to advise on good practice in arts *sponsorship*. Members, which include IBM, W H Smith, Barclays Bank and Channel 4, can take advantage of a range of services, including advice on sponsorship policy, consultancy, networking and attending specialist events. Since 1984, ABSA has administered the government-funded Business Sponsorship Incentive Scheme, which matches new sponsorship funds with government grants.

Association for Conferences and Events (ACE) is a trading name of the Association of Conference Executives Ltd., which was established in 1971 to act as a forum for member organisations who are involved in all facets of the industry. ACE offers a range of services to its members, including a helpline for advice and information, mailings of job vacancies, a regular letter and a series of workshops. In 1992, ACE was involved in the development of *National Vocational Qualification (NVQs)* for the business travel sector and has since been involved in extending the NVQ system into the events services sector.

ASTA: see *American Society of Travel Agents*

ATB: see *ATB Landbase*

ATB Landbase: an organisation involved in assessing training needs and providing courses for the land-based industries, such as agriculture, horticulture, equine management, *rural tourism* and *recreation, conservation* and forestry. Previously known as the Agricultural Training Board, ATB Landbase works with *Training and Enterprise Councils (TECs)* and colleges to meet the need at local level for practical, supervisory and management training.

ATLAS: see *European Association for Education in Tourism, Leisure and the Arts*

ATOL: see *Air Travel Organisers' Licence*

ATTF: see *Air Travel Trust Fund*

attractions are one of the three core components of the *tourism* industry, along with *transportation* and *accommodation*; indeed they are often the very reason why visitors decide to venture out. *The British Tourist Authority (BTA)* estimates that there were around 350 million visits to attractions in the UK in 1992, Blackpool Pleasure Beach being the number one UK tourist attraction with approximately 6.5 million visitors. Attractions can be classified into those that are naturally occurring and those that are man-made. Throughout time, *natural attractions* have always been a powerful motivating force behind people's desire to travel. On an international scale, the Himalayas, the Amazon Rain Forest, the Sahara Desert, the Alps, the Black Sea, the Rocky Mountains and the Victoria Falls, to name but a few, have all welcomed visitors in their millions. Closer to home, the National Parks in England and Wales, the Scottish Highlands and the Giant's Causeway are still important visitor destinations. *Man-made attractions* are purpose-built facilities designed to provide fun, excitement and entertainment.

ATTT: see *Association of Tourism Teachers and Trainers*

audit: an independent investigation into the financial or operational aspects of an organisation, often prior to a change in *policy* or operation, or in response to a problem. Audits are most often associated with the financial resources of an organisation, but may also be concerned with environmental or health and safety matters. (See also *environmental audit.*)

Audit Commission: a government agency responsible for ensuring that local authorities, *quangos* and other national bodies receiving public funds are effectively and efficiently managed, and that the public is getting value for money from the provision of a range of services, including *leisure* and *recreation* facilities.

authoritarian leadership: see *autocratic leadership*

authority: the right to take actions and make decisions. In the workplace, authority is often delegated from managers to their subordinates, but managers are, at the end of the day, accountable for their own actions and ultimately responsible for the actions of the staff under their control. (See also *delegation, accountability, responsibility.*)

autocratic leadership is a leadership style most commonly associated with *centralised, hierarchical organisational structures* (*steep pyramids*), where decision making rests with a small number of senior staff. This may be because senior managers distrust their staff or because they are unwilling to delegate responsibility down the hierarchy. Autocratic leadership, sometimes called authoritarian leadership, can often lead to a demoralised workforce.

Automobile Association (AA): one of the foremost motoring organisations in Europe, which, in 1912, introduced a star-rating system for *hotels* and other *accommodation* in the UK. Today the AA *accommodation grading scheme* has developed to encompass one to five star appointments for hotels and a 'listing' category for private hotels, guesthouses, farmhouses and inns. AA inspectors make unannounced visits on an annual basis to accommodation establishments within the classification scheme, in order to ensure that standards of service and quality of facilities are being maintained. Hotels that consistently provide outstanding levels of hospitality, service, food and comfort are recognised by the awarding of one to five red stars, the AA's ultimate accolade for quality.

AVC: see *additional voluntary contribution*

average room rate (ARR) is an important *performance indicator* used in the *man-*

agement of *hotels* and other accommodation establishments, since it shows the average price paid by guests on a particular day or other period of time. It is calculated by dividing the value of rooms sold by the total number of rooms occupied, e.g.

$$\frac{£2400}{40 \text{ rooms}} = \text{an ARR of £60}$$

Once the ARR has been calculated, comparisons can be made between different time periods and even different establishments.

REVISION: There is a set of revision lists at the back of this book to help you prepare for GNVQ unit tests. See pages 246–250 for unit tests in GNVQ Advanced Leisure and Tourism.

B

BAA: see *British Airports Authority*

BABA: see *book-a-bed-ahead*

back of house: see *back office*

back office is a term used to denote certain organisational functions that are carried out 'behind the scenes', away from direct contact with customers and the public in general. Sometimes referred to as 'back of house', these functions include accounting, security, maintenance, *stock control* and *marketing*. There must be a strong link between these back office functions and the *front office*, denoting the reception point in a leisure or tourism facility. For example, when a guest books into a hotel at reception, information must be conveyed, either manually but more likely via a *computer* system, to other departments that need to know, such as housekeeping, accounts, food and beverage, laundry and marketing. The concept of a back office is widespread in leisure and tourism, not just in hotels but also in *leisure centres*, entertainment complexes and *tourist information centres*.

- Staff training
- Marketing and publicity
- Stock control
- Health and safety
- Security
- Maintenance
- Food preparation
- Personnel
- Accounting
- Membership systems
- Cash control

Typical 'back office' functions

back-to-back: the practice of a single *charter* aircraft flying to an overseas *destination* with a full load of passengers and returning with another full load of passengers who have just completed their holiday. Back-to-back arrangements ensure that an airline maximises its capacity at all times, thereby reducing its costs.

BACT: see *British Association of Conference Towns*

bad debt: an unpaid bill or account that has not been settled and which is unlikely ever to be repaid, perhaps because the *debtor* has ceased trading. It is important for an organisation to keep a tight control of its debtor situation by chasing late payments and not granting credit too freely. Bad debtor control can have a serious effect on a company's *cash-flow* position.

baggage allowance is the weight of luggage that airline passengers are allowed to take with them without incurring an excess charge. Currently the allowance is 20 kg (44 lb) for economy passengers and 30 kg (66 lb) for those travelling first class.

BAHA: see *British Activity Holiday Association*

balance of payments is a statement of the inflows and outflows of currency to and from a particular country earned from its *imports* and *exports*. A nation's balance of payments is divided into its capital account and current account, which can be thought of as being similar to an individual's savings and current accounts. The capital account is made up of investments, grants and loans, while the current account is sub-divided into *'visible'* and *'invisible' items*. Travel, tourism and leisure are 'invisible' items on the current account. The difference between a country's receipts from *incoming tourism* and the expenditure by its residents on travel abroad is shown separately as the *travel* (or *tourism*) *balance*.

balance sheet: a statement of an organisation's *assets, liabilities* and *capital* and a summary of its financial position at a given point in time, usually the last day of the financial year. Balance sheets are constructed at least on an annual basis and often more frequently than this, depending on an organisation's financial systems. An organisation's ability to pay off outstanding debts can be assessed by comparing *current assets* with *current liabilities*, as shown in the balance sheet. It can also be used to determine the extent to which an organisation is able to borrow funds from external sources without straining its capability to service its debts. An example of a balance sheet is given below.

Balance sheet for 'Spangles' café

FIXED ASSETS	£	£
Lease on premises	25,000	
Fixtures and fittings	7,000	
Kitchen equipment	4,000	
Van	3,500	39,500
CURRENT ASSETS		
Stock	2,000	
Debtors	1,500	
Bank	6,000	
Cash	200	
Total current assets	9,700	
CURRENT LIABILITIES		
Creditors	3,000	
Total current liabilities	3,000	
NET CURRENT ASSETS		6,700
TERM LOAN		(3,000)
		43,200
OWNER'S CAPITAL EMPLOYED		
At start	15,000	
Profit for period	28,200	
		43,200

Example of a balance sheet

banker's draft: a *cheque* drawn by a bank, as distinct from a personal cheque written by an account holder. Sometimes called certified cheques, they give the payee a greater degree of security, particularly when payment is needed quickly and there is no time to go through the normal cheque clearing process. Banker's drafts are an easy way of accepting payment in a foreign currency.

Bank Holidays were first introduced in the UK during the *Industrial Revolution*, under the Bank Holiday Act of 1871, which created four public holidays per year. They became the magnet for trips to the countryside and coast, with Brighton welcoming 132 000 visitors on Easter Monday in 1862. Today, changes in working practices, greater mobility and changes in trading laws mean that Bank Holidays are no longer viewed by many people as a time to relax, but rather a chance to go *shopping* to the many out-of-town retail complexes around the country, e.g. Lakeside, Meadowhall and Metrocentre.

bar chart: a useful way of presenting data to give an immediate comparison between variables, e.g. the trend in overseas visits to a country or the monthly sales figures for a *leisure centre*. Bar charts can be drawn either vertically or horizontally, with the heights of the bars corresponding to the values indicated.

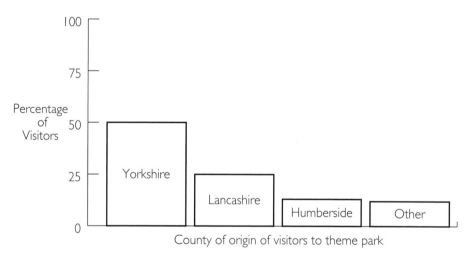

Example of a bar chart

BATO: see *British Association of Tourism Officers*

BCC: see *Bus and Coach Council*

BCG: see *Boston Consulting Group matrix*

bed and breakfast is a type of *serviced accommodation* offered in private households, popular because it offers excellent value-for-money and allows guests to experience the way of life of the owners of the establishment. It is particularly popular with *overseas visitors* to Britain who want to sample the 'real' British way of life, whether it is on a Welsh or Scottish farm or in an historic city such as York or Bath. Bed and breakfast is also an accommodation and meal arrangement offered by all types of serviced accommodation comprising a room and British or continental breakfast. (See also *Continental Plan*.)

below-the-line promotion refers to marketing activity for which *commission* is not normally paid to an *advertising agency*, but the work is carried out on a fee basis instead, e.g. an agency may charge a fee of £2 000 to carry out a small *direct mail* campaign for a travel company. As well as *direct mail*, other below-the-line activities include *public relations, sales promotions* and *merchandising*.

benchmarking is a process of setting industry standards of performance based on the achievements of the most efficient companies in the sector. It is beginning to be applied to the *UK tourism* industry, under an initiative developed by the *Confederation of British Industry (CBI)*.

benefits statement: part of the *sales process* in *leisure* and *tourism* when a sales person indicates specifically what a product or service can do for an individual customer. The information given is selected on the basis of the customer's *needs* and should, if presented in a positive fashion, persuade him or her to commit to a sale. The sales person can then make the necessary arrangements to *close the sale*. (See also *features statement, advantages statement*.)

Bermuda Agreement: an *air travel* protocol developed between Britain and the USA, which restricted air carriage between the two countries to the national carriers alone. Agreed initially in 1946, soon after the *Chicago Convention on Civil Aviation*, the Bermuda Agreement was subsequently modified in 1977.

berth: the term used to describe a bedspace on a ship or train. May also be used to mean the place where a ship comes to rest in a harbour.

BFI: see *British Film Institute*

BHTS: see *British Home Tourism Survey*

BISL: see *Business in Sport and Leisure*

BITOA: see *British Incoming Tour Operators' Association*

Blue Flag Campaign: a scheme that provides a comparison between standards of cleanliness and *management* at European resort beaches. Launched in 1987, the European Year of the Environment, a Blue Flag is awarded to resort beaches which have achieved the guideline standard of the *EU Bathing Water Directive*. There is some concern in the UK at the way in which the Directive has been implemented, and tourism organisations are pressing for a simplified system of operation for the future. The Blue Flag scheme is co-ordinated in the UK by the *Tidy Britain Group*. (See also *Seaside Award*.)

BNTS: see *British National Travel Survey*

BOA: see *British Olympic Association*

body language is a common type of *non-verbal communication (NVC)*, involving the transmission of messages through gestures of the body, such as a shrug of the shoulders to show indifference, banging a table to display anger, a particular facial expression, eye contact or bodily contact.

booking systems are an essential requirement in the leisure, travel and tourism industries, as a way of monitoring sales, controlling access to facilities and events, and ensuring financial and other *resources* are used effectively. Booking systems may be either manual, based on charts and card files, or computerised. Many organisations that formerly used manual systems have transferred their *data* onto *computers*, because of the greater speed and storage capacity they offer.

borough council: see *district council*

boarding pass: authorisation issued to a traveller to allow him or her to board an aircraft, cruise ship or ferry. Passengers are sometimes required to show their boarding passes when making *duty-free* purchases on board. Boarding passes used on ships are sometimes called embarkation passes.

bonding is concerned with providing financial security in order to compensate travellers in the event of a *company* failure. *ABTA tour operators* and *travel agents*, for example, must deposit a bond on joining the Association, so that travellers can be financially compensated should there be a problem with a holiday. (See also *ABTA bond*.)

bonus: a regular or one-off payment to an employee in appreciation of hard work and effort, or in relation to the completion of a specific project or campaign. *Overseas representatives* may be paid a bonus by their *tour operator* at the end of the season, hotel workers sometimes receive a bonus at Christmas and a manager of a major *tourist attraction* may be paid a bonus at the end of an exceptionally successful year.

book-a-bed-ahead (BABA): a booking service offered by *tourist information centres (TICs)* in the UK, whose staff will make a reservation in a hotel or other type of accommodation through another TIC anywhere in the country, in return for a small fee or *commission* (normally 10 per cent).

Boston Box: see *Boston Consulting Group matrix*

Boston Consulting Group (BCG) matrix: a model that can be used by *marketing* managers to analyse their likely *strategies* for future survival and expansion. Developed in the early 1960s in the USA, and sometimes also referred to as the Boston Box or the Boston Matrix, the BCG is a type of *portfolio analysis* that allows an organisation to judge how its current products and services are performing and what changes, if any, need to be made to its *product portfolio* to ensure future success.

The figure overleaf shows that the matrix compares the rate of market growth of particular products with their relative share of the market. 'Stars' are those products and services that enjoy a high market growth rate and a high *market share*, while at the other end of the spectrum, 'dogs' have both a low market growth rate and a low share of the market. In between are the *'cash cows'*, products that have a high share of a stable market, and 'question marks', where the rate of growth is high but market share is low.

Boston Matrix: see *Boston Consulting Group matrix*

BR: see *British Rail*

BRA: see *British Resorts Association*

BRAD: see *British Rate and Data*

brainstorming is a way for members of a group to solve problems or develop new ideas by saying the first things that come into their heads. This spontaneous action sometimes leads to innovative ideas and solutions, which standard *management* decision-making practices may miss. Having 'brainstormed' a list of ideas, the group

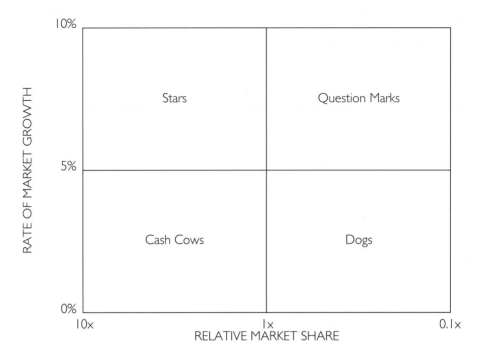

Boston Consulting Group matrix

members can then consider each in detail and make further recommendations for action.

brand: an identifiable product or service name or *image* offered by a company, e.g. Harvester, Reebok or Avis.

brand awareness is the extent to which a customer recognises one particular *brand* over another, e.g. the fact that a customer is aware of the difference between *British Airways'* First Class service and Virgin Atlantic's Upper Class service. Brand awareness is measured through *surveys* and other *market research* techniques and can lead to alterations in the way that products and services are promoted.

brand leader: the product or service that has the greatest volume of sales in its particular product category. Eurocamp, for example, is the brand leader in self-drive camping holidays to the Continent, since it sells more of this type of holiday than any other operator. In order to remain the brand leader, an organisation must hold onto its *market share.*

brand loyalty is shown when *customers* continue to purchase a particular product or service on a regular basis. A couple, for example, may book their annual holiday with the same *tour operator* every year, or choose the same car hire firm for business trips. Encouraging brand loyalty makes very good business sense, since research in the USA has shown that it takes five times as much effort, time and money to attract a new customer than it does to keep an existing customer. Companies may offer incentives to existing customers to develop their brand loyalty, e.g. airline *frequent flyer programmes.*

branding is the practice of giving a product or service a distinctive name or logo, in the hope that it will become easily identifiable from its competitors and take on a certain identity. Branding is linked to the concept of *market segmentation*, with *brands* being developed to meet the needs of different segments of the market. Common brand names used in leisure and tourism include Harvester, Avis, Reebok, Holiday Inn, Forte and Slazenger, to name but a few. Organisations hope that customers will show *brand loyalty*, by buying their particular products above all others.

break-even denotes the point at which an organisation's sales generate just enough *revenue* to cover *fixed* and *variable costs*, with no *profit* nor any loss. The break-even point is often shown on a break-even chart, as follows:

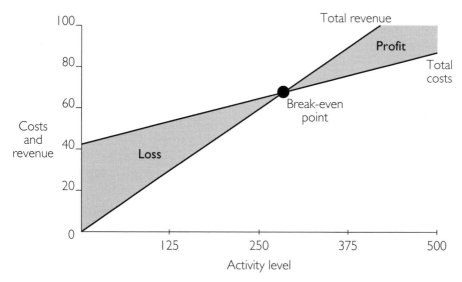

Break-even chart

break-even load factor is a measure of the number of seats that need to be sold on an airline flight, as a proportion of total seats available, before all operating, *marketing* and administrative costs are covered. It is not uncommon on charter flights for the break-even factor to be set as high as 90-95 per cent, so as to bring down the actual cost per seat to a level which will encourage people to buy. It is only when the break-even load figure has been reached that the airline will begin to make a profit on the flight.

bridleway: a *public right of way* suitable for use by horse riders, walkers and cyclists, but not by vehicles.

briefing: a meeting at which an individual or group of people are given information prior to taking part in an *event* or attending a meeting. A briefing session will not only convey factual information, but may also advise which course of action to take in particular circumstances, e.g. an emergency at an outdoor event. (See also *debriefing*.)

Britain consists of England, Wales and Scotland and is sometimes more fully described as Great Britain. Islands around Britain that are part of the *United Kingdom* include the Orkneys, Shetlands, Isles of Scilly, Anglesey and the Isle of Wight. The Isle of Man and Channel Islands have their own administrations.

Britain in Bloom is an annual environmental enhancement competition co-ordinated by the *Tidy Britain Group*. The scheme is divided into a number of different categories depending on the population size of a city, town or rural area.

British Activity Holiday Association (BAHA) was formed by a number of *outdoor activity centre* operators in 1986, with the express intention of establishing operating guidelines for the safe and efficient management of activity centres. Since that time, BAHA has developed a *code of practice* for members, activity guidelines and an inspection scheme. The Association has also contributed to the debate on safety at outdoor activity centres generally and is a member of the *Activity Centre Advisory Committee (ACAC)*. Members of BAHA include PGL Adventure Holidays, Holiday Club Pontin's and Millfield Village of Education.

British Airports Authority (BAA) is a former government-controlled organisation that was privatised in 1987. Now a *public limited company (PLC)*, BAA owns and operates seven UK airports – Heathrow, Gatwick, Stansted, Glasgow, Edinburgh, Aberdeen and Southampton. Together, these airports handle 71 per cent of UK air passenger traffic and 81 per cent of air cargo in the UK, with Heathrow alone handling some 52 million passengers per year using more than 200 scheduled routes, confirming its status as the world's busiest international airport. BAA also manages the commercial facilities at its airports, including shops, restaurants, bars, bureaux de change and car parks. BAA is campaigning hard to ensure the construction of a fifth terminal at Heathrow, to increase the airport's capacity by a further 30 million passengers a year.

British Airways (BA) is the world's leading international passenger airline with a scheduled network covering some 169 destinations in 80 countries. The company had a turnover in 1994–95 of nearly £7.2 billion, employed more than 53 000 staff and carried more than 35 million passengers. In seeking to achieve its mission of being 'the best and most successful company in the airline industry', BA has embarked upon a major *globalisation* programme, which it calls its Global Alliance. As part of this Alliance, BA has negotiated agreements with a number of major airlines, including USAir and Qantas, giving a total coverage of 492 scheduled destinations in 99 countries across the world's major markets, offering an average of 7 000 departures every day.

British Association of Conference Towns (BACT) is a professional association representing all the major, and many of the smaller, conference *destinations* in the British Isles. Founded in 1969, BACT now represents more than 100 local authorities and convention bureaux in Britain, Northern Ireland, the Isle of Man and Channel Islands. BACT's primary objective is to promote the British Isles as a destination for conferences, exhibitions and *incentive travel*. The Association also organises *CONFER*, an exhibition currently held annually in London.

British Association of Tourism Officers (BATO) is a network of *tourism* professionals based in the *UK*, whose main common purpose is to come together and share best practice in the tourism industry, discuss topical issues and matters of concern, develop new ideas and act as an advisory organisation to government and other agencies. Most members of BATO, which is a member of the European Union of Tourist Officers, work in local authority tourism departments and other *public sector* bodies. BATO is to be dissolved in 1996 and replaced by the new Tourism Management Institute.

British Film Institute (BFI): an independent organisation that aims to encourage the development of the art of film in Great Britain and Northern Ireland, and to promote its use as a record of contemporary life. Established in 1933, the BFI also seeks to encourage the best use of *television* in the UK and to foster the study and appreciation of films for television and television programmes generally.

British Holiday and Home Parks Association: the nationally recognised representative body of the parks industry, including park homes, caravan holiday homes, chalets, touring caravans, tents and all forms of park *self-catering accommodation.* The Association works for the benefit of park owners and managers, servicing and representing their interests and promoting the *image* of the industry as a whole. It is a strong lobbying organisation, with access to decision makers in Westminster, Whitehall, Brussels, Strasbourg and their local authority offices.

British Home Tourism Survey (BHTS): see *United Kingdom Tourism Survey*

British Hospitality Association (BHA): formerly the British Hotels, Restaurateurs and Caterers' Association, the BHA is an independent organisation established in 1910 to represent the interests of its members and the wider *hospitality industry* in general. The BHA lobbies government and the *European Commission* on matters of specific relevance to the industry, including taxation, proposed domestic legislation, the *Package Travel Directive* and changes to the *Crown Classification Scheme*. BHA acts as a campaigning voice for its members by liaising with the *trade press*, organising mailshots to members and co-ordinating stands at major exhibitions.

British Incoming Tour Operators' Association (BITOA) is an independent membership organisation representing around 100 *incoming tour operators* in the UK. Founded in 1977, BITOA aims to provide a forum for the exchange of information and ideas, to follow an accepted code of conduct and to act as a pressure group in dealing with government and other bodies in the UK with a common interest in tourism matters.

British Isles: refers to the *United Kingdom* and the Republic of Ireland. (See also *Britain.*)

British National Travel Survey (BNTS): an annual survey conducted by the *British Tourist Authority (BTA)* giving details of British residents' holiday habits, including length of stay, most popular *destinations*, types of accommodation used and *seasonality* of trips. BNTS is carried out in November and involves personal interviews with a random sample of adults living in Great Britain. It is concerned only with holiday travel and not with travel for other purposes.

British Olympic Association (BOA): a national, voluntary organisation made up of representatives of the UK governing bodies of the sports included in the *Olympic Games*. Founded in 1905, the BOA aims to encourage, particularly in the young, the ideals of the Olympic movement, to co-ordinate British participation in the Games and to assist the governing bodies in their preparation. The BOA also acts as a forum for consultation on issues related to the Games, including drug abuse and the introduction of new Olympic sports.

British Rail (BR): the public corporation that owns the UK rail network and is responsible for providing passenger and freight services nationwide. Services are operated on a city-to-city and regional basis, the former known as InterCity and the latter Regional Railways. The rail network is about to be privatised, with *franchises* being offered to train-operating companies, while the track itself is managed by a government-funded agency called Railtrack. Under the terms of the proposed privatisation, the different train-operating companies will pay Railtrack for the use of rail networks and stations. The government believes that a *private sector* railway system will offer the travelling public a more efficient service than has hitherto been supplied by the public sector. Opponents of rail privatisation consider that rural and other rail lines that are used infrequently will disappear, since they will not be an attractive investment for the private sector.

British Rate and Data (BRAD) is a monthly publication that contains up-to-date information on *advertising* opportunities in a wide range of *media*, including national and provincial newspapers, magazines, transport advertising, commercial radio and television, billboards and direct mail. BRAD, which is used extensively by *advertising agencies*, lists detailed information on prices, contacts, copy deadlines and circulation figures. Some libraries will hold copies of BRAD, but it is an expensive item.

British Resorts Association (BRA): an independent organisation representing *local authorities, tourist boards* and other organisations with common aims within the UK, Isle of Man and Channel Islands. Formed in 1921, the aim of the Association is to function as a national organisation promoting the mutual interests of all member resorts and tourist regions. Membership is currently in the order of 55 local authorities and 9 tourist boards. BRA provides an information service to members on such matters as European *legislation*, marketing and customer care, and is active in *lobbying* interested parties to highlight the economic importance of tourism.

British Spas Federation (BSF) celebrates its 75th anniversary in 1996. Led originally by the British Medical Association, more recently the work of the BSF has been funded and co-ordinated by its 12 spa town members, with interest from private health resorts. The aim of BSF is to promote British spas as centres for *tourism, leisure* and health, while at the same time increasing the awareness of mineral waters and preserving the historic fabric of the spa towns.

British Sports Association for the Disabled (BSAD) was established in 1961 to provide and encourage *sport* and *recreation* for people with disabilities. With over 50 000 individual members in approximately 550 clubs, schools and associations throughout England, and a further 14 000 members in Wales, Scotland and Northern Ireland, BSAD works in partnership with other organisations, such as the British Paralympic Association, *Sports Council* and *governing bodies* of sport, in order to achieve its aims.

British Standards Institution (BSI): an organisation, funded through government and voluntary subscription, which sets minimum standards for quality and safety of products and services. Organisations are awarded BSI 'kitemarks' for products and services that meet these minimum requirements. In *leisure* and *tourism*, the increasing importance of quality has meant that many organisations have sought *British Standard (BS) 5750*, now more commonly known as *BS EN ISO 9000*.

British tourism: see *UK tourism*

British Tourist Authority (BTA): established under the 1969 *Development of Tourism Act*, the BTA is responsible for promoting *Britain* to *overseas visitors*. Its principal *objectives* are:

- to maximise the benefits of tourism to Britain from abroad, while working in *partnership* with the *private* and *public* sector organisations involved in the industry and the *English Tourist Board, Scottish Tourist Board* and *Wales Tourist Board*
- to identify the requirements of *visitors* to Britain, whatever their origin
- to stimulate the improvement of the quality of tourism *products* on offer
- to spread the economic benefits of tourism to Britain more widely, particularly to areas with tourism potential and higher than average levels of unemployment
- to encourage tourism to Britain in *off-peak* periods
- to make the most cost-effective use of its *resources* in pursuing its *objectives*

In order to meet these objectives, BTA works in close co-operation with *National* and *Regional Tourist Boards, local authorities, media* and the *travel trade.* As well as running the British Travel Centre in London, BTA operates a network of 34 overseas offices and representatives worldwide.

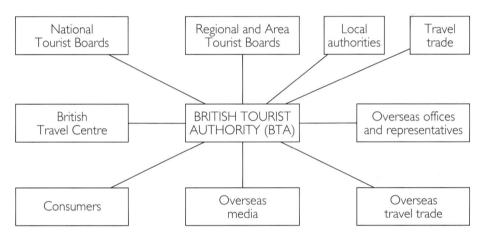

British Tourist Authority (BTA)

British Travel Educational Trust: an educational charity formed in 1970 with the aim of promoting education in *tourism* in its widest context. The Trust provides funding for both international research projects undertaken by individuals and projects related to tourism education undertaken by organisations. Those working in any sector of the *British tourism* industry or holding an academic post at a further or higher education establishment in the UK are eligible to apply for Trust funding.

British Travel Trade Fair (BTTF) is an annual *travel trade* exhibition focusing on *UK tourism* products. It gives the suppliers of a wide range of UK products, including hotels, *destinations,* travel companies and attractions, the chance to meet with potential buyers, who may be conference organisers, coach operators, overseas buyers, tour operators or travel agents. The buyers need up-to-date information on new products on offer and the Fair is a cost-effective way of doing business. BTTF is organised by the *English Tourist Board*, in co-operation with *WTB, STB* and *NITB*.

British Trust for Conservation Volunteers (BTCV): a voluntary body that offers people the chance to take practical steps to improve their environment. It provides advice, training and support to more than 60 000 volunteers each year, working on environmental projects throughout Britain, including repairs to dry stone walls, footpath clearance and beach cleaning. BTCV also operates a programme of more than 600 *conservation* holidays each year, which it calls 'Natural Breaks'.

British Universities Accommodation Consortium (BUAC) was set up in 1971 to promote the residential/non-residential exhibition, catering and meeting facilities available at member universities or university colleges throughout England, Wales, Scotland and Northern Ireland. There are now more than 60 universities in membership and BUAC is entirely funded by membership subscriptions.

British Waterways Board (BWB) is a nationalised industry sponsored by the *Department of Environment.* Often referred to simply as British Waterways, the mission of BWB is the efficient management of the inland waterways system in Britain for the increasing benefit of the nation. The carrying of freight is still important on the 2 000 mile network of canals managed by BWB, but their future lies increasingly in the fields of *leisure* and *recreation,* specifically fishing and cruising. Britain's canal network welcomes more than 7 million visitors each year for informal recreation and nearly 1 million anglers.

Britrail Pass: a rail ticket giving *overseas visitors* to Britain unlimited travel on train services. The ticket is not available in the UK, but must be purchased in the visitors' home country before travelling to Britain. It is aimed mainly at the independent traveller who wishes to explore the lesser-known parts of the country by public transport.

broadcast media: generally refers to *television* (terrestrial, cable and satellite) and commercial radio, but is increasingly being used to include global communications systems such as the *Internet.*

brochure: an essential promotional tool for most leisure, travel and tourism organisations, since they are mainly involved in selling *intangible* products, such as holidays, *short breaks* and coaching sessions. Brochures must be both informative and persuasive, and should follow the *AIDA* principle in their design. A well-designed brochure should aim to convert an enquiry into a sale.

brunch: a meal taken mid-way between breakfast and lunch times. First conceived in the USA, brunches are now commonplace in *hotels* throughout the world, particularly at weekends when many people prefer to get up late in the mornings and so miss normal breakfast serving times.

Brundtland Report: an influential document which resulted from the World Commission on Environment and Development, organised by the *United Nations* in 1987, which focused on the concept of global sustainability and the threats to the world environment. The report, named after the Norwegian Prime Minister who chaired the Commission, defined sustainability as 'meeting the needs of the present without compromising the ability of future generations to meet their own needs'. The report is significant in being the first attempt to address global environmental problems. It has been a significant influence on the development of the concept of *sustainable tourism.* (See also *Earth Summit.*)

BS 5750: see *BS EN ISO 9000*

BS 7750: a BSI Standard that focuses on *environmental management* systems. Following similar processes to *BS 5750*, BS 7750 requires an organisation to document all its systems and measure its environmental performance. The Standard is designed to be equally applicable to service industries, such as leisure and tourism, and manufacturing concerns. Central to certification to BS 7750 is the need to consider the whole organisation, which means that the environmental management systems can be based on many of the principles of *total quality management (TQM)*.

BS EN ISO 9000: a quality standard (also known as BS 5750) that aims to ensure consistently high levels of product and service delivery. Developed initially for manufacturing industry, this British Standard (BS) is now increasingly applied to service industries, including *leisure* and *tourism*. The underlying objective of BS EN ISO 9000 is to make sure that all administrative and management systems are fully documented and audited, leading to high standards of quality at all times. Critics of the Standard argue that it is overly bureaucratic and that simply having well-documented procedures does not necessarily lead to high quality standards.

BSAD: see *British Sports Association for the Disabled*

BSF: see *British Spas Federation*

BSI: see *British Standards Institution*

BTA: see *British Tourist Authority*

BTCV: see *British Trust for Conservation Volunteers*

BTEC: see *Business and Technology Education Council*

BTTF: see *British Travel Trade Fair*

BUAC: see *British Universities Accommodation Consortium*

bucket shop: a non-appointed *travel agency* that specialises in selling discounted air tickets, for both *charter* and *scheduled services*. Commonplace in the 1970s and 1980s, bucket shops were used by major airlines to sell off seats at short notice (a process known as 'dumping'). The role of bucket shops has declined markedly in recent years, particularly since discounted fares are now made available legitimately to *ABTA* and *IATA* appointed agents and specialist brokers.

budget: a forecast of expected income and expenditure over a given period of time. At an organisational level it is an action plan for the coming financial period, which can be used to delegate *responsibility* to departmental managers. In practice, it is likely that a leisure or tourism organisation will have many budget heads, i.e. many products and activities that will attract income and incur costs. Each of these budgets will be consolidated into one master budget for the organisation, which will detail its overall short-term financial plan. The budget is the principal tool for allowing managers to co-ordinate and control the activities of their organisation. Two of the most useful financial control measures are the *sales budget* and the *expenditure budget*. (See also *budgetary control*.)

budgetary control is the process of comparing actual *costs* or expenditure with budgeted figures to identify any *variances*, and taking appropriate action to put matters right. Budgetary control is an essential part of the job of a manager in leisure and tourism. The investigation of any deviations from the budgeted figures is known as *variance analysis*.

Worked example: budgetary control through variance analysis

All figures in £000s

	January			February			March		
	Budg	Act	Var	Budg	Act	Var	Budg	Act	Var
Revenue	85	80	(5)	95	86	(9)	110		
Materials	36	34	2	42	39	3	46		
Fixed costs	42	44	(2)	45	45	–	45		
Profit	7	2	(5)	8	2	(6)	19		

Bus and Coach Council (BCC): see *Confederation of Passenger Transport UK (CPT)*

'bus stop' arrangement: a term used in aviation when an aircraft takes off from one airport and stops at another to pick up passengers, before flying on to its final destination airport. This arrangement is carried out in order to maximise capacity on the aircraft and may be preferable to *consolidation*, which would involve one set of passengers travelling by road to meet their flight at another airport.

Business and Technology Education Council (BTEC): an independent, self-financing awarding body, which aims to promote and develop high quality vocational education and training programmes, to prepare people for the world of work and for progression to higher study. Accountable to the *Department for Education and Employment (DFEE)*, BTEC is a major partner in the development of *National Vocational Qualifications (NVQs)* and *General National Vocational Qualifications (GNVQs)*.

business environment: a general term used to denote the local, regional, national and international world in which an organisation functions and the factors that will have some bearing on its operation. The business environment is often divided into those internal influences over which an organisation has some degree of control (the *micro environment*) and those that form part of the wider world and which are normally outside of its control (the *macro environment*).

business house agency: a *travel agency* that specialises in providing a range of services for business clients, including airline tickets, *visas* and currency requirements.

Business in Sport and Leisure (BISL) was established in 1991 with the aim of *lobbying* for changes to the *fiscal* and *statutory* climate for sporting and leisure developments in the UK. It is an independent umbrella organisation, representing more than 50 private sector companies in *sport* and *leisure* and acts as a forum for the exchange of information between members.

business objectives are the commercial aims that an organisation sets itself, as opposed to any *social objectives* it may be seeking to achieve. They will relate to *profitability*, *sales revenue*, *market share*, etc., and will be the basis on which the organisation's overall *strategy* and *business plans* are developed.

business plan: a document that sets out the future financial and operational aspects of a current or proposed venture. Business plans are commonly prepared by new businesses seeking external funding and support, as a way of convincing external agencies, such as banks, planning authorities and potential sponsors, that a project is viable. Large organisations will prepare overall business plans, plus plans for different departments within the organisation. A business plan should include detailed information about:

- the *objectives* of the venture
- financial costs and revenues
- market *demand*
- legal aspects
- *management* expertise

While an organisation's *strategic planning* process will give a blueprint of its overall aims, business plans should be seen as short- to medium-term working documents, reviewed on an annual basis and constantly monitored.

business tourism is the category of the *travel and tourism industry* concerned with travel for business purposes, rather than travel for leisure purposes (*leisure tourism*). Business tourism includes travel for meetings, exhibitions, trade fairs, conferences, conventions and *incentive travel*. Business tourism is an increasingly important sector of the industry since it is often high value, earning hoteliers, carriers and caterers significant revenue. The *Gulf War* had a major impact on international business travel, with many countries only just returning to their former market positions. Some travel agents specialise in dealing with business travel and are known as *business house agents*.

Butlin: the name of the world's pioneer of *holiday camps*. The first holiday camp was opened in Skegness in 1936 by Billy Butlin. Butlin's camps soon spread across the country, working on the principle that if the children were happy, their parents would be as well. Today, Butlin's holiday centres (known as Butlin's Holiday Worlds) attract around 500 000 holidaymakers every year, in accommodation that has been updated to meet current demands. Butlin's, now part of the *Rank Organisation*, also operates hotels and is the leading contractor of star entertainers in the UK.

BWB: see *British Waterways Board*

by-laws are local regulations implemented by *district* and *county councils*, covering the proper use of *public open spaces*, footpaths and recreation grounds.

C

CAA: see *Civil Aviation Authority*

CAB: see *Citizens' Advice Bureau*

cabotage refers to airline and shipping routes within a country's national territory, e.g. flights between London and Glasgow, and even London and Gibraltar. Such routes are not subject to international agreements on fares, making residents of the country eligible for reduced rate tariffs, sometimes called cabotage fares. It is intended that when full *airline deregulation* occurs in the *European Union (EU)*, the routes between member states will be considered cabotage routes.

Cadw is a department of the Welsh Office responsible for the protection, *conservation* and appreciation of the built *heritage* in Wales. Created in 1984, Cadw performs similar functions in Wales to those undertaken by *English Heritage* in England. Its duties include *planning* responsibilities for ancient monuments and historic buildings, grant-aiding their repair and managing 131 ancient monuments in Wales, including Chepstow Castle, Tintern Abbey and Conwy Castle.

Camelot: the company chosen by *OFLOT* to operate the *National Lottery*, from a final short list of eight applicants. Camelot Group PLC is a consortium of the following companies: Cadbury Schweppes, De La Rue, G Tech, Racal and ICL.

campaign has two meanings in *leisure* and *tourism*. The first is concerned with *advertising* and *promotion*, and is a planned activity aimed at increasing sales of products and services, e.g. an advertising campaign tied in with a major sporting event. The second is an activity undertaken by a pressure group to highlight an issue or stop a planned development, e.g. the campaign to halt the extension of the M3 motorway at Twyford Down in Hampshire.

Campaign for the Protection of Rural Wales (CPRW) is a national charity founded in 1928 as the Council for the Protection of Rural Wales. Today it organises concerted action to protect the beauty of the coast and countryside in Wales. CPRW has branches throughout Wales, whose aim is to protect the local environment while encouraging sustainable rural development. Funded by members' subscriptions and supporters' donations, CPRW is a source of information and guidance on *conservation* issues in Wales to politicians, the *media* and rural bodies.

capital: the funds invested in a business in order to acquire the *assets* which it needs to be able to trade. The principal sources of capital are *shareholders* and lenders (*loan capital*).

capital allowance: the proportion of the cost of *fixed assets* that can be charged to profit each year, thereby reducing a company's tax liability, e.g. a company vehicle costing £5 000 may be eligible for a 25 per cent capital allowance per year, resulting in the business being able to offset £1 250 against its taxable income.

capital expenditure represents expenditure on the acquisition or improvement of *fixed assets*, such as buildings, machinery and plant.

capital gearing: see *gearing*

car ownership has risen dramatically since the end of the Second World War. There were 2.3 million cars on the roads in 1950, 11 million in 1970 and around 21 million in 1995. The private car is the predominant mode of travel for tourists in Britain, whether UK residents or *overseas visitors*. The car accounted for 76 per cent of all holiday trips in 1993. The growth in car use is putting severe strain on Britain's main tourist areas, including the *National Parks*, historic cities and *seaside resorts*.

Caravan Club: founded in 1907, the Caravan Club represents the interests of over 285 000 members in the UK. It operates the largest private network of sites in the British Isles, with 200 Club sites and over 3 000 *Certificated Locations (CLs)*. The Club offers a comprehensive range of services to its members, including a travel and insurance service, and places environmental and safety issues to the fore in its work.

caravanning is a popular type of *self-catering* holiday, accounting for a quarter of all *accommodation* used on main holidays in Britain by British people in 1994. Caravan holidays either use towed vehicles or take place in static vans on holiday parks.

careers in leisure and tourism offer a variety of benefits, including job satisfaction to those who like helping other people make the best use of their *leisure time*, opportunities for travel at home and abroad, excellent prospects for promotion and scope for initiative, flair and imagination. In return, the industries look for staff who like working with people, who are not afraid of hard work (when most people are 'at leisure'), who are prepared to learn quickly, who present themselves well and who can take on *responsibility*, often at a young age. (See also *employment in leisure and tourism*.)

- Hotel management
- Sports coaching
- Casino/betting shop management
- Sports administration
- Contract catering
- Event management
- Teaching/lecturing
- Airlines and airports
- Tour operators
- Tourist attractions
- Coach operators
- Tourist information centres
- Ferry and cruise companies
- Arts administration
- Pub or restaurant management
- Countryside management
- Outdoor pursuits
- Conference planning
- Leisure centre management
- Sportsman/woman
- Travel agencies
- Local authority tourism departments
- Hotels and other accommodation
- Car hire companies
- Guiding
- Training

The wide range of possible careers in leisure and tourism

carnet: a French term describing an official document that allows the temporary importation of goods into a foreign country, without the payment of any levies or duties. This could be related to a vehicle, promotional items of no commercial value or *duty-free* goods.

carrier: the term used in the *travel and tourism industry* to denote any individual or *company* that offers transportation services for passengers or goods. Airlines, car hire companies, coach operators, taxi firms, railway operators and ferry companies all fall within the category of 'carrier'.

carrying capacity: the maximum number of people that a resort, site or other area can sustain, before there is a reduction in the quality of the visitor experience or adverse effects on either the physical environment or the *host community*. The concept is at the heart of the debate surrounding *sustainable tourism*. It is a difficult concept to put into practice, because people will have different threshold levels above or below which the quality of their experience will suffer. Carrying capacity is sometimes divided into distinct types:

- physical capacity – the most straightforward type indicated, for example, by a finite number of bedspaces or car parking spaces
- psychological or perceptual capacity – relates to a decline in the quality of the visitors' experience
- biological capacity – concerns environmental damage to flora and fauna
- social capacity – relates to adverse pressures on the host community

cartel: an arrangement whereby a number of providers of goods and services agree to either regulate supply or fix prices in order to maintain their *profitability*. An example in the *travel and tourism industry* would be two ferry companies operating on the same route both agreeing to keep their prices artificially high, rather than getting involved in a price war. A cartel is a form of restrictive practice that is outlawed in most countries, since it is considered to be against the public interest.

cascading is the process of disseminating information and ideas within an organisation down the hierarchy. Often associated with staff development and *training*, cascading is a cost-effective way of informing a large number of people from a small initial base. An example of cascading would be a senior manager in a leisure or tourism organisation attending a training course on new *computer* systems, and running a session for other managers within the organisation on his or her return. They in turn would brief their staff, thereby informing more employees until the whole organisation is made aware of the details.

'cash cow': a product or service that enjoys a high relative share of a market that is either static or declining. The 'cash cow' generates surplus cash that can be invested in other areas to help other products and services grow. Organisations will try to maximise the prices of their 'cash cows', while keeping expenditure to a minimum. The term is used in *portfolio analysis*, in particular the *Boston Consulting Group matrix*.

cash-flow is the money coming into a business from sales receipts and other *revenue* sources, and going out of the business in the form of fixed and variable costs, such as payments to suppliers, employees and interest charges.

cash-flow forecast: an estimate of the expected future cash inflows and outflows of an organisation, usually presented on a monthly basis. Banks and other lenders will expect to see a cash-flow forecast before granting a *loan* or extending an organisation's *overdraft* facility.

cash-flow statement: a statement of the flow of funds into and out of a business for a given period of time, usually twelve months. An organisation's cash-flow statement provides a link between its *profit and loss account* and its *balance sheet*. It forms part of the audited accounts and shows the funds that have entered a company, how they have been used and how any net surplus or deficit in short- and long-term funds has been applied.

	October (£000's)	November (£000's)	December (£000's)
Cash at start	52	62	72
Total cash inflows	180	160	140
Total cash outflows	170	150	170
Net cash-flow	+10	+10	−30
Cumulative cash	62	72	42

Quarterly cash-flow forecast

Castlefield Urban Heritage Park was developed in the Castlefield region of Manchester to contribute to the area's economic regeneration programme. The Park has two key attractions, the Museum of Science and Industry and Granada Studios, plus a range of smaller attractions. The Park is a good example of a private and public sector *partnership* aimed at improving the standards of *management* of the area and improving visitor facilities and services. The Park operators stage an extensive programme of *events* throughout the year.

catchment area: the geographical limit from within which a leisure or tourism facility draws its customers. The size of the catchment area will depend on a number of factors, such as the availability and quality of transport links, the uniqueness of the facility and the population density of the area. The use of *market research* data will enable a facility to estimate the total size of a *target market* in its catchment area.

catering: the sector of *leisure* and *tourism* that is concerned with the preparation, distribution and serving of food. It includes cafés, *fast-food outlets*, restaurants, motorway service areas, pubs, school meals and contract catering services. (See also *hospitality*.)

CBA: see *cost-benefit analysis*

CBI: see *Confederation of British Industry*

CCPR: see *Central Council of Physical Recreation*

CCT: see *compulsory competitive tendering*

CCTV: see *closed-circuit television*

CCW: see *Countryside Council for Wales*

CD-ROM stands for compact disk read-only memory. It is a method of information storage and retrieval using a *personal computer (PC)* with the appropriate hardware and software. Increasingly, *secondary research* information, including newspapers, directories, encyclopaedias and *databases* are being made available on CD-ROM. Computers installed with a CD-ROM drive can accept advanced software with sound and video effects superior to normal *floppy disk software*.

CDW: see *collision damage waiver*

CEI: see *Centre for Environmental Interpretation*

census: a survey in which data about every individual in a 'population' is recorded, as distinct from *sampling*, when only a proportion is surveyed. In the UK, the Census of Population is carried out every ten years by the *Office of Population Censuses and Surveys (OPCS)*, the most recent having been undertaken in 1991. It provides useful data for leisure and tourism organisations on such matters as the economic and social characteristics of the population, e.g. levels of car ownership, number of one-parent families, etc.

Center Parcs is a company, owned by Scottish & Newcastle brewery, with its origins dating back to the late 1960s in the Netherlands, when the idea of 'a villa in a forest' was born. The Center Parcs concept revolves around providing a relaxing, high quality, natural holiday environment, where city dwellers can escape from the pressures of everyday life. The company now operates three sites in the UK, near Nottingham, Cambridge and at Longleat in Wiltshire, all of which have covered leisure pools and *self-catering accommodation* in woodland settings.

Central Council of Physical Recreation (CCPR) was founded in 1935 with two particular objectives:

- to encourage as many people as possible to participate in all forms of *sport* and *recreation*
- to provide the separate *governing bodies* of the individual sports with a central organisation that would represent and promote their interests

CCPR claims to be 'the voice of sport', since it is the only organisation that speaks for the interests of some 20 million British sportsmen and women. It is a non-governmental voluntary organisation, which is largely self-financing and whose officers and executive committee are elected by the membership as a whole. At present, the membership of the CCPR consists of 65 English and 199 British sporting organisations, including the Football Association, the Royal Yachting Association and the Institute of Swimming Teachers and Coaches, to name but a few.

The CCPR also provides a number of services for its member bodies, including a press service, help with *sponsorship*, legal advice and assistance with fund-raising. In 1982, the CCPR launched the *Community Sports Leaders Award* to harness greater community involvement in sport.

central reservation system: a centralised booking facility used by leisure and tourism companies to offer an efficient service to the *customer*, while at the same time minimising its costs. Examples include central reservation systems operated by hotel chains, *tour operators* and airlines. Such systems are usually computerised, so as to be able to offer greater flexibility of choice to the customer and provide links with other network systems. (See also *computerised reservation systems*.)

centralised structures: *organisational structures* in which power and decision making rest with a small number of senior managers. Organisations with a *'steep' pyramid* structure are often run on very centralised lines, with many tiers of management, often powerless to make decisions on a day-to-day basis. Centralised structures can lead to a demoralised workforce and a senior management team that is out of touch with its staff. They are also criticised for being too bureaucratic. Advocates of centralised structures argue that they have the advantage of promoting a clear *corporate identity* for an organisation and facilitate the implementation of common policies across very large enterprises. (See also *decentralisation*.)

Centre for Alternative Technology (CAT): an environmentally based *tourist attraction* in Wales, which is, unusually, a *public limited company (PLC)*. It decided to change its status and issure shares to the public to finance a capital building programme.

Centre for Environmental Interpretation (CEI): a non-profit making organisation set up in 1980 by the Carnegie UK Trust as a national centre for environmental and *heritage interpretation*. With offices in Manchester and Edinburgh, CEI has the largest UK collection of published and unpublished material on the subject of interpretation. CEI staff run a series of short courses on the subject throughout the UK and provide in-house training for a range of agencies including the *National Trust, Groundwork Trusts* and *local authorities*.

Certificate of Travel Agency Competence (COTAC): an examination-based qualification for those working, or seeking employment, in the *travel industry*. Awarded by City and Guilds, COTAC was replaced in 1994 by the *ABTA Travel Agents Certificate (ABTAC)*, bringing the qualification more in line with *National Vocational Qualifications (NVQs)*.

Certificated Location (CL): a network of more than 3 000 caravan sites in Britain, licensed by the *Caravan Club*. CLs originated when the Caravan Club was granted exemption under the 1960 Caravan Sites and Control of Development Act, which allowed the Club to grant certificates to landowners to provide these small, informal sites for not more than five vans at any one time. Found mostly on farms, CLs offer users a range of basic facilities and an opportunity to 'get away from it all'.

certified cheque: see *banker's draft*

chain of command: the declared lines of *authority* within an organisation through which *communication* takes place and decisions are conveyed. In large private sector organisations with a *hierarchical* structure, the chain of command begins at the top with the *directors*, through senior managers and middle managers, to the employees.

chair: see *chairman*

chair of board: see *chairman*

chairman: an individual who takes on the role of chairing the meetings of an organisation. The chairman of a *company* will have a much wider role than simply chairing meetings of the board of directors. He or she may also take responsibility for developing the *mission* and *policies* that the company will follow, in conjunction with other directors and senior staff. In many leisure and tourism organisations, the chairman, sometimes known simply as the chair or chair of board, becomes the public face of the organisation, e.g. Richard Branson of Virgin and Colin Marshall of *British Airways*.

Champion Coaching is a *National Coaching Foundation (NCF)* government-funded initiative which aims to deliver quality coaching to children between the ages of 11 and 14 who show an above average level of ability in a particular *sport* or sports. The mission of Champion Coaching is to 'promote quality-assured youth sport coaching for performance-motivated children within a co-ordinated community structure'. Begun originally in 1991/92 as a pilot study, the initiative has spread to some 44 different regions and covers a wide range of sports, including volleyball, cricket, tennis and hockey. The children recruited onto the scheme are nominated by their school's PE teacher and attend for a period of six weeks, normally in out-of-school hours. As well as developing a range of useful skills, they are given the chance of gaining various coaching awards.

change management is the process of anticipating, investigating, *planning* and managing enforced or unenforced changes to any of an organisation's *resources* and operating mechanisms. Managing change is a constant process in the dynamic leisure and tourism industries, where customers' needs and expectations alter constantly, and competitive pressures force companies to adopt new working practices and management styles. People are inherently resistant to change, making change management a process that must be undertaken with a very sensitive touch. Factors in an organisation's *internal* and *external environment* will combine to trigger change on a regular basis in virtually all leisure and tourism organisations.

Channel Tunnel: one of the biggest civil engineering projects of the century, opened to passenger and freight traffic in 1994. Built by *Eurotunnel,* a joint English-French consortium of construction companies, the Tunnel offers a rail passenger service, known as *Eurostar,* linking London Waterloo with Paris, Brussels and other major European cities. The Tunnel also operates a passenger- and vehicle-carrying facility, called *le Shuttle,* where cars, coaches and lorries are loaded onto shuttle trains running every 15 minutes at peak times. Although a tremendous engineering achievement, the Channel Tunnel is facing serious financial problems, and must capture a greater share of the market for cross-Channel travel if it is to prosper.

charge cards allow payment by plastic card on *credit* in place of cash, but, unlike *credit cards,* they offer no extended credit facility, i.e. accounts must be settled in full each month. Their use in leisure and tourism facilities is mainly for business and corporate customers. Diners Club and *American Express* are two of the best known charge cards, accepted across the world.

charter flight: an aircraft commissioned for a set period of time, flying to a particular destination and able to offer reduced fares by setting high *load factors.* Most *package holidays* that include air travel will use charter flights (known as *inclusive tours by charter*). (See also *scheduled air services.*)

Charter Mark: an award scheme set up by the government to reward excellence in public services, including *leisure* and *recreation,* under the *Citizens' Charter* initiative. Applicants have to demonstrate to the satisfaction of the Prime Minister's Advisory Panel on the Charter that they have achieved measurable improvements in the quality of their service over the previous two years, and that their customers are satisfied with their services. Winners of a Charter Mark keep it for three years and can gain useful publicity for their organisation.

Chartered Institute of Marketing (CIM) was founded in 1911 and is the leading organisation for *marketing* and sales professionals in Europe, with over 50 000 members and registered students worldwide. Awarded a Royal Charter in 1989, the principal aim of CIM is to establish marketing as a universally recognised, understood and accepted profession, reflecting the levels of quality, standards and principles expected of a chartered body. It has more than 40 industry groups, including CIMTIG, the *Chartered Institute of Marketing Travel Industry Group.*

Chartered Institute of Marketing Travel Industry Group (CIMTIG) is one of 40 sector groups belonging to the *Chartered Institute of Marketing (CIM).* Made up of CIM members working in *public* and *private sector travel* and *tourism,* CIMTIG holds regular meetings for members and non-members on issues relating to sales and marketing in the industry.

Chartered Institute of Public Finance and Accountancy (CIPFA) is a professional body representing accountants and financial administrators working in the public sector. Every year CIPFA publishes comparative data on the operating costs of *public sector leisure* service departments and leisure facilities across the country.

check-in is the procedure of registering a guest at a *hotel* or other *accommodation* establishment on his or her arrival. Check-in can also mean the process of completing the necessary formalities before travelling on an airline, some forms of rail travel (e.g. *Eurostar*), boarding a ferry or cruise ship, or picking up a hire car.

check-out: the procedure for guests vacating their rooms, paying their bills and leaving a hotel or other *accommodation* establishment. Some hotels offer a fast check-out facility, particularly suited to the needs of business travellers wishing to depart early in the morning.

cheque: a method of payment without the use of cash, used by both individuals and businesses. Cheques are a relatively convenient way of paying for goods and services, backed up by a *cheque guarantee card*. The use of *debit cards*, such as Switch and Delta, is having a considerable impact on the number of cheques issued.

cheque guarantee card: a card used in conjunction with a *cheque* to guarantee that the amount written on the cheque, assuming it is less than the face value of the card, will be paid by the bank or building society which issued the card. Most cards honour cheques up to the value of £50, but it is becoming increasingly common to find £100 cheque guarantee cards. Staff should only accept cheques that are accompanied by a current card, with the same signature as on the accompanying cheque.

Chicago Convention on Civil Aviation: an international symposium held in 1944 which agreed the five *freedoms of the air* and established the *International Civil Aviation Organisation (ICAO)*. (See also *Bermuda Agreement*.)

CIM: see *Chartered Institute of Marketing*

CIMTIG: see *Chartered Institute of Marketing Travel Industry Group*

cinema attendances have been rising since 1985, with 62 per cent of all those aged seven and over claiming to have visited a cinema in 1992. The Cinema Advertising Association estimates that there were 103 million visits to the cinema in 1992, which rose to an estimated 110 million in 1993, the highest for 14 years. These figures have to be viewed in the context of a long-term downward trend in visits since 1960. For example, the number of visits made to UK cinemas in 1992 represented only 8 per cent of the visits made in 1956. The recent growth in audiences has coincided with the introduction of *multiplex* cinemas, some containing up to 14 screens of entertainment.

CIPFA: see *Chartered Institute of Public Finance and Accountancy*

circulation: the number of copies of a newspaper or magazine distributed by its publishers. Advertisers need to know circulation figures when devising *advertising campaigns*, as well as the socio-economic profile of the readers, in order to target customers most effectively. It is generally the case that the larger the circulation of a newspaper the more expensive its costs of advertising. In Britain currently, the highest daily circulation is held by the Sun, while the most popular Sunday newspaper is the News of the World. The Readers' Digest has the highest circulation of any magazine with net sales of 1.6 million copies. Details of circulation figures can be found in *BRAD* *(British Rate and Data)*.

Citizens' Advice Bureau (CAB): a voluntary organisation that operates a chain of centres throughout the country offering free advice on a range of matters including legal disputes, financial problems and housing issues. People who have had problems with products and services, for example faulty sports goods or *holidays* that have gone wrong, sometimes visit a CAB to find out how to complain and investigate their consumer rights.

Citizens' Charter: a scheme launched by the government in 1991 with the aim of raising the standard of public services and making them more responsive to the needs of consumers. To date, 40 separate Charters have been published covering a wide range of public services, including *British Rail*, the NHS and the Parents' Charter. Although successful in some areas, critics of the scheme consider it to be more of a public relations exercise than a genuine attempt to raise standards. (See also *Charter Mark*.)

City Challenge: a competition operated by the *Department of the Environment (DoE)* to stimulate investment in *urban regeneration* projects in England. Cities are encouraged to develop projects, which often include leisure and tourism facilities, and to bid on a competitive basis for City Challenge funds.

city farm: a facility that allows people living in towns and cities to have first-hand experience of looking after animals and learning about nature. Schools will often use the city farm as a learning resource.

Civic Trust: a charitable organisation that aims to improve and regenerate the environment where people live and work, particularly in urban areas, and to promote high standards of *planning*, design and *conservation*. With the help of a network of local groups, the Trust makes annual awards for appropriate development of all kinds.

Civil Aviation Authority (CAA) has been serving the needs of UK air travellers since it was established under the Civil Aviation Act of 1971. It is both a public service enterprise and a regulatory body, whose responsibilities include:

- air safety – air worthiness and operational safety
- air traffic control and telecommunications
- economic regulation – including air transport licensing and *Air Travel Organisers' Licences (ATOLs)*
- advice to government on civil aviation matters
- consumer interests in relation to civil aviation

The CAA in the 1990s is a business with a turnover of £500 million a year, employing some 7 600 people at over 100 locations throughout the UK. It is financed by the users of its services and does not receive any subsidy from the government.

CL: see *Certificated Location*

class: see *social class*

classified advertisement: an announcement in the *trade* or *consumer press* usually charged on a per line or per word basis. It is a relatively cheap form of *advertising*, since, unlike *display advertisements*, no pictures or headlines are included. Many smaller leisure and tourism companies advertise their services in the classified advertisements of newspapers and magazines.

> **Majorca:** self-catering villa close to Arenal. Sleeps 6. Available July–Oct. From £320 per wk. Tel. 0171 682 6225
>
> **Majorca:** cheap flights and villas. Call (0162) 71835
>
> **Menorca:** luxury villas and apartments. From £450 inc. pools and maid service. Menorca Alive. Tel. 0182 68665

Classified advertising for holidays abroad

climate plays a crucial role in how people use their *leisure time*. British people will often travel thousands of miles to escape the cool temperate climate, in favour of 'guaranteed' sunshine. Within Britain itself, there are marked differences in climate, with the west and south generally experiencing warmer summers and less severe winters than the north. This is due in part to the warming effects of the Gulf Stream, a mild air current that originates in the Gulf of Mexico and reaches the west of Britain on our prevailing westerly winds.

closed-circuit television (CCTV) has a number of uses in leisure and tourism, including helping organisations improve the security of their buildings, equipment and staff. CCTV is also a useful management tool, particularly in large leisure and tourism facilities, where it can be used to observe visitor and traffic flows, e.g. in a *theme park* or large outdoor event. It is also useful for staff training sessions, for example *interviewing* and *interpersonal skills* training.

closed question: one that invites a specific reply, often negative, from within a small selection of responses, rather than allowing a respondent to give an expanded reply, as is the case with an *open question*. Examples of closed questions are 'can I help you?' and 'can I get a brochure for you?', both of which invite the reply yes or no. In a sales situation, the use of closed questions makes it difficult to establish rapport with the customer. Closed questions are, however, useful for *questionnaire* surveys, since they can speed up the analysis stage of the survey.

'closed shop': an arrangement in the workplace whereby employees must join a trade union when taking up their post. The Employment Acts of 1980, 1982, 1988 and 1990, plus other related employment legislation, contained clauses to outlaw the 'closed shop' arrangement, which was considered to be undemocratic.

closing a sale is a selling technique used to persuade a *customer* to make a commitment to purchase a particular product or service. It is a key stage in the *sales process*, when staff should be looking for buying signals from the customer to trigger the process of closing the sale. Statements from the customer such as 'that sounds fine' or 'yes I like that', clearly indicate a desire to purchase. When such signals are evident, the member of staff should begin to finalise the deal, perhaps by taking a customer's money, cheque or credit card details. Sales staff should always remember, however, that customers should never be forced into a sale that they may later regret. Closing the sale is all about helping a customer move from 'I'd like' to 'I'll buy'.

coach travel is a relatively cheap form of transportation, favoured by students and young people, and senior citizens. Young people use the scheduled services operated by companies such as *National Express*, while older people use these services, but also go on organised coach holidays to scenic parts of Britain, including the Lake District, Snowdonia and the Highlands of Scotland, organised by companies such as Shearings and Frames Rickards.

code of conduct: a set of guidelines that an industry association or regulatory body devises, laying down minimum standards within which its members will operate, or face sanctions if they transgress. In leisure and tourism, the *Association of British Travel Agents (ABTA)* operates codes of conduct for both travel agency and tour operator members, governing their relationship with the paying customer. The *Office of Fair Trading (OFT)* advises industry organisations on the content and implementation of codes of conduct.

code of practice: see *code of conduct*

collateral is the American term for the *security* that is usually required before a *loan* can be made by a financial institution.

collision damage waiver (CDW): an extra *insurance* payment made by a person hiring a motor vehicle, in order to exempt the hirer from further costs in the event of an accident resulting in damage to the vehicle.

commercial mortgage: a long-term *loan* from a bank or building society for the purchase of land and buildings, which are used as *security* in case the lender defaults on the agreement. A leisure or tourism organisation may take out a commercial mortgage for the purchase or extension of retail premises, a sports facility or other business premises.

commission is a payment made to an agent for selling the products and services of a *principal*, e.g. a *travel agent* is paid a commission for selling a tour operator's package holidays. The commission is usually an agreed percentage of the selling price, which may be increased for higher sales levels (*override commission*). Sales staff in a company may be paid commission in addition to their basic salary, as an incentive to increase sales.

Commission for Racial Equality (CRE) was established under the *Race Relations Act of 1976*, combining the functions of the two former statutory bodies, the Race Relations Board and the Community Relations Commission. The CRE works towards the elimination of discrimination, promoting equality of opportunity and good relations between different racial groups generally.

committee: a group of people who work together to achieve a common purpose, operating under a set of rules (the constitution) and with elected officials. As a minimum, a committee can operate with two officials, a *chairman* to control meetings and a secretary to take the minutes of meetings and handle correspondence. In reality, it is likely that the committee will also need a treasurer and people to organise publicity and fund-raising. If a committee has been formed to organise an *event,* it is a good idea to invite sponsors onto the committee, as well as representatives of the emergency services.

commoditisation is the notion that *tourism* products and even *destinations* can be sold in the same way as other commodities. Tour operators' brochures depict resorts from Bali to the Bahamas using similar *images* and descriptions. The 'packaging' and selling of tourist destinations, however, can have long-term environmental and socio-cultural effects on *host communities;* sensitive planning and management is needed to ensure their future well-being.

communication is the interaction between individuals and their exchange of information and opinions. Service industries, such as leisure, travel and tourism, rely heavily on effective communication both within organisations (*internal communication*) and with the outside world (*external communication*). Communication may be either *formal,* such as a letter to a client, or *informal,* e.g. a chance conversation with a colleague in the corridor. Communication does not only involve written and spoken words. *Non-verbal communication (NVC)* is when we use gestures and body language to make our feelings known or emphasise a point. (See also *one-way communication, two-way communication, marketing communications.*)

communication barrier: an obstacle preventing the smooth flow of information through an organisation. Examples include distortion to messages as they pass through many layers of bureaucracy, managers with poor *interpersonal skills* and individuals suffering from *information overload.*

communication channels: the routes through which individuals communicate with one another. Typical communication channels in leisure and tourism organisations include formal meetings and staff liaison committees.

communication networks are charts that show the communication structure within an organisation. Three of the most common networks are the circle, the chain and the wheel. The wheel is considered to be the most effective for simple tasks, the chain the slowest, but the circle tends to give employees the most job satisfaction, as it gives the greatest amount of interaction between employees.

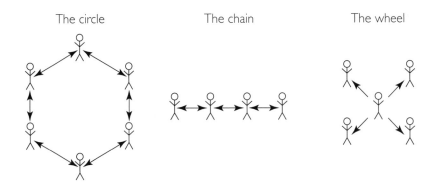

| The circle | The chain | The wheel |

Examples of communication networks

communication systems: the equipment and procedures that an organisation uses to disseminate information between employees and to maintain contact with outside agencies. The main types of communication systems used by leisure and tourism organisations include *written, verbal* and *electronic* communication systems. They help an organisation to manage its flow of information, act as an aid to decision making, help monitor organisational performance and facilitate links with external bodies.

community arts is made up of individuals, organisations and practices that give all members of a community the opportunity to take a full part in their local arts scene and express themselves creatively. Community arts organisations are funded by local authorities, the *Arts Council* and the *Regional Arts Boards (RABs)*.

Community Charge: a tax which replaced household rates and which was levied on individuals rather than being related to the value of their house. Colloquially known as the 'poll tax', the Community Charge was introduced by the Conservative government in 1990 and levied on all adults over the age of eighteen, with reductions for students, pensioners and people on state benefits. The tax proved very unpopular, not least because the very wealthy were often paying the same Community Charge as the very poor. The government scrapped the tax in 1992–93 in favour of the *Council Tax*, again based on the value of property.

community council: the lowest tier of local government, coming below *county* and *district councils*, and the one which many would say is the closest to the people it represents, namely those living in small rural or urban communities. Sometimes referred to as a parish council, the community council is responsible for managing some local facilities, such as sports fields, but generally lacks the power and resources of either the district or county councils to be able to get things done. Instead, the role of the community council is often that of a local sounding board, bringing items for attention to the notice of the respective authorities.

community recreation is an important sector of the UK *leisure and recreation industry*, concerned with meeting the leisure needs of all members of society, irrespective of class, income, gender, age, religion, education, ethnic origin, ability or mobility. Studies conducted since 1970 have shown that the majority of users of leisure facilities tend to be white, male, car-borne and middle class. Bodies such as the *Sports Council* have sought to redress the balance through campaigns such as *Sport for All*, while the *CCPR* introduced its *Community Sports Leaders Award* in 1982. (See also *sports equity*.)

Community Sports Leaders Award (CSLA): created by the *CCPR* in 1982 in recognition of the contribution of sport to the social well-being as well as the sporting life of the nation. The idea behind the CSLA is to develop existing voluntary effort by recruiting from local communities people who might care to extend their involvement by training to become leaders in their own chosen activity. It is awarded at three progressive levels and is recognised as a qualification for the voluntary service element of the *Duke of Edinburgh's Award Scheme*. Since the launch of the CSLA in 1982, more than 2 500 courses have been organised, producing some 35 000 qualified sports leaders.

Companies Act 1985: the principal piece of UK legislation concerning the formation of *companies* and their operation. The Act stipulates the documentation and records that all limited companies must keep, including the *Memorandum of*

Association and *Articles of Association*. Parts of the 1985 Act were amended in 1989 to bring them into line with European legislation.

company: see *limited company*

compensation: money or other benefits given to an individual as a result of poor service, problems with products and services, or to make up for inconvenience or anxiety. In leisure and tourism, *tour operators*, airlines, leisure operators, etc. will, from time to time, agree to pay compensation to aggrieved customers, sometimes under the terms of a *customer charter* or *code of conduct*.

competition is a common feature of the *leisure* and *tourism* industries, especially since the majority of organisations operate in the private sector, with profit maximisation as their primary *objective*. In an attempt to increase their *market share*, companies will sometimes enter into merger talks with potential partner organisations, leading sometimes to *vertical* or *horizontal integration* in the industries. The government has sought to encourage competition within leisure and tourism through *privatisation* and *compulsory competitive tendering (CCT)*.

competitive advantage is a position that an organisation strives to achieve over its competitors, perhaps through a wider range of products, more effective *promotion* or higher standards of *customer service*.

competitive pricing: a pricing method, sometimes referred to as 'the going rate', which assumes that, where products and services are similar, the organisation will match the prices of its competitors. This method often leads to very low profit margins and, in the long run, the collapse of some organisations, e.g. *tour operators*, who find that their *profitability* is too low.

competitive tendering is the process of inviting bids for the provision of goods and services. It is common practice in both *private* and *public sector leisure and tourism* to ask suppliers to tender, often to find the supplier who can do the job for the lowest price. As part of a general move towards privatisation and the contracting out of services, local councils are required to invite tenders for a range of their services which were previously provided by council employees, a practice known as *compulsory competitive tendering (CCT)*.

complaints are adverse reactions or comments by *customers* who are unhappy about a product or service they have bought, or the standard of service they have received. Common areas for complaints in leisure and tourism include tour operators changing details of package holidays at the last minute, retail staff being unhelpful towards customers and problems in getting through on the telephone to a *tourist information centre (TIC)*. All staff must be trained in handling customer complaints and learn to treat them as a form of *feedback* which will help improve standards in the future.

compulsory competitive tendering (CCT) is the process of inviting tenders from commercial operators for the management of services and facilities that were previously carried out by public agencies. CCT was first adopted following the Local Government and Planning Act 1980, which required competition for building and highways construction and maintenance. The Local Government Act of 1988 extended the 1980 Act by requiring local authorities to subject a number of services to competitive tendering, including:

- refuse collection
- schools and welfare catering
- vehicle maintenance
- management of sports and leisure facilities

Within the *leisure* and *recreation* sector, all local authorities in England and Wales were required to have put the management of their sports and leisure facilities out to tender by the end of 1993. Facilities falling within the scope of CCT include sports centres, leisure centres, athletics grounds, cycle tracks, bowling greens, artificial ski slopes and golf courses. The principle underlying CCT is that increased competition should provide an improved service and better value-for-money for the local population. Critics of CCT argue that it may lead to certain services and facilities being phased out since they are unprofitable, but nonetheless fulfil an important local need, e.g. facilities for disabled people. There is no doubt that CCT has provided local authorities with major challenges, not least in terms of the efficiency of organisational structures, as well as cost and revenue factors.

computerised reservation system (CRS): an automated facility that allows leisure and tourism companies to provide up-to-date information on product availability and offer customers the opportunity of finalising a purchase of a range of products, including holidays, flights and car hire. Specialist leisure and tourism companies will have 'stand-alone' systems, often operating on tailormade software, e.g. *leisure centres*, coach companies and specialist tour operators. Larger organisations, such as airlines and mass market tour operators, have extensive systems that can often be accessed directly by travel agents using a *'gateway'* facility, in order to check availability and make reservations. Such systems are interactive, ensuring that there is constant updating of product availability and no problem of the same stock being offered for sale by more than one person at a time.

Airlines have invested heavily in global computerised reservation systems, which provide not only accurate data on airline flights and costs, but also information on other travel services, including car hire, resort information, exchange rates, weather data, sporting events and resort excursions. Probably the best known system is American Airline's *Sabre* CRS, although there is competition from European systems such as *Galileo* and *Amadeus*.

computers: see *personal computer (PC)*

concentrated marketing: a type of *marketing strategy* where an organisation chooses to compete in only one sector of a market, developing the most effective *marketing mix* for that sector. Many smaller operators in leisure and tourism choose this option and gain in-depth information on their *customers* and their requirements. Eurocamp is a UK company that adopts a concentrated marketing strategy, focusing on a narrow sector of the market for family camping holidays.

concentration ratio refers to the share of the market taken by the largest companies in a particular industry, e.g. between them, *Thomson*, Airtours and First Choice Holidays have around 60 per cent of the total market for outbound *package holidays*.

concession: an individual or organisation that is given the opportunity to trade within an existing facility, such as a *tourist attraction* or *hotel*, in return for a fixed fee or percentage of their profits being given to the facility owner. Concessionaires are also found at events, providing services such as catering and retail units. The owners and operators of facilities need to ensure that the concessionaires meet certain minimum quality and safety standards to make sure that their reputation is not compromised.

concierge: a French term used to denote a member of hotel staff with responsibility for the movement and storage of guests' luggage, car parking and the provision of information.

conciliation: another name for *arbitration.*

conditions of employment: details such as salary, holiday arrangements, hours of work, *pension* entitlement, etc. that are included in an employee's *contract of employment.*

condominium: an apartment in which individual living units are owned separately, but the land and building in which they are housed is in the collective ownership of the residents. Condominiums are often found in resort areas and may be used as *second homes.*

Confederation of British Industry (CBI) is the representative body for industry in *Britain,* embracing the manufacturing and service sectors of the economy. Its mission is to promote the long-run competitiveness of British business. It is seen by government and the *European Commission* as the principal mouthpiece for industry in Britain across the whole range of policy issues. The CBI has a Tourism Advisory Group made up of representatives of a number of leading commercial organisations and public sector tourism bodies.

Confederation of Passenger Transport UK (CPT) is an independent association representing the interests of UK bus and coach operators. Formed in 1974 as the Bus and Coach Council (BCC), CPT acts as the voice of the bus and coach industry in representations at national and European level. It has drawn up a *code of conduct* for professional operators, covering bonding arrangements and safety.

CONFER: an annual trade exhibition organised by the *British Association of Conference Towns (BACT).* The aim of the exhibition is to give organisers of conferences, exhibitions and *incentive travel* the opportunity to obtain up-to-date information on the services and facilities offered by BACT member destinations.

conference: a gathering of people for the purpose of information exchange, analysis and discussion. Academics and people working in the *leisure* and *tourism* industries hold regular conferences, sometimes called conventions or congresses, in order to keep up to date on industry developments and develop contacts. Conferences in general, across all sectors of industry, are an important element in *business tourism,* bringing economic benefits to regions and countries around the world.

conflict in teams can have serious implications for an organisation if it is not managed effectively. Conflict can be either inter-team, i.e. between two or more teams in the same organisation, or intra-team, i.e. develops within a team. It can lead to a number of problems, including high staff turnover, increased absenteeism, reduced staff morale and poor levels of *customer service.*

conglomerate is the name given to a large organisation that owns and operates a number of smaller subsidiary enterprises, each of which contributes to overall profitability. In leisure and tourism, the Pearson Group is a good example; it operates

Madame Tussaud's, *Alton Towers* and Warwick Castle as independent business units, with a co-ordinating role for itself as the parent company. (See also *multinational corporation.*)

congress: see *conference*

conservation: the practice of protecting artefacts, buildings, habitats and natural landscapes for future generations to enjoy and appreciate. *Tourism* and *recreation* often come into conflict with *conservation*, leading to problems of erosion, pollution and the spoiling of landscapes. Careful management is needed to ensure that visitors do not destroy the very thing they have come to enjoy. Organisations such as the *Countryside Commission* and the *British Trust for Conservation Volunteers (BTCV)* offer practical solutions to countryside conservation problems, while the *Civic Trust* promotes the conservation of urban areas.

consolidation: the practice in the *charter* airline industry of combining the passengers on a flight from one departure airport with those from another departure airport, so as to produce one plane load of passengers. Consolidation occurs when the take-up of seats on an aircraft is low, i.e. there is a low *load factor*. It is in the interest of the airline or tour operator to consolidate, since it helps their productivity. Passengers, however, are often inconvenienced by the practice, particularly when the *transportation* to another departure airport results in a delay in them catching their flight or starting their holiday.

consortium: a grouping of independent businesses or other organisations working together for a common purpose or benefit. A group of farmhouse *accommodation* owners, for example, may pool their resources to develop a *joint marketing* scheme or buy their collective supplies in bulk at discount prices. Best Western Hotels is a good example of a marketing consortium in the leisure and tourism industries; individual hoteliers pay to become members of the consortium and benefit from inclusion in a national *brochure, advertising* and *promotion*, and the services of a *central reservation system*. Consortia are also found in the visitor attractions sector, e.g. the *Assocation of Leading Visitor Attractions (ALVA)*.

constraint: a factor that limits the extent to which an organisation is able to achieve its full potential. Constraints may be *internal*, over which the organisation has some degree of control, or *external*, i.e. those that occur in the wider world and over which it has little control.

Consumer Credit Act 1974: government *legislation* designed to protect *customers* who enter into a credit agreement when buying products and services. The Act has a wide scope and covers *credit cards, hire purchase* arrangements, any type of cash *loan* and bank *overdrafts*. One important part of the Act is the requirement that all publicity material concerning a credit arrangement must clearly state the *annual percentage rate (APR)* charged by the lender.

consumer press refers to magazines, newspapers and journals targeted at members of the general public. (See also *trade press.*)

consumer protection: the process of ensuring that consumers are treated fairly, honestly and safely when they buy goods and services. Consumer protection is most commonly achieved through government legislation, but can be carried out on a voluntary basis, e.g. a voluntary *code of practice* or *code of conduct*. Legislation designed to protect consumers includes the *Consumer Protection Act 1987*, the *Trades Description Act 1968* and the *Food Safety Act 1990*. Consumer protection legislation is enforced by central government and local authority officials, including *Environmental Health Officers (EHOs)* and *Trading Standards Officers (TSOs)*. There is an increasing amount of consumer legislation coming from the *European Commission*, e.g. the *Package Travel Directive*.

Consumer Protection Act 1987: government legislation that addresses a number of consumer issues, including the clear display of prices for goods and services, the safety of products and the liability of suppliers if things go wrong. In the case of travel and tourism, many of these issues are now contained in the *Package Travel Directive*.

consumerism is a developing movement which encourages people to be better informed of their legal rights as consumers and empowers them to challenge suppliers of goods and services. The popularity of *television* and radio programmes such as Watchdog and You and Yours, plus the growth of groups such as the *Consumers' Association*, is evidence that people are no longer willing to accept poor standards of products and service. This applies equally well to leisure and tourism products and services, whose providers need to be constantly aware of consumer tastes and preferences.

Consumers' Association: a membership organisation that champions consumer rights and carries out independent testing on a range of products and services, to determine safety levels and value for money. Perhaps best known for its monthly publication *Which?*, the Association also carries out extensive research on holidays and associated products, with these results published in a sister publication called *Holiday Which?*. The Association also campaigns on behalf of its members for changes to government *legislation*.

Continental Plan: an accommodation arrangement consisting of bed and continental breakfast. (See also *American Plan, Modified American Plan, European Plan*.)

contingency plan: a set of procedures, planned in advance of an event, which can be put into operation if certain circumstances arise, e.g. the failure of the electricity supply at a major outdoor event, the failure of a key member of staff to turn up or an accident to visitors. All event organisers must ensure that they have plans in place to deal with a range of contingencies, particularly those affecting health and safety.

continuing professional development (CPD): the practice of giving employees the opportunity, through different types of *staff training* and development, to improve their work skills and develop themselves as individuals. When linked to *staff appraisal*, CPD can be an effective way of developing an organisation's human resources and empowering individuals to be effective members of staff. As part of a planned programme of continuing professional development, staff may attend in-house training courses, go to conferences and seminars, 'shadow' other members of staff or study for formal qualifications.

contract of employment: a written, legal document that sets out the terms and conditions under which a member of staff is expected to work. Under the Trade Union Reform and Employment Rights Act of 1993, employees who are eligible to be given a contract of employment must receive it within two months of starting their employment. The contract will contain details of a number of conditions of employment, including the names of both parties to the contract, the job title, the date when employment began, details of remuneration, hours of work, holiday entitlement, termination arrangements and *grievance procedures*. The current trend in UK employment is away from permanent contracts for employees in leisure and tourism, towards short-term contracts and casual working.

contribution pricing: the practice of setting prices for products and services on the basis that as long as the prices set cover the *variable costs*, then the product or service is making a contribution towards the *overheads* of the business. It is sometimes referred to as marginal costing. (See also *loss leader*.)

Control of Substances Hazardous to Health (COSHH): a set of regulations that add to an employer's duties concerning the use of harmful substances, as laid down in the *Health and Safety at Work, etc. Act*. Under the COSHH Regulations, employers must assess the likely exposure to all hazardous substances on their premises and put in place control measures and monitoring procedures as appropriate. A 'hazardous substance' can be solid, liquid, gaseous, vapour, dust or fumes. The use of chemicals in the leisure and tourism industries falls within the scope of the Regulations, for example the treatment of swimming pool water, storing and using disinfectants, controlling insects and vermin, and the marking and management of sports fields.

convention: see *conference*

convention bureau: an organisation responsible for promoting an area to *tourists*. Convention bureaux in the UK, e.g. Sheffield Visitor and Convention Bureau and Manchester Visitor and Convention Bureau, are often *partnerships* between public and private sector organisations, pooling their resources to gain maximum impact. Most convention bureaux will offer an *accommodation* reservation service, arrange conferences and offer tourist information. Many bureaux are members of BACT, the *British Association of Conference Towns*.

conversion rate: a term used in *marketing* to denote the ratio of enquiries that are converted into sales in reponse to a promotional *campaign*, e.g. 20 holiday bookings arising out of 200 enquiries for brochures would give a conversion rate of 1:10.

co-operative: a type of business enterprise which is owned and managed by its workforce and operated on democratic lines. The number of co-operatives in leisure and tourism is small, but they are to be found in community ventures such as art galleries, music workshops, street theatre and countryside groups. They operate on the basis of one person, one vote, with *objectives* being determined by the workforce and profits distributed equitably.

co-operative marketing: an arrangement between two or more organisations who agree to pool their resources and share costs, in the hope of achieving a better response to a promotional *campaign* than if they advertised individually. Sometimes called joint marketing, it is best suited to sectors of the leisure and tourism industries that are not in direct competition with each other, e.g. hotels and airlines, tourist boards and ferry companies. Fifty/fifty marketing is a particular type of co-operation in which, for example, travel agents and tour operators share advertising space in the *consumer* or *trade press*, each paying half of the total cost.

corporate fitness describes a company's efforts to improve the fitness levels of its employees, in the hope that fitter staff will work more effectively and ultimately bring benefits to the organisation. This could include the provision of sports grounds, fitness suites and indoor gyms.

corporate hospitality: refers to entertaining existing and potential business clients with the expectation of making new contacts and increased business *opportunities*. Corporate hospitality events range from lavish occasions at Wimbledon or Henley Regatta, to the owner of a business inviting his or her bank manager for a meal in a local restaurant.

corporate identity is the image that an organisation portrays to the outside world, as shown by its *logo*, business stationery, vehicles, staff uniforms, premises and *advertising*, all of which may be co-ordinated to reinforce the identity. Establishing a corporate identity will help to project an image that is recognised easily and establish a consistent level of quality and service in the minds of *customers*.

corporate image: another name for *corporate identity*

corporate objectives: see *business objectives*

corporation tax is a direct tax paid by *companies* on their profits, in the same way that individuals pay *income tax* on their income and investments. There is a lower rate of corporation tax for small and medium-sized businesses.

corrective maintenance: see *maintenance*

COSHH: see *Control of Substances Hazardous to Health*

cost-based pricing is a pricing policy that sets the prices of products and services purely on the basis of the cost of their production, taking no account of market factors and conditions. In the highly competitive leisure and tourism industries such a policy rarely exists, except where there is little direct *competition*. *Market-led pricing* is the norm in leisure and tourism. (See also *cost-plus pricing*.)

cost-benefit analysis (CBA) is a planning process which considers all the financial, operational, environmental and social costs and benefits of a proposed project or other course of action. It is a systematic technique that tries to look beyond the purely commercial costs and benefits and into the wider social and community issues that may arise. A CBA of a major airport expansion, for example, would certainly consider the extra *revenue* and jobs that the project would generate, plus the extra costs, but also the effects on the local people of extra noise and disturbance, the loss of amenity land and the likelihood of extra accidents and their associated costs. These costs, which may be hard to quantify, are sometimes known as *social costs*.

cost centre: a readily identifiable location, department or function within an organisation, against which its *costs* of operation can be charged. For example, the *marketing* department of a large *tour operator* is likely to have a number of cost centres, including:

- *market research*
- brochure production
- brochure distribution
- agency sales support
- agency marketing
- *merchandising*

Each cost centre will be allocated a unique cost code to make sure that all its costs are identified correctly.

cost control is the process of managing an organisation's expenditure within pre-determined limits. Budgeting allows the comparison of actual and budgeted costs and allows management to take corrective action over any *variances* found.

cost-plus pricing is a simplistic pricing method that totals all an organisation's *fixed* and *variable costs*, and adds a small profit margin to arrive at the final price to charge. Sometimes called *'accountant's pricing'*, cost-plus pricing assumes that an organisation can calculate its costs accurately, which a large leisure complex, for example, may find difficult. It also ignores market conditions, thereby denying an organisation a potential profit opportunity. It does, however, have the advantage of protecting a firm's profit margin, since it assumes that any increases in costs will be passed on to the customer.

costs are the items of expenditure incurred by an organisation in the production of its goods and services. Costs may be classified by nature, i.e. *fixed* (remaining constant despite the level of business activity), or *variable* (changing in proportion to the level of activity). Classification by type is also common, dividing costs into *direct* and *indirect*. For purposes of budgeting, costs are sometimes allocated to *cost centres* or the departments that incur them. *Cost control* is an essential element of the work of managers in leisure and tourism.

COTAC: see *Certificate of Travel Agency Competence*

couchette: basic sleeping *accommodation* provided on trains in some continental European countries and consisting of a *berth* in a shared compartment, each with a supply of linen but no washing or toilet facilities.

Council of Europe was established in 1949 with the aim of promoting greater unity between its members and achieving economic and social progress. The Council is not a *European Union (EU)* body, but many of its members are EU member states, including the *United Kingdom*, Spain, Greece and Germany. The Council promotes co-operation in a number of areas, including health and social services, youth activities, consumer protection and the harmonisation of laws within Europe.

Council of Ministers: an important institution of the *European Union (EU)* which decides on all the laws that set up Union policies. The Council consists of government ministers from the fifteen member states, accountable to their own parliaments, representing national interests on the subjects under discussion, e.g. trade, agriculture, social policy, etc. Each member state takes a six-month turn to hold the Presidency of the Council, setting the agenda and chairing meetings.

Council for National Parks was established in 1936, before Britain's *National Parks* were designated, as the Standing Committee for National Parks, as a way of ensuring that the environment within the National Parks was both protected and made available for the public to enjoy. Today the Council works to continue the original aims of the Standing Committee by campaigning for protection of the National Parks, fighting issues of national importance, such as mineral extraction in the National Parks, and encouraging good practice, including environmentally friendly farming projects and schemes to protect the cultural *heritage* of local communities.

Council for the Protection of Rural England (CPRE): established in 1926, CPRE is the only independent environmental group working for the whole of the English countryside. It fights against the onset of urban development in the countryside, works for better *conservation* measures and a stronger system for the protection of the landscape. CPRE also encourages better *management* of woodland and farmland, and advocates more efficient use of energy resources. Its membership of 46 000 is drawn from all over the country and there are branches in every English county.

Council Tax: a tax levied by local authorities on people living in their area, in order to supplement national government funding for local services. Council Tax, which replaced the unpopular *Community Charge* (poll tax) in 1992–93, is used by local authorities to provide a range of services, including refuse collection, library services and *leisure* facilities. The amount of Council Tax a person pays is based on the value of the property in which they live; the higher the value of the property, the greater the Council Tax.

Country Park: an area designated for outdoor *recreation* and located close to urban areas. Country Parks were established under the *Countryside Act of 1968* as a way of giving town dwellers a chance to enjoy their leisure in the open without travelling too far and adding to congestion on the roads. The designation of Country Parks is the responsibility of the *Countryside Commission*, although they are maintained by *local authorities*.

Countryside Act 1968: government *legislation* concerned with *conservation* and *access* to the countryside for leisure and recreation. The Act established the *Countryside Commission* and designated *Country Parks*, nature trails, picnic sites and bird sanctuaries.

Countryside Commission: a government-funded *quango* that works to keep the countryside of England properly protected and managed, now and in the future, and to make it accessible to the 30 million people who visit every year. Established under the *Countryside Act of 1968*, the Commission's work has three broad aims:

- to conserve and enhance the scenic, natural, historic and cultural qualities of the whole countryside
- to secure and extend opportunities for people to enjoy and use the countryside for open air-recreation
- to promote understanding of the countryside, its life and work

The Commission has a wide-ranging programme of work, including running demonstration projects of good practice in countryside management, advising on strategy for the *National Parks*, working with local authorities to protect the *Areas of Outstanding Natural Beauty*, supporting practical work on the *Heritage Coasts* and developing community forests close to major towns and cities.

Countryside Council for Wales (CCW) is the government-funded body formed as a result of the merger between the Nature Conservancy Council and the Countryside Commission in Wales. With its headquarters in Bangor, the Council is the statutory adviser to government on sustaining natural beauty, wildlife and the opportunity for outdoor enjoyment in rural Wales and its inshore waters. The purposes of CCW are to conserve the quality of the Welsh landscape and its inshore waters, conserve the variety of wildlife and habitats, create opportunities for everyone to enjoy and understand the countryside, and to consider the culture and economy of Wales in all its day-to-day work.

countryside recreation is a growing sector of the UK *leisure and recreation industry*, encompassing both informal and formal activities. Informal activities, such as walking and rambling are among the most popular pastimes in Britain, while the growing interest in health and fitness has encouraged many people to take up formal recreational pursuits in the countryside, e.g. mountain biking, orienteering and rock climbing. The increasing numbers of people seeking enjoyment and recreation in the countryside are putting some rural areas of Britain under extreme pressure, especially the *National Parks*, where managers are constantly trying to maintain a balance between the needs of the visitors and the *conservation* of the natural environment.

Countryside Recreation Network (CRN) is a network providing an easy means of access to individuals and agencies concerned with countryside and related *recreation* matters. The Network reaches a variety of organisations and individuals in the public, private and voluntary sectors. It helps the work of agencies and individuals by helping to meet the needs of its members for advice, information and research. CRN also promotes co-operation between member agencies and encourages the dissemination of good practice in *countryside recreation.*

county council: the tier of local government responsible for providing services to the people and businesses in the 47 Shire counties of England and Wales. County councils tend to operate at more of a strategic level than *district councils*, and are responsible for developing *Structure Plans*, the provision of roads, education and social services facilities, and *tourism policy.*

courier: a representative of a travel company who is employed to assist *customers* during their holiday or business trip. Couriers, sometimes called resort representatives, are most usually associated with *tour operators*, with the responsibility for the care of clients on a package holiday abroad. Typical courier duties include arranging transfers between airports and *accommodation*, organising excursions from resorts and generally helping to provide customers with an enjoyable experience. Couriers are usually only employed for the holiday season and may be specifically recruited to work with children on holiday.

cover is a term used in the catering industry to denote the number of places available for customers who are eating in a restaurant or *hotel*, i.e. a restaurant with 100 covers will seat and serve 100 customers.

CPD: see *continuing professional development*

CPRE: see *Council for the Protection of Rural England*

CPRW: see *Campaign for the Protection of Rural Wales*

CPT: see *Confederation of Passenger Transport UK*

Crafts Council: a government-funded body established in 1979 to ensure that crafts can be enjoyed by as wide a cross-section of the public as possible. The Council works with the *Regional Arts Boards (RABs)* and provides funding for crafts in the regions. It also advises crafts people on such matters as business development and training, and represents the interests of crafts generally at government level.

CRE: see *Commission for Racial Equality*

credit is when goods and services are supplied but the request for payment is delayed. The actual period of time granted is known as the *credit period*. Credit is accepted practice in all dealings between organisations and sometimes between *companies* and their *customers*. Credit may be given freely (the so-called 'free credit' often seen on consumer purchases) or may attract an interest payment. *Credit cards* offer a free credit period before settlement is due.

credit card: a plastic card, issued by banks and other financial organisations, that gives its holder a period of free credit, subject to certain conditions. Credit cards are a convenient way of making a large purchase, and are in widespread use in *hotels*, restaurants and other catering outlets, and for booking *holidays* and flights. Credit cards can also be used for postal and telephone bookings, allowing instant purchases of, for example, theatre and concert tickets. The two most common cards in use in Britain are Access and Visa.

credit control: the process of managing an organisation's *debtors* so as to minimise *bad debts* and the time within which payments are due.

credit period: the amount of time granted by a supplier within which payment is expected to be made. Credit periods are typically 30, 60 or 90 days, depending on the value of the goods and services supplied and the working relationship between the two parties concerned.

creditor: a person or individual to whom you owe money for the supply of goods and services. Creditors form part of an organisation's *current liabilities*, as shown on its *balance sheet*. It is common practice in leisure and tourism for companies to grant periods of *credit* before payment is due.

crisis management is the response of an organisation to an unexpected or unplanned event or incident, such as a fire or major accident. All organisations should have *contingency plans* to cover such occurrences, with clear lines of *responsibility* and *communication*, so as to implement emergency procedures as quickly as possible. In the event of an incident of national importance, an organisation should implement a *public relations* plan to minimise adverse publicity.

critical path analysis (CPA): a technique used in *operations management* to simplify decision making by breaking a project into its component activities. CPA sets out to:

- identify all the tasks and activities involved in the project
- place them in an appropriate sequence
- set timescales and allocate work tasks
- calculate the best critical time path for the project

By so doing, CPA can be used to plan, schedule, monitor and control the project. It is used particularly in the *management* of large building projects, such as the development of a new *theme park* or hotel complex. It is also applicable to planning marketing campaigns and developing new products.

CRN: see *Countryside Recreation Network*

Crown Classification Scheme: a voluntary national *accommodation grading scheme* for *serviced accommodation* in Britain. Launched in 1987, the scheme classifies the facilities offered by establishments into one of six categories, from 'listed' for basic, clean facilities to 'five crowns' for hotels with ensuite facilities in all bedrooms, a restaurant serving breakfast, lunch and dinner, the availability of a night porter, room service, etc. In 1990, the Crown Scheme was refined to include an assessment of the quality of the accommodation as well as the 'listed' and one to five crown ratings. The quality gradings were as follows:

- approved – an acceptable overall standard of quality
- commended – a good overall standard of quality
- highly commended – a very good overall standard of quality
- de luxe – an excellent overall standard of quality

An establishment can fall into any of the four quality gradings regardless of whether it is 'listed' or has been awarded any number of crowns. The Crown Classification Scheme is administered by the *National* and *Regional Tourist Boards* in Britain, who inspect premises regularly to make sure they meet the standards. (See also *Key Classification Scheme.*)

CRS: see *computerised reservation system*

cruising is considered by many to be the ultimate *holiday* in a floating hotel. It is currently experiencing something of a revival, with new generation ships and mass market tour operators beginning to offer cruise holidays at affordable prices to a new segment of the market. Apart from round-the-world cruises, the most popular destinations are the Caribbean, the Mediterranean and the Baltic. (See also *fly-cruise.*)

CSLA: see *Community Sports Leaders Award*

CSQ: see *customer satisfaction questionnaire*

CTC: see *Cyclists' Touring Club*

cultural recreation: see *arts and entertainment*

cultural tourism is 'travel with a purpose', for those seeking artistic and cultural inspiration. It includes history tours, *museum* visits, wine and food appreciation holidays, trips to art galleries and music tours.

Cumbria Tourist Board is the official *Regional Tourist Board* covering the county of Cumbria, centred on the Lake District *National Park.*

currency refers to notes and coins used as the medium of exchange in a country. Some countries impose restrictions on the amount of currency that can be taken into and out of the country, so as to protect their exchange rate. Fluctuations in international currencies can have a marked effect on the demand for tourism, e.g. a fall in the French franc against the pound sterling will make French holidays more expensive for British people. (See also *hard currency.*)

current assets are items owned by a business, where the value is changing constantly, e.g. stock, cash and *debtors* (those who owe money to an organisation), and which are likely to be converted into cash before the date of the next *balance sheet*, generally within twelve months. The balance of current assets over current liabilities is known as the *working capital*, which finances an organisation's everyday operations.

current liabilities are amounts owed by an organisation that are likely to be repaid before the date of the next *balance sheet*, usually within twelve months. Typical current liabilities include *creditors* (those to whom money is owed), loans, overdrafts and dividends.

current ratio: see *liquidity ratio*

curriculum vitae (CV): a written statement of an individual's career history, which may be sent to a prospective employer in response to a job advertisement. A CV should include personal details, such as name, address, telephone number, details of education and qualifications obtained, as well as brief information on past employment, notable achievements and the names of referees. Some organisations prefer to ask for a CV rather than a completed job application form, while others make it very clear that a CV is not acceptable in place of an application form.

- Name
- Address
- Telephone number
- Date of birth
- Education to date
- Academic and vocational qualifications
- Employment record
- Skills
- Notable achievements
- Interests and hobbies
- Names and addresses of referees

Information normally included in a CV

customer: an individual with a unique set of characteristics who buys or uses *leisure* and *tourism products* and services. Customers are the lifeblood of an organisation and usually the very reason for its existence. Customers will have very different needs and will expect high levels of *customer service* from leisure and tourism providers. (See also *internal customer*.)

customer care: a specific component of *customer service* that focuses on training staff to provide *customers* with a high quality service at all times. High standards in customer care will give an organisation a competitive edge, while at the same time reducing the burden on *management* associated with customer and staff dissatisfaction.

customer charter: a written document that sets out the minimum levels of service and standards of facilities that *customers* can expect when they use a facility or buy a particular product or service. The charter will indicate clearly what the organisation is trying to achieve and sometimes what is expected of customers in return. Customer charters are gaining in popularity in all sectors of the UK economy, even at government level with the introduction of the *Citizens' Charter* and the awarding of *Charter Marks*.

customer comment form: a technique for giving visitors an immediate opportunity to tell the management what they think of the service and facilities they have used. Unlike *CSQs*, which give people the chance to comment in depth, customer comment forms often contain only a few questions and can be found in a wide range of leisure and tourism facilities, including hotels, restaurants, fast-food outlets, visitor attractions, ferries and leisure centres. The forms are checked regularly by management and appropriate action taken as necessary to improve standards.

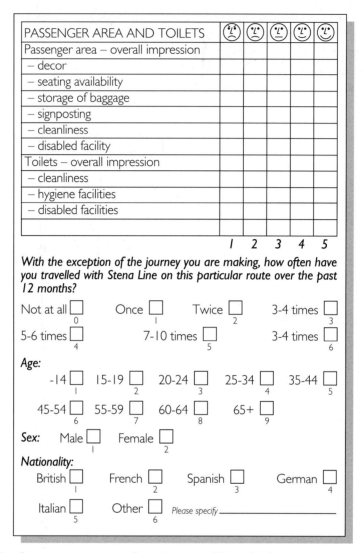

PASSENGER AREA AND TOILETS	☹	☺	☺	☺	☺
Passenger area – overall impression					
– decor					
– seating availability					
– storage of baggage					
– signposting					
– cleanliness					
– disabled facility					
Toilets – overall impression					
– cleanliness					
– hygiene facilities					
– disabled facilities					
	1	2	3	4	5

With the exception of the journey you are making, how often have you travelled with Stena Line on this particular route over the past 12 months?

Not at all ☐ Once ☐ Twice ☐ 3-4 times ☐
0 1 2 3

5-6 times ☐ 7-10 times ☐ 3-4 times ☐
4 5 6

Age:

-14 ☐ 15-19 ☐ 20-24 ☐ 25-34 ☐ 35-44 ☐
1 2 3 4 5

45-54 ☐ 55-59 ☐ 60-64 ☐ 65+ ☐
6 7 8 9

Sex: Male ☐ Female ☐
1 2

Nationality:

British ☐ French ☐ Spanish ☐ German ☐
1 2 3 4

Italian ☐ Other ☐ *Please specify* _____
5 6

An example of a customer comment form (courtesy of Stena Line)

customer needs: see *needs*

customer orientation is the *management* philosophy and practice that puts *customers* at the heart of the operation of any leisure, travel or tourism organisation. Rather than focusing purely on what is supplied to customers *(product orientation)*, customer orientation is concerned with making sure that all levels within an organisation have a clear commitment to providing products and services that customers will want, as well as excellence in the standards of *customer service* offered.

customer profile: the precise characteristics of the *customers* who buy a particular product or service, such as age, gender, employment status and income level. Customer profile information is a vital starting point for product development and *promotion*.

customer satisfaction questionnaire (CSQ): an important *market research* tool used by most leisure and tourism organisations. CSQs invite customers to make comments on the quality of service and standards of facilities they have experienced on their holidays or other leisure or travel arrangements. It is common practice for airlines, tour operators and hotel companies to use CSQs in order to improve the levels of service they offer their customers. CSQs are sometimes referred to as customer service questionnaires.

customer service concerns all aspects of the interface between a *customer* and an organisation. Recognition of its importance is relatively new to leisure and tourism, although most organisations now offer some form of *customer care* training. The key issues to be addressed by any organisation that is committed to the highest standards of customer service include:

- identifying customer *needs*
- developing the right mix of products and services
- ensuring high quality delivery systems
- measuring customer satisfaction
- carrying out staff *training*

Obstacles to good customer service include poor *communication* within an organisation, lack of management commitment and inadequate *resources*.

The benefits of developing a customer service approach

customer service questionnaire: see *customer satisfaction questionnaire*

Cyclists' Touring Club (CTC): established in 1878, the CTC is Britain's largest cycling organisation, promoting recreational and utility cycling. It provides its members with technical advice, touring services, *insurance* and legal aid. CTC campaigns to improve facilities and opportunities for all cyclists.

CV: see *curriculum vitae*

D

data: factual information of any kind, including statistics, financial information and details on markets. The term is often used in connection with *computer* programs and systems.

Data Protection Act 1984 (DPA): government *legislation* introduced to safeguard the public from problems relating to the inaccuracy of any information held about them on *computer* records. Under the terms of the Act, all organisations that hold data about individuals on automated systems must register with the Data Protection Registrar and comply with a set of Data Protection Principles, which are a set of good practice guidelines. Individuals who have computer data held on them have a number of rights in civil law, including right of access to the data, rights to *compensation* for inaccuracy of data or its wrongful disclosure, and rights to have any inaccuracies in the data rectified.

database: a collection of files, *data* and records, stored manually or on a computer-based or electronic system, and used for a range of *management* purposes. Common uses of databases in leisure and tourism are travel companies compiling lists of their customers and leisure centres holding details of their suppliers on computer. The main advantage of using a computerised database, such as Dbase or MS Access, is that once data has been entered onto the system, it can be retrieved, amended or sorted easily, much more quickly than by using a manual system. Also, searches of the database can be made for specific purposes, e.g. the details of all customers living in a particular town or taking a short break in a particular country.

database marketing is the use of information held in a *database*, usually computerised, for *marketing* and promotional purposes. An example of database marketing would be a tour operator sending a *brochure* to all the clients who travelled to a particular destination the previous year. It is a rapidly growing part of the marketing industry, helped by advances in computer *software* and networks.

Date Line: see *International Date Line*

day visitor: see *excursionist*

DCF: see *discounted cash flow*

debenture: a method by which a company can finance long-term *capital* projects. It is a form of long-term *loan* at a fixed annual rate of interest, secured on the *assets* of a company, often land and buildings. Debentures are sometimes issued by golf clubs and operators of stadia, as a way of financing their expansion plans. If the company defaults on the loan, the *security* can be sold to repay the lender.

debit card: a card used in place of a *cheque*, with the cardholder's bank account being debited usually within three working days. Debit cards offer greater convenience than writing a cheque and, since their introduction, the number of cheques written by current account holders has fallen dramatically. Debit cards should not be confused with *credit cards*, since they offer no free credit period. Examples of debit cards are Switch and Delta. (See also *cheque guarantee card.*)

debriefing is the process of reflecting on an *event* or meeting after it has finished and relaying information to a third party. It is important that debriefing sessions take place immediately after the event or meeting, while information and views are still fresh in the mind.

debtor is an individual or organisation that owes you money. Debtors form part of an organisation's *current assets*, i.e. those items whose value is changing constantly and which will be converted into cash in the normal course of trading. It is important for an organisation to keep tight control of its debtor situation by chasing late payments and not granting *credit* too freely. Bad debtor control can have a serious effect on a company's *cash-flow* position. (See also *creditor*.)

decentralisation: the process of distributing power and *responsibility* away from a central source to smaller management units, e.g. the head office of a major travel agency chain deciding to allow its branch managers to take some management decisions that were previously the responsibility of head office personnel. Within an organisational structure, senior managers may introduce a more decentralised or 'hands-off' approach to management, by shedding layers of bureaucracy and creating a *'flat' pyramid* structure. If managed properly, decentralisation can lead to faster decision making, better *communication*, more senior management involvement in day-to-day activities and improved staff motivation and morale. In large, multi-centre enterprises, decentralisation can, however, lead to a lack of uniformity of business operation, which may prove to be less cost effective.

deferred demand consists of those people who are not currently using or buying a particular product or service, because of a problem on the supply side. This could be a lack of *accommodation* in the resort of their choice, no tickets left for the theatre or a fire at a restaurant. At some stage in the future, it is expected that the customers will get what they want, i.e. deferred demand, sometimes called latent demand, will be converted into *effective demand*. (See also *potential demand*.)

delegation: the process of assigning work tasks to subordinates. Delegation is an essential element of *management*, but one which many managers find difficult to carry out. The structure of an organisation will have a bearing on the degree of delegation that takes place; a *centralised structure* will limit the extent of delegation, since the senior managers will be unwilling to pass decision-making powers down the hierarchy. While specific tasks can be delegated to subordinates, it must be remembered that the *responsibility* for ensuring that they are carried out satisfactorily must lie with the manager. (See also *authority*.)

delivery note: a form sent by a *supplier* to a *customer* at the time of delivery giving details of items supplied. The person receiving the goods is asked to sign the delivery note, which acts as confirmation of delivery and receipt. An *invoice*, showing the costs of the items supplied, usually follows the delivery.

Delphi technique: an approach to the long-term *forecasting* of events based on the combined judgements of a group of experts, rather than by using more objective statistical methods. The technique could be used, for example, to predict the likely trends in *tourism development* in a number of countries.

demand is considered by economists to be one half of a marketplace for goods and services, supply being the other. It is the driving force of a market economy, with producers developing goods and services to satisfy the demand. Demand for leisure and tourism products will be influenced by a number of factors, often categorised into *determinants* and *motivators*. The actual number of people buying or using a product or service is known as *effective demand*, while *suppressed demand* is made up of individuals who are currently not buying or using a particular product or service, either because there is a problem on the supply side (*deferred demand*) or because their current circumstances do not allow them to buy or use a particular product (*potential demand*).

demarketing is the technique of withdrawing *marketing* activity from a product or service so as to dissuade *customers* and thereby reduce *demand*. In leisure and tourism, demarketing can be applied to a *destination* that has become too popular and is giving rise to complaints of overcrowding and damage to the environment. Demarketing usually goes hand-in-hand with increased marketing effort for other products so as to switch demand.

demographics are factors concerning the characteristics of the population of a country or region, e.g. *age structure*, proportion of males and females, social class, level of income and employment status. Researching the demographic profile is an important step in *market segmentation* and can also be used to forecast changes in demand, e.g. the trends for people to live longer and retire from work earlier will affect the demand for holidays and other travel products in the future. Demographic data is available from a number of sources, including *Social Trends*, the *General Household Survey (GHS)* and specialist leisure and tourism consultancy reports.

demonstration effect is seen most often in *developing countries*, when members of the *host communities* begin to imitate the patterns of behaviour of their (often) wealthier Western visitors. Some residents are curious about and may yearn for the consumer goods belonging to the tourists, e.g. cameras, personal stereos and radios. At its worst, the demonstration effect can lead the hosts into crime and violent behaviour against the tourists.

Department for Education and Employment (DFEE): government department formed from the merger of the former Education Department and Employment Department. The DFEE's main areas of responsibility include schools and further/higher education policy, vocational education and training, plus the work of a number of agencies, such as the *Health and Safety Executive* and the *Advisory Conciliation and Arbitration Service (ACAS)*.

Department of the Environment (DoE): government department responsible for a variety of issues, including *planning*, new towns, inner cities, countryside issues, environmental protection and *conservation*. *Policies* adopted by the DoE can have wide-ranging implications for those who live and work in the countryside, and who visit it for active and passive recreation. Particular responsibilities of the DoE include the *National Parks, Areas of Outstanding Natural Beauty* and *public rights of way*.

Department of National Heritage (DNH) was created after the general election of April 1992 as a totally new ministry, which would aim to co-ordinate the many different activities that go to make up *leisure* and *tourism* in Britain. The DNH, which is headed by a cabinet minister, the Secretary of State for National Heritage, has responsibility for:

- broadcasting
- the arts
- *sport*
- *tourism*
- national *heritage*
- the film industry
- the *Millenium Fund*

Before the DNH was formed, these activities were the responsibility of many different government departments. The following chart shows the organisational structure of the DNH. The budget of the DNH is approximately £1 billion per year.

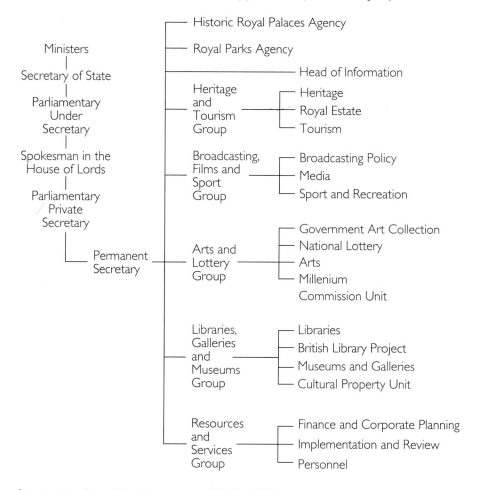

Organisation chart of the Department of National Heritage

Department of Trade and Industry (DTI): government department with a very wide sphere of activities, including *grants* to industry and small businesses, export promotion, *European Union* initiatives, *consumer protection* and company legislation. The DTI operates a regional framework of offices, supported by other satellite offices and agencies.

Department of Transport (DoT): government department responsible for land, sea and air transport, including safety of passenger-carrying vehicles, motorways and trunk roads, domestic and international civil aviation, the rail network and services, transport *deregulation* and road safety.

departmental structures: *organisational structures* based on clearly defined functions and activities. A mass market tour operator, for example, will have a structure based on a number of departments, including marketing, research, contracting, flights, brochure production, reservations, etc. These type of structures benefit from a clear division of *responsibilities*, but may hamper inter-departmental liaison.

deplane is the term used to denote passengers leaving an aircraft. (See also *enplane.*)

depreciation: a measure of the falling cash value of *fixed assets* over a period of time. For tax purposes, assets such as equipment and vehicles are able to be 'written off' over an agreed number of years, with tax relief claimable on their depreciating value.

deregulation is the withdrawal of local or central government control over industries to encourage greater *competition* between companies. Although its advocates argue that deregulation will provide *customers* with better products and services, some people fear that deregulated industries will lose interest in achieving *social objectives* and be concerned only with generating profits. *Airline deregulation* in Europe is currently high on the agenda, following on from the experience in the USA, where the Airline Deregulation Act was passed in 1978. The UK operates a deregulated coach travel industry.

desk research: see *secondary research*

desktop publishing (DTP) is a sophisticated *word processing* system that is capable of producing very high quality documents from a standard *personal computer*. DTP allows the user to manipulate text, pictures and graphics on screen and download the finished result to a printer. By so doing, it is possible to arrange printed pages in the same format as for a newspaper or magazine. New word processing software now incorporates many features that were once only found in DTP packages.

destinations are the end points of people's journeys, whether they are travelling for leisure or business purposes. It is often a destination, its *images* and the way in which it is promoted, that stimulates an individual to want to visit, thus energising the whole of the *travel and tourism industry*. Destinations are the focus of much tourist activity and the point at which many components of leisure, travel and tourism come together. Attracting visitors to destinations is a very competitive business, given the economic and social benefits that tourism can bring to a wide range of national, regional and local destinations.

destination life cycle: a *model* based on the *product life cycle* concept, but applied to the way that destinations grow and/or decline over time. Sometimes referred to as the tourist area life cycle (TALC), the destination life cycle suggests that all tourist regions will undergo a similar pattern of growth over a given period of time. They will pass through a number of stages, from initial exploration, through *development*, into stagnation and eventual decline. Majorca is considered to be a classic example of the destination life cycle concept, having enjoyed steady growth between the mid-1970s and the end of the 1980s, only to be faced with a decline in visitor numbers at the beginning of the 1990s. It was considered that Majorca had reached the stagnation point in the cycle. The tourist authorities have responded to the drop in popularity by investing in *hotels* and *infrastructure* to help regain its appeal as British travellers' most popular overseas holiday destination. Like the product life cycle concept, the major weakness of the destination life cycle is that it describes what has already taken place and cannot be an accurate *forecasting tool.*

destination marketing: the processes and techniques concerned with attracting visitors to a *destination*, whether it be a continent, country, region, town, country area or single *visitor attraction*. Destination marketing is a complex issue, often undertaken by *public sector* agencies, since it involves the *promotion* of many different leisure and tourism products in the same area, most of which will be under different ownership and control.

determinants are the economic, social, political and technological factors that influence a person's *demand* for travel and leisure products, irrespective of any motivations they may have. These will include:

- the political regime under which they live
- demographic factors, e.g. an ageing population
- socio-cultural factors, e.g. types of community (urban/rural)
- geographical factors, e.g. living in cold and hot climates
- economic factors, e.g. the wealth of a country as measured by its *GDP/GNP*

Determinants can be regarded as the 'base' factors that influence travel; people living in a *developing country* with a low GNP are unlikely to have the necessary financial *resources* to travel abroad, when compared with, say, people living in the UK or Germany. Determinants are usually considered along with *motivators*, the inner feelings and needs of individuals.

developing countries: nations of the world with relatively low levels of economic and social development, and low standards of living. They are, however, visited in increasing numbers by tourists from Western developed nations and are beginning to realise that tourism can bring economic and social benefits if planned and managed properly. However, in developing countries, sometimes known as Third World nations, there are concerns about the harmful *environmental* and *socio-cultural impacts* of unplanned tourism *development.*

development: a wide-ranging term that can mean both the building of a single facility, such as a hotel or leisure complex, and the longer-term process of a country acquiring *infrastructure* and *superstructure* developments as part of its economic development. Development can be a very emotive term, with individuals and groups campaigning against new road developments and large facilities, while *developing countries* often criticise the role played by *multinational corporations* in exploiting their resources for development. Most leisure and tourism developments are regulated, to a greater or lesser extent, by central and local governments.

Development Commission: see *Rural Development Commission*

Development of Tourism Act 1969: the first piece of UK *legislation* dealing specifically with *tourism*. The Act, which still applies today, covers four main areas:

- the establishment of the *British Tourist Authority, English Tourist Board, Wales Tourist Board* and *Scottish Tourist Board*

- the introduction of *section 4 grants* for tourist developments
- the establishment of the hotel development grants scheme
- legislation to introduce a compulsory registration scheme for *accommodation*

The part of the Act concerning compulsory registration of accommodation has not been fully implemented, with the industry instead preferring to follow a system of voluntary *accommodation grading*. The *Northern Ireland Tourist Board* was not included in the 1969 Development of Tourism Act, having already established its own *tourist board* under the Development of Tourist Traffic Act (N Ireland) in 1948.

development plan: a term which has a number of meanings in *leisure* and *tourism*, including a detailed scheme for a single project, e.g. the building of a major *tourist attraction*, or an overall long-term plan for land use developments in a country or region. Development plans are drawn up by private and public sector bodies, and are constantly reviewed in the light of changing circumstances. Some agencies include reference to techniques such as *critical path analysis (CPA)* and *PERT* in their development plans.

DFEE: see *Department for Education and Employment*

DG XXIII is the department of the *European Commission* with special responsibility for *tourism*.

differentiated marketing is a type of *marketing strategy* that tailors specific marketing approaches and activities to different sectors of a market, rather than adopting the same approach to everybody, as is the case with *undifferentiated marketing*. A mass market tour operator, for example, will have different strategies for reaching families, young couples and senior citizens, and will develop a range of products to suit each group's individual *needs*.

differential pricing: a technique used to influence *demand* for products and services, and ultimately maximise *revenue*, by offering variable prices at different times or for different market segments. It is common, for example, for leisure facilities to offer discounted prices outside peak times, in the same way that holidays are often more expensive in the *peak season*.

'dinky': stands for 'double income no kids', a term first used widely in Britain during the Thatcher years of the 1980s. 'Dinkies' are couples who both follow professional careers and who do not, by choice or otherwise, have children. They enjoy an affluent life style, with high *disposable incomes* to spend on a range of consumer durables and expensive leisure pursuits. 'Dinkies' are an important target market for some leisure and tourism organisations. (See also *'yuppie'*.)

direct costs relate to expenditure incurred as a direct result of the production of an organisation's products and services. Sometimes called prime costs, an example of direct costs would be the expenditure associated with running an extra series of health and fitness courses, e.g. the wages for an extra instructor, publicity, postage, telephone costs, etc. (See also *overheads*.)

direct mail is the most common and fastest-growing type of *direct marketing* used in leisure and tourism. It is a technique that uses a *mailing list* of names and addresses to send promotional materials to selected individuals or organisations. Its uses in leisure, travel and tourism are extensive, for example:

- a *tourist attraction* sending details of its group rates to selected coach operators
- a travel agent mailing a newsletter to existing clients
- a *local authority* sending out leaflets about its leisure facilities with *Council Tax* bills

Large direct mail campaigns can make use of sophisticated *database marketing* systems, such as *ACORN*, as a way of targeting customers more effectively.

direct marketing is the term used to describe the various techniques that an organisation can use to sell its products and services on a personalised basis direct to the consumer, without the need for an *intermediary*. It is an important element of *promotion* in leisure and tourism, with the benefit of being able to target *customers* effectively and precisely. The most common direct marketing techniques used in leisure and tourism include *direct mail, telemarketing, door-to-door distribution* and *direct response advertising*.

direct response advertising is any type of *advertising*, in any medium, that asks a customer to respond in some way, perhaps by ringing a telephone number, completing a coupon or calling in to a shop to pick up a *brochure* or free gift. Some organisations use freecall numbers such as 0800 or 0500, reduced rate 0345 numbers or a freepost address, in order to stimulate more responses to the advertising.

direct sell is when an organisation sells its products and services direct to the consumer, rather than through an *intermediary*, sometimes called a 'middle man'. A hotelier, for example, may choose to advertise his establishment in local and national newspapers and handle all enquiries and bookings himself, rather than using the services of an agent. The hotelier will not have to pay any fee or *commission* to an agent when he sells direct, but he will have to pay the costs of advertising and staff time for handling enquiries and taking bookings. In the package holiday industry, direct sell operators, such as Portland Holidays and Eclipse Direct (formerly Tjaereborg, Sunfare and Martin Rooks), suggest that they can sell holidays more cheaply since they don't have to pay any commission to travel agents.

direct services organisation (DSO): a *local authority* in-house team that submits a *tender* in competition with commercial organisations for the right to manage leisure services and facilities. Under the terms of *compulsory competitive tendering (CCT)* legislation, the DSO must keep separate accounts for this aspect of the local authority's work. Successful DSOs may bid for the management of facilities in nearby districts, thereby increasing their spheres of activity.

direct tax: a levy on a person's income and the profits of an organisation. Individuals pay *income tax*, while companies pay corporation tax on their profits. Since 1979, the burden of *taxation* has shifted away from direct to *indirect taxes*, such as *value added tax (VAT)*.

director: a senior manager within an organisation, elected by the *shareholders* as their representative on the board of directors, the main policy-making committee. The duties of directors, who may be *executive* or *non-executive*, are to exercise their power, influence and authority for the good of the organisation. They are expected to act in a professional manner at all times when managing the affairs of the organisation.

disadvantaged groups: categories of people who, for a number of reasons generally outside of their control, are unable to participate fully in leisure activities and tourist trips. These groups, which include women, ethnic minorities, disabled people, rural dwellers and unemployed people, have been targeted for priority treatment by bodies such as the *Sports Council*, the *Holiday Care Service* and *Countryside Commission*. (See also *community recreation*.)

disciplinary procedures: the steps that the *management* of an organisation takes to deal with staff whose behaviour, work performance or absenteeism are giving cause for concern. The process normally starts with a *verbal warning*, followed by a *written warning*. If the problem persists, the management may issue a final written warning, which may ultimately lead to *dismissal*. It is important that organisations follow the disciplinary procedures to the letter, so as to ensure fairness for the employee and to reduce the likelihood of a claim for *unfair dismissal*.

discount: a reduction in the published price or *rack rate* for a product or service. Discounts are normally available for bulk purchases, so that a *tour operator* will be able to negotiate discounted rates for *accommodation* with hoteliers, on the basis of a high volume of business.

discounted cash-flow (DCF): a method of investment appraisal used to measure the desirability of an investment project, by converting future monetary values into current figures. (See also *investment appraisal*.)

discretionary income: see *disposable income*

dismissal: the termination of an employee's *contract of employment* by his or her employer, with or without notice. This may be as a result of *gross misconduct* or *redundancy*. (See also *unfair dismissal*.)

Disney: arguably the most successful *leisure* corporation of all time, based on the world's most popular *theme parks* founded by Walt Disney in the USA, the first being opened in California in 1955. Today, Disneyworld in Florida welcomes more than 25 million visitors every year, making it the world's number one tourist attraction. Disney ventured into the European theme park market in 1993 with the opening of Disneyland Paris, originally known as *EuroDisney*. Disney resorts and theme parks have set the industry standard for levels of *customer service* and *customer care*.

Disneyland, Paris: see *EuroDisney*

displacement effect is when tourism *development* has the effect of taking employment and other economic *resources* away from other industries, e.g. the development of tourism in some Mediterranean countries has taken jobs away from *primary sector* industries, such as fishing and agriculture. This may have long-term consequences for the health of a nation's economy.

display advertisement: an announcement in the *consumer* or trade *press* that includes headlines, graphics and/or pictures to create an impression with readers. Display advertisements tend to be larger than *classified advertisements* and are more expensive, being charged on a pro-rata basis for the space they take up.

display screen equipment: the Health and Safety (Display Screen Equipment) Regulations 1992 were developed as a direct result of the *EU Directives on health and safety*, to cover the safe use of such equipment as *computers* and *VDUs*. Work with

An example of a display advertisement (courtesy of Golley, Slater & Partners, Cardiff)

display screens is not generally hih risk, but it can lead to muscular and other physical problems, eye fatigue and mental stress. Under the regulations, employers have a duty to:

- assess workstations and reduce risks that are discovered
- make sure that workstations meet minimum requirements
- plan work so that there are breaks or changes of activity
- provide information and training for staff who use display screen equipment

Given that staff in the leisure and tourism industries use computers and VDUs on a daily basis, these particular regulations may have serious implications for particular organisations.

disposable income: the amount of money left over when all necessary household and personal expenses have been met. Disposable income, sometimes called discretionary income, is money that people can choose to spend as they wish, for example on *leisure* pursuits and *holidays*.

distance learning: a type of *off-the-job training* that involves study without the need for face-to-face contact with teachers or trainers. It can involve the use of written study materials, videos, audio cassettes, radio and television programmes. Sometimes referred to as a correspondence course, distance learning gives the student the advantage of working at his or her own pace. Some distance learning programmes, such as those run by the Open University, offer students telephone support from tutors, refresher seminars and summer schools.

distribution channels are the methods used to make products and services available to *customers*. Since many leisure and tourism products are *intangible*, with consumption taking place at the point of production, there is no need for a standard distribution system, as would be the case with, for example, sports goods and food.

The way that *package holidays* are sold shows clearly how distribution channels operate in leisure and tourism. *Tour operators* liaise with hoteliers and airlines to buy hotel bedspaces and airline seats. They then produce a *brochure* of their holidays which is stocked by travel agents, who sell the packages for a *commission*. Customers book their holidays from the travel agents or can sometimes book direct with *direct sell* operators. In this process, the tour operator acts as the wholesaler and the travel agent as the retailer.

district council: the tier of local government concerned with providing services to people living in one of the 333 non-metropolitan districts in England and Wales. District councils are responsible for providing a wide range of services, including libraries, refuse disposal, environmental health, planning and building control. District councils, some of which are known as borough councils, also play a vital role in the provision of leisure and tourism facilities, such as sports and *leisure centres*, parks and gardens, playing fields, museums, tourist information centres and theatres. Some of these may be dual use or *joint use*, when a facility is shared between the local community and schools or colleges to maximise its use.

diversification is the process of introducing new facilities, products and services into an organisation in order to increase sales and/or reduce the reliance on too narrow a range of products. There are many examples of diversification in leisure and tourism, including a tour operator buying a chain of hotels and a leisure centre offering to carry out fitness testing for employees in a nearby firm. Three distinct levels of diversification can be identified in leisure and tourism:

- diversification into and out of the industry, e.g. Lord Thomson initially built his empire on publishing, but diversified into tour operations in 1965
- diversification into different sectors of leisure and tourism, e.g. the *Rank Organisation* has interests in films, television, holidays, hotels, entertainments and leisure
- diversification within an individual organisation, e.g. a couple running a farm *bed and breakfast* enterprise deciding to convert a redundant building into *self-catering accommodation*

An important aspect of diversification is that an organisation is able to spread its risks across a number of different operations, thereby reducing the likelihood of overall business failure.

dividend: a payment to a *shareholder* from the profits of a *company*. Dividends are paid on both *ordinary shares* and *preference shares*, and are a type of investment from which the shareholder hopes to benefit, although there is no guarantee of a fixed return with ordinary shares. Dividends on ordinary shares will vary from one year to another, depending on the profitability of the company.

DNH: see *Department of National Heritage*

DoE: see *Department of the Environment*

'dogs': see *Boston Consulting Group matrix*

domestic tourism is when people take holidays, *short breaks* and business trips in their own country. For example, a family from York taking a two-week holiday in a caravan in Cornwall or a group of academics from London attending a conference in Chester are both examples of domestic tourism. Figures from the *British National Travel Survey* show that British people took an estimated 57.75 million long holidays (4+ nights) away from home in 1994, of which 31.5 million were in Britain (domestic tourism) and 26.25 million were abroad (*international tourism*). Altogether, they spent more than £4.6 billion on domestic tourism. The West Country is the most popular *destination* for UK domestic tourism, with 23 per cent of all long holidays spent in this region.

The domestic tourism industry in the UK has faced fierce competition in recent years from overseas package holidays. There is a general belief that many UK tourist regions have not invested sufficiently in accommodation, *infrastructure*, training and product development, and that they must be flexible enough to respond to the changing nature of the market for UK holidays. (See also *UK tourism.*)

domestic visitor: see *visitor*

door-to-door distribution: a method of *direct marketing* that involves the distribution of leaflets or other promotional materials to selected households. Door-to-door distribution is popular with hotels, restaurants, attractions and leisure facilities that are keen to capture a local market. A certain amount of *market segmentation* is possible with this distribution method, with particular postcode areas being targeted in terms of social class, age characteristics, family composition, etc. Local free newspapers often offer a leaflet distribution service to local companies.

DoT: see *Department of Transport*

DPA: see *Data Protection Act*

DSO: see *direct services organisation*

DTI: see *Department of Trade and Industry*

DTP: see *desktop publishing*

dual use: see *joint use*

Duke of Edinburgh's Award Scheme: a voluntary scheme aimed at encouraging young people between the ages of 14 and 25 to develop their talents, help their local communities, make new friends and learn new skills. They can progress from the Bronze Award, through Silver to the Duke of Edinburgh Gold Award, by completing specific tasks and expeditions.

duty-free refers to goods that are purchased free of all duties. Subject to certain limits, they may be bought in shops abroad and brought back into this country, or purchased at duty-free outlets at airports and ports, or on board aircraft and ships.

REVISION: There is a set of revision lists at the back of this book to help you prepare for GNVQ unit tests. See pages 246–250 for unit tests in GNVQ Advanced Leisure and Tourism.

E

Earth Summit: a major international conference held in Rio de Janiero in 1992 to consider global development and its impact on the world environment. Attended by the majority of world leaders, the Summit was a natural progression from the World Commission on Environment and Development held in 1987, which gave rise to the *Brundtland Report.* The Summit agreed a set of principles for future sustainable development, known as Agenda 21, which has since been interpreted and expanded at national, regional and local level in many countries. Many communities in the UK have developed their own action plans, referred to as Local Agenda 21. The role of tourism in global economic development was debated at the Earth Summit, leading to further debate on the concept of *sustainable tourism.*

East Anglia Tourist Board is the official *Regional Tourist Board* covering the counties of Essex, Suffolk, Norfolk, Cambridgeshire, Bedfordshire and Hertfordshire.

East Midlands Tourist Board is the official *Regional Tourist Board* covering the counties of Derbyshire, Lincolnshire, Nottinghamshire, Leicestershire and Northamptonshire.

EC stands for European Community, the grouping of member states renamed the *European Union (EU)* in 1993. The European Community was originally called the European Economic Community (EEC) when it was established in 1958.

Economic and Monetary Union (EMU): the process by which all member states of the *European Union* would agree to a single interest rate and exchange rate policy, rather than each country determining its own. At the final stage, there would be a *single currency* for all partcipating countries. The proposed deadline for EMU is 1999, but there are doubts in some countries as to whether this is achievable, or even desirable.

economic impacts of leisure and tourism refers to the positive and negative effects of the industries on national and local communities. One of the principle positive impacts is income generation for private individuals, local authorities, companies, voluntary bodies and national governments. Leisure and tourism also create jobs, with tourism alone employing more than 120 million people worldwide. Investment in leisure and tourism can also help *urban regeneration* projects and add to regional and national prosperity. Negative economic effects include the fact that local people may resent paying part of their taxes to provide facilities for visitors and land and property prices may rise as a result of tourist activity in an area.

economies of scale: the benefits that a large organisation gains by virtue of its size and scale of operation. *Multinational corporations,* for example, are able to pool the resources of their subsidiary companies and gain favourable discounts from *suppliers.* Smaller enterprises that enter into *co-operative marketing* activities can do likewise.

ecotourism is defined by the *Ecotourism Society* as 'purposeful travel to natural areas to understand the cultural and natural history of the environment, taking care not to alter the integrity of the ecosystem, whilst producing economic opportunities that make the conservation of natural resources financially beneficial to local citizens'. There is some concern that ecotourism, rather than being beneficial to local communities, can, because of its exploratory nature, actually have a more harmful effect than *mass tourism*, whose harmful effects tend to be confined to small areas of a country.

Ecotourism Society: an independent membership organisation that promotes the concept and practice of *sustainable tourism*, aimed particularly at visitors to natural areas of the world who wish to explore cultural and natural history.

ECU: see *European Currency Unit*

educational trip: see *familiarisation trip*

EEA: see *European Economic Area*

EEC: see *EC*

EFCT: see *European Federation of Conference Towns*

effective demand is the actual number of people using or buying a particular product or service, e.g. the number of people visiting a *theme park* over a six-week period or the number of people buying *package holidays* to Greece. Commercial organisations will be aiming to increase the effective demand for their products so as to increase their *market share*. (See also *suppressed demand*.)

effectiveness is a measure of how well an organisation has met its objectives. Measuring effectiveness presupposes that the organisation has developed *objectives* that are both realistic and measurable. Measurement is undertaken by developing and implementing a range of *performance indicators* and financial ratios. Effectiveness is also a function of *management style* and leadership.

efficiency is the wise use of an organisation's *resources*, i.e. the maximum output from the resources used. It can be measured in many ways, including by using *performance indicators*, e.g. the number of visitors per member of staff at a *tourist attraction*, and *financial ratios*, e.g. the *return on capital employed (ROCE)*. By using techniques such as these, an organisation can measure its financial efficiency, operational efficiency and overall efficiency.

EFTA: see *European Free Trade Association*

EFTPOS: see *electronic funds transfer at point-of-sale*

EHO: see *Environmental Health Officer*

EHOS: see *English Hotel Occupancy Survey*

EIA: see *environmental impact assessment*

EIB: see *European Investment Bank*

eighty/twenty rule: see *Pareto principle*

elasticity of demand: an economics term that measures how much the *demand* for a product or service is affected by changes in its price. Goods and services whose demand stays constant even if prices rise are said to be demand inelastic, e.g. staple foods such as bread. Those whose demand falls when the price rises are said to be demand elastic, e.g. some leisure and tourism products, such as entry prices at tourist attractions and package holidays.

Electricity at Work Regulations 1989: a set of statutory regulations that cover all aspects of electrical installations, equipment and maintenance in all places of work, including leisure and tourism premises. The regulations cover such items as earthing, connections, isolation of supply, protection from excess current and the competence of members of staff. *Management* must follow a clear programme of action to minimise risks from electrical plant and installations, including regular inspections and *training* for staff.

electronic communication: a range of techniques and equipment that allows the rapid transfer and receipt of information. Based on the premise that electronic communication is faster and more efficient than paper-based alternatives, worldwide communications are now available to all leisure and tourism organisations, regardless of their size. Electronic communication systems allow organisations to communicate internally and externally, using facilities such as *electronic mail, facsimile (fax) transmissions, ISDN* and the *Internet.* Electronic communication is set to transform business operations up to and beyond the year 2000.

electronic funds transfer at point-of-sale (EFTPOS): an electronic payment system, triggered by a plastic card, that automatically transfers money from a customer's bank account and credits the sum of money to the company selling the goods or services. The transaction is carried out at the *point-of-sale,* providing the *customer* with greater convenience and the retailer with greater security, since there is less cash to handle. EFTPOS systems accept both *credit cards* and *debit cards.*

electronic mail (E-mail): a computer-based system that allows the transfer of messages and information between registered E-mail users on a *network.* Most E-mail systems operate within large organisations, such as the headquarters of airlines and tour operators, but it is possible to send E-mail messages anywhere in the world via a number of worldwide communication systems such as Compuserve. E-mail provides instantaneous communication and also cuts down on the amount of paper used in an organisation.

electronic point-of-sale (EPOS): an electronic sales and *stock control* system that automates many of the tasks previously performed by sales staff, allowing them to concentrate on providing high levels of *customer service.* EPOS systems are commonplace in shops and supermarkets, where they will perform all of the normal functions of a cash register, but also log all transactions with time, date, items sold, cost, method of payment and the name of the member of staff who served the customer. In leisure and tourism, EPOS systems are found in pubs, clubs, arenas, entertainment complexes, cinemas, bars and fast-food outlets, where staff use 'touchpads', small touch-sensitive panels located behind the bar or counter and pre-programmed with prices. EPOS also allows automated control of stock and re-ordering procedures.

E-mail: see *electronic mail*

embargo: refers most commonly in leisure and tourism to a date or time before which a *press release* cannot be used. For example, a press release about the launch of a new tourism initiative may be circulated to the news media 24 hours before it actually takes place, with an instruction that the contents of the release should not be made public until after the launch has actually taken place. More generally, an embargo may be an order forbidding trade with a particular country or a stop on the release of information.

embarkation pass: see *boarding pass*

employment contract: see *contract of employment*

employment in leisure and tourism is one of the principal economic effects that countries and local areas gain from investment in the industries. Figures from the *World Travel and Tourism Council (WTTC)* estimate that there are approximately 118 million people working in the tourism industry worldwide. Closer to home, there are around 1.5 million people employed in tourism-related industries and 470 000 jobs in sport alone. Trends suggest that employment in the leisure and tourism industries will continue to rise up to and beyond the year 2000. (See also *careers in leisure and tourism.*)

'empty leg': an airline flight that has no passengers aboard. 'Empty legs' are the usual consequence of a *flight series charter* arrangement, when there will be an empty flight home at the beginning of a season, having dropped passengers off, and an empty flight out at the end of the same season to pick up passengers.

EMS: see *European Monetary System*

EMU: see *Economic and Monetary Union*

empowerment is the process of giving individuals ownership of the means to improve their personal and work-related development. Empowering people in the workplace can result in a more motivated and effective workforce, with greater confidence to try new ideas and exploit any new *opportunities* that may come along.

enclave: see *tourist enclave*

English Heritage is the government's official adviser on *conservation* legislation concerning historic buildings and ancient monuments. Established under the National Heritage Act 1983, it provides the major source of public funds for rescue archaeology, town schemes and repairs to historic buildings and ancient monuments. It is also responsible for preserving and presenting around 400 national historic properties, including Stonehenge, Dover Castle, Battle Abbey and Tintagel Castle. Financed mainly from government funds, English Heritage has a membership of around 275 000 and is the largest independent organisation responsible for heritage conservation in the country.

English Hotel Occupancy Survey (EHOS) is a joint venture between BDO Hospitality Consulting and the *English Tourist Board*, which provides data about hotel *occupancy rates* and overseas arrivals at UK hotels. It is presented in twelve monthly reports, as well as an annual summary.

English Nature is a government-funded body set up under the Environmental Protection Act of 1990, replacing the former Nature Conservancy Council. Its purpose is to promote the *conservation* of England's wildlife and natural features. The most visible signs of English Nature's work is its ownership or control of *National Nature Reserves* and the designation of *SSSIs (Sites of Special Scientific Interest)*.

English Sports Council (ESC): one of the new bodies set to replace the *Sports Council* on 1 April 1996. The ESC will concentrate its resources on helping grass-roots sport and the *governing bodies* of sport to achieve their objectives.

English Tourist Board (ETB) is the official *tourist board* for England, established under the *1969 Development of Tourism Act*. With its headquarters in London, shared with the *BTA*, its principal objectives are to:

- encourage people living in the UK to take holidays in England
- stimulate the provision and improvement of facilities for tourists to England
- advise government and public bodies on all matters concerning tourism in England
- produce and distribute information on tourism to the travel trade and consumers
- ensure that England's character and heritage is protected through the sensitive management of tourism

In order to achieve these objectives, ETB is engaged in a wide-ranging programme of work with *public* and *private sector* organisations, which includes marketing to the public and the travel trade, co-ordinating the network of *tourist information centres (TICs)* and advising on national and local tourism planning and development. ETB also undertakes and commissions research, publishing a range of statistical data related to tourism. ETB is financed from central government, through the *Department of National Heritage.* Since the early 1990s, ETB has seen its government funding cut severely from £15.6 million in 1992/93 to £9.1 million in 1995/96.

enplane is the term used to denote passengers boarding an aircraft. (See also *deplane.*)

Enterprise Neptune is the *National Trust's campaign* to save Britain's threatened coastline. Launched by the Duke of Edinburgh in 1965, with a target of raising £2 million towards the purchase of the remaining 900 miles of unspoilt coastline in England, Wales and Northern Ireland, Enterprise Neptune's fund now stands at more than £22 million. To date, 368 miles of coastline have been brought under the protection of the National Trust with the help of Neptune funds, in addition to the 187 miles the Trust previously owned, making a total of 555 miles under protection. As well as raising funds to acquire coastline, Enterprise Neptune also aims to draw attention to the pressures facing this threatened habitat.

entertainment facilities: a wide-ranging term used to describe a variety of products and services offered by public, private and voluntary sector *leisure* and *recreation* providers. They can be divided into those facilities provided outside the home, e.g. cinemas, bingo halls, social clubs, theatres, etc., and a range of *home-based leisure* facilities and products, such as television, board games, computer games, video recorders, hi-fi systems, etc. Private sector entertainment facilities can be further subdivided into those that require active participation, including dance halls, ballrooms, nightclubs, etc., and those that offer performances to audiences, e.g. arenas, concert halls, theatres, etc. (See also *arts and entertainment, community recreation.*)

entrepreneur: an individual who is prepared to take a risk and accept a challenge or undertake a venture that has no guarantee of success. Entrepreneurs often run their own businesses and can be an inspiration to others to follow the route of enterprise. Richard Branson, *chairman* of the Virgin Group, is often cited as a good example of an entrepreneur.

environmental audit: an investigation of an organisation's *policies, management* and practices from the point of view of their impact on the local and global environment. Many leisure, travel and tourism organisations, large and small, are beginning to look at their activities and put in place measures to reduce their environmental impact, e.g. the use of low-energy lighting systems, unleaded fuels, recycling programmes and biodegradable materials. Although often a voluntary exercise, many companies are, nonetheless, keen to display their 'green' awareness, as well as using their concern for the environment as a *marketing* tool.

Environmental Health Officer (EHO): an official employed by a *local authority* to monitor a range of environmental issues in a locality, including the handling and storage of food in shops, restaurants and hotels, air and water pollution, and excessive noise at events such as outdoor concerts and sporting matches.

environmental impacts of leisure and tourism can be both positive and negative. On the positive side, we see initiatives such as the *Britain in Bloom* competition and the *Seaside Award* helping to improve local environments for both locals and visitors. Problems associated with the environmental impacts of leisure and tourism include litter, pollution, physical erosion and loss of habitats. Careful visitor and traffic management can go some way towards minimising many of these problems, although areas such as the *National Parks* are under particular pressures.

environmental impact analysis: see *environmental impact assessment*

environmental impact assessment (EIA): a technique for carrying out an appraisal of the costs and benefits of a particular development from an environmental point of view. Sometimes called an environmental impact analysis, an EIA may be necessary before the building of a major *hotel* or leisure complex is given the approval to proceed. The EIA is a structured process which aims to establish who will lose and who will gain if a development goes ahead, examine alternative courses of action and their likely impacts, and consider ways of reducing impacts if a project is given the green light. Increasing concern for the environment will mean that EIAs will become more common in determining future leisure and *tourism* projects.

environmental management: the practice of managing *resources* in such a way as to cause least harm to the environment and promoting sustainability. This may involve organisations in carrying out an *environmental audit, environmental impact assessment (EIA)* or applying for external certification under *BS 7750*.

Environmentally Sensitive Area (ESA): an area of countryside where the *Ministry of Agriculture, Fisheries and Food (MAFF)* is working with farmers to conserve characteristic landscapes, wildlife habitats and historic features. The ESA scheme was introduced in 1987, with ten designated areas, including Breckland, Clun, North Peak and the South Downs. After several years of operation, the original schemes have been enhanced and expanded, and now include provision for public access for walking on enclosed farmland. The 22 ESAs in place today range in character from coastal marshland to rolling chalklands, river valleys and open moorland.

EOC: see *Equal Opportunites Commission*

EPOS: see *electronic point-of-sale*

equal opportunities is concerned with giving all people, regardless of their gender, age, race, religion, ability, employment status, income level and mobility, equal rights in society. This extends to equal rights in the workplace and employment issues generally, as well as equal access to *leisure* and *tourism* facilities and opportunities. *Legislation* such as the *Equal Pay Act* and *Race Relations Act* has sought to make discrimination illegal, while bodies like the *Sports Council* and *Countryside Commission* are actively promoting equal access for all.

Equal Opportunities Commission (EOC): an organisation set up under the auspices of the *Sex Discrimination Act 1975* to promote good practice in eliminating discrimination in the workplace on the grounds of gender. The EOC now has a wider remit, being involved with a range of equality issues and advising individuals and employers on the development of codes of practice and other mechanisms for reducing discrimination.

Equal Pay Act 1970: legislation introduced to abolish discrimination between men and women in pay and other terms of their *contracts of employment*. The Act was amended in 1983 to give all workers the right to equal pay for work of equal value when:

- the work being carried out by both male and female employees is the same or broadly similar (this is known as 'like work')
- the work of employees undertaking different jobs is of 'equal value'
- a *job evaluation study (JES)* has been carried out

Employees who feel that they should be receiving equal pay can apply to an *industrial tribunal* at any time during their employment, or up to six months after leaving.

equity is a financial term referring to the owners' stake in a business as *shareholders*, plus the profits from previous years that have not been distributed. Equity is a form of risk capital, since there is no guarantee that shareholders will receive any dividend on their investment in a company. Principal sources of equity are a company's owners, private shareholders, banks and providers of *venture capital*.

ERDF: see *European Regional Development Fund*

ERM: see *Exchange Rate Mechanism*

ESA: see *Environmentally Sensitive Area*

ESF: see *European Social Fund*

estimates are projections made by *local authorities* of their likely *revenue* and expenditure for the forthcoming year. Councillors will debate whether estimates for particular departments will need amending and must agree the estimates before the officers can begin preparing their operating budgets. The estimates are usually based on the previous year's budgets, with an adjustment made for *inflation*.

ETB: see *English Tourist Board*

ETC: see *European Travel Commission*

ethics: the moral codes and values that should underpin any decision making by individuals and organisations. They represent an acceptance that a *company* decision which would generate most profit is not necessarily in the best interests of society as a whole. A tour operator, for example, may identify an opportunity to develop *package holidays* to a remote part of South America, which would prove financially profitable in the long term. There may, however, be risk of environmental or cultural damage to the indigenous people. It may decide not to go ahead on ethical grounds.

Sponsorship is another area that sometimes causes ethical problems. Should a sports club or individual sportsman or woman accept sponsorship money from a company that promotes smoking or other harmful practices? *Pressure groups* sometimes become involved in these situations and force companies to think again.

ethnic minority: the term used to describe a small number of people of a particular cutural background living in an area or country where the majority of the population follows a different cultural or religious code. There is general concern that ethnic minorities in Britain may not be getting equal access to *leisure* and *sport* facilities. Bodies such as the *Sports Council* have targeted people from within these groups as priorities for action to improve the situation.

EU: see *European Union*

EU Bathing Water Directive: this *EU Directive* sets quality standards for bathing waters in all member countries of the *European Union*. The Directive requires each country to identify the stretches of coastline most popular with holidaymakers and these are tested regularly during the bathing season. In the UK, the testing is carried out by the *National Rivers Authority (NRA)*. All EU countries have to make sure that their bathing waters meet the standards set down in the Directive and take measures to rectify any deficiencies. The results of the tests are made available to the general public. Since its introduction in 1976, the Directive has been the subject of much controversy in the UK. Proposals have been put forward to simplify the testing procedure and provide a more streamlined service. (See also *Blue Flag Campaign*.)

EU Directive: a law or regulation which is binding on all member states of the *European Union (EU)*. Proposals for EU Directives come initially from the *European Commission*, are debated by the *European Parliament* and given final approval by the *Council of Ministers*, after consideration by their national parliaments. Examples of EU Directives are the *Package Travel Directive* and the *EU Bathing Water Directive*.

EU Directives on health and safety: six new sets of health and safety at work regulations came into force at the beginning of 1993, to meet the requirements of six European Union (EU) Directives on health and safety. The Directives are part of the EU's programme of action on health and safety, which is an essential ingredient of the move towards a *Single Market* in Europe. Most of the requirements of the Directives are not completely new, meaning that any leisure or tourism organisation that is already complying with the *Health and Safety at Work, etc. Act* should not find the new regulations daunting. The regulations cover:

- *health and safety management*
- *work equipment safety*
- *manual handling of loads*
- *workplace conditions*
- *personal protective equipment*
- *display screen equipment*

All leisure and tourism organisations are likely to be affected in some way by one of more of the new regulations, with implications for finance, staffing and *management*.

EU Package Travel Directive: see *Package Travel Directive*

Eurocheque: a form of *currency* used throughout Europe which allows the holder to withdraw money from banks and write *cheques* in any local currency. Just as with a standard cheque used in the UK, Eurocheques must be supported by a valid Eurocheque guarantee card. Eurocheques have not been used extensively by UK travellers who prefer to use *travellers' cheques* and *credit cards.*

EuroDisney: the *Disney* resort opened in 1993 near Paris, now known as Disneyland Paris. After a disastrous start from a financial viewpoint, the theme park is beginning to show signs of improvement, both in visitor numbers and revenue. Disney has had problems in selling an essentially American concept to the European market.

European Association for Education in Tourism, Leisure and the Arts (ATLAS) is an association of higher education institutions throughout Europe that provide courses in *tourism, leisure* and the arts. Established in 1991, ATLAS exists to:

- promote the teaching of tourism, leisure and the arts throughout Europe
- encourage the exchange of staff and students between member institutions
- promote links between professional bodies in tourism, leisure and the arts and to liaise on issues, curriculum development and professional recognition of courses
- promote transnational research which helps to underpin the development of appropriate curricula throughout Europe

Membership of ATLAS is open to any institution of higher education or professional bodies in Europe with an interest in these areas.

European Commission: an important institution in the *European Union*, which makes proposals for European laws and ensures that EU policies and practices are followed by member states. The Commission fulfils a similar role to that of the civil service in the UK, except that the Commission actually proposes legislation. Any proposals for new EU laws or regulations pass from the Commission to the *European Parliament* for debate and then on to the *Council of Ministers* for approval or rejection. The Commission is made up of a number of separate departments, known as Directorates General (DGs). The department concerned most with tourism issues is DG23, although the work of many other DGs has a bearing on the industry, e.g. DG7 which handles transportation matters.

European Community (EC): the former name of the grouping of European countries now known as the *European Union.*

European Council is the name given to the European Union Heads of State or Government, which usually meets twice a year to give overall direction to the Union's work. The Heads of State take it in turns to chair the meetings of the European Council. (See also *Council of Ministers.*)

European Court of Justice: a *European Union* institution that interprets and adjudicates on Union law. There are fifteen judges, one from each member state, plus one extra to prevent deadlock, and six Advocates General who advise the Court. The Court is assisted by a Court of First Instance, which handles certain cases brought by individuals and companies.

European Currency Unit (ECU): an artificial currency made up of the trade-weighted averages of the currencies of the *EU* member states. The ECU is the basis on which the *European Union's* transactions are carried out, so that any payments to assist member countries with structural or economic developments are made in ECUs. The ECU may form the basis of a European common currency in the future, if *Economic and Monetary Union (EMU)* becomes a reality.

European Economic Area (EEA): the trading zone set up under an agreement signed in 1991 by the member states of the *European Union (EU)* and the *European Free Trade Association (EFTA).* The agreement allows greater access to EU countries for EFTA members, while at the same time promoting the harmonisation of legislation between countries belonging to the two organisations.

European Economic Community (EEC): see *European Union*

European Federation of Conference Towns (EFCT) is a Brussels-based membership organisation representing the interests of conference towns throughout Europe. EFCT provides advice and guidance to meeting planners and conference and incentive group organisers who seek a venue anywhere in Europe. For conference towns which meet its criteria, EFCT membership is a resource which helps to spread information about their *destinations*, centres, hotels and services. EFCT members in the UK include Birmingham, Eastbourne, Brighton, Edinburgh and London.

European Free Trade Association (EFTA) was set up in 1960 to encourage the free movement of goods between its member countries, which originally included the *UK*, Austria, Finland, Iceland, Denmark, Norway, Sweden and Switzerland. Since countries cannot be members of both EFTA and the *European Union*, the UK, Denmark, Austria and Sweden have subsequently left the Association. In many respects EFTA is a rival organisation to the European Union, but there is close co-operation on matters concerning the movement of people, goods, services and capital and both bodies have agreed to work towards the formation of an integrated trading zone known as the *European Economic Area (EEA).*

European Investment Bank (EIB) is the *European Union's* bank for financing capital investment projects that promote the balanced development of Europe. The Bank works with both public and private sector organisations and has funded a variety of *tourism* projects throughout the EU.

European Monetary System (EMS): a system introduced in 1979 that aims to harmonise the currencies of the member states of the *European Union (EU)* prior to full *Economic and Monetary Union (EMU).* The two principal elements of the EMS are the *ECU (European Currency Unit)* and the *Exchange Rate Mechanism (ERM).*

European Parliament: the institution in the *European Union* which debates and amends legislation put forward by the *European Commission.* The European Parliament is made up of 626 Members of the European Parliament (MEPs), directly elected every five years from within the member states. Seats are shared out between member states broadly according to the size of the country. The Parliament sits in both Brussels and Strasbourg.

European Plan: an *accommodation* arrangement consisting of a room only, with no meals included in the tariff. (See also *American Plan, Modified American Plan, Continental Plan.*)

European Regional Development Fund (ERDF): an *EU* Structural Fund which is primarily used by member states to improve the *infrastructure* in their countries. Eligible tourism and leisure projects include airport developments, hotel building and extensions, road projects, conference centres, museums, sports centres, archaeological sites and leisure developments. The ERDF is only able to support capital projects in designated areas of the UK.

European Social Fund (ESF): a *European Union* training fund, which concentrates on helping young people who are out of work and the long-term unemployed in the EU member states. Certain ESF projects are connected with leisure and tourism, for example skills *training* in the hotel and catering sector.

European Travel Commission (ETC): a voluntary body established in 1948 to promote the whole of Europe as a single tourist destination to the rest of the world. ETC's stated aims are to increase the level of *tourism* from other parts of the world to Europe, as a result of its marketing activities, and to provide a forum for individual member countries to exchange ideas and experiences for the benefit of each member of the group. The work of the ETC is supported by the *European Commission*, which sees tourism as an industry of growing economic importance throughout Europe and beyond.

European Union (EU) is a grouping of 15 countries, known as member states, who have joined together to safeguard peace and promote economic and social progress in Europe. The EU originated in 1957 as the European Economic Community (EEC) with six original members: France, Italy, West Germany, Belgium, Netherlands and Luxembourg. Membership increased to nine in 1973 when Ireland, the United Kingdom and Denmark joined. In 1981 Greece became the tenth member state, followed by Spain and Portugal in 1986. The most recent members are Austria, Finland and Sweden who became full members of the EU in 1995.

With a population in excess of 400 million, the EU is the world's largest trading entity. The EU is made up of a number of interlinked institutions, the most important of which are the *European Commission*, the *Council of Ministers*, the *European Parliament*, the *European Council* and the *European Court of Justice*. The Treaty of Rome sets out the Union's legal framework. It was amended by the Single European Act in 1986, while the Treaty of Maastricht incorporated further changes.

The EU is involved with a number of issues which concern leisure and tourism in Europe, including the abolishing of frontier controls, liberalisation of air travel, the *Package Travel Directive*, harmonisation of *VAT* rates and the deregulation of coach travel.

European Year of Tourism 1990 was conceived by the *European Commission* with the general aim of promoting greater knowledge among *EU* citizens of the cultures and life styles of other member states. Specific objectives of the initiative were the staggering of holidays, the development of new tourist destinations, the creation of alternatives to mass tourism, the promotion of tourism within EU member states and the development of tourism to Europe from non-EU countries. Altogether there were more than 2 000 events held in the UK alone in support of the initiative.

Eurostar is the passenger train service that operates through the *Channel Tunnel*, as opposed to *le Shuttle*, which is the vehicle-carrying service using shuttle trains.

Eurostar reaches Paris in 3 hours and Brussels in 3 hours and 15 minutes from the new Waterloo International Terminal in London. These timings are likely to reduce considerably when the high-speed rail link between London and the Channel Tunnel is completed soon after the year 2000. Eurostar offers a range of *APEX* and standard fares and some *tour operators* are now featuring short breaks on the continent travelling on the service.

Eurostat is the official body that collects, analyses and publishes statistical data on matters concerning the *European Commission* and member states of the *European Union (EU)*. Officially known as the Statistical Office of the European Communities, Eurostat publishes two main sets of documents:

- statistical documents – comprehensive, reference data intended for specialists and made available in paper form or on diskette, magnetic tape or CD-rom
- general publications – intended for a wider audience and grouped in subject areas, including education, health, transport, travel and tourism

Eurostat also publishes a variety of yearbooks which are a useful starting point for initial research. Eurostat's data on tourism shows which are the main *generating* and *receiving* countries in Europe.

Eurotunnel: the joint English-French consortium of companies that built and now operates the *Channel Tunnel*. (See also *Eurostar, le Shuttle.*)

evaluation is the process of looking back on an event or management decision to gauge if, with the benefit of hindsight, matters were handled as effectively as possible. In *leisure* and *tourism*, there are many circumstances in which evaluation is undertaken, including:

- to see if an event has met its *objectives*
- to establish whether visitors are happy with a facility or standard of service
- to find out whether financial and staffing *resources* are being used to best effect
- to compare performance with competitor organisations
- to identify weaknesses and strengths in *management* and administrative systems

Evaluation is often the final stage of a cyclical management process, e.g. *management by objectives (MBO)*.

evaluation process: see *evaluation*

event co-ordinator: a person who takes the lead role in overseeing the *planning* and organisation of an event. Events play an important part in leisure and tourism, making the appointment of an effective co-ordinator a very important decision. Although every event is unique, there are basic skills and qualities that any good co-ordinator should possess, including excellent leadership qualities, good written and oral *communication* skills, persuasive negotiation skills and the ability to delegate. The co-ordinator will often chair the planning meetings set up to ensure the smooth running of an event.

event evaluation is the process of reflecting on the planning and staging of an event to analyse whether its *objectives* were met and *resources* were used to best effect.

It tries to answer a number of questions, such as 'was the organisational structure workable?', 'were those who attended satisfied with the event?' and 'were all eventualities covered?'. The event organiser and organising committee should hold a debriefing session with all staff and helpers after the event, before a final *report* on the event is prepared and distributed to interested parties, with one copy being retained for future reference.

event objectives are the aims that an individual or organisation will hope to achieve from running an event. Event organisers need to be clear at the outset exactly why an event is being staged and what outcomes are expected of them and their helpers. As with all goals, event objectives need to be measurable, realistic and achievable.

Precise objectives will vary depending on the nature of the event and whether the organiser lies in the *public, private* or *voluntary sector*. Public sector organisations will stage events to fulfil their social and community objectives, rather than attempting to make a profit. A local council, for example, often feels that events improve the quality of life for local people. Private companies will usually be looking to make a profit from running an event, although an event in itself may be seen as a good way of promoting a facility or product. Voluntary bodies organise events to raise funds and publicise a specific cause, perhaps a local playgroup or an environmental concern.

event planning is a crucial early phase in the running of a successful event. Once a decision to proceed has been made, an individual or, more commonly, a group of people will get together to plan timescales and the best use of their *resources*. The key stages in the planning process for a large event are likely to include:

- making the decision widely known
- setting budgets
- appointing a co-ordinator
- assembling a *committee*
- creating an organisational structure
- clarifying objectives
- setting timescales and deadlines
- devising *contingency plans*

It is sometimes helpful if the plan is set out as a *critical path analysis (CPA)*, indicating the precise order of tasks and where responsibilities lie.

events are an important part of the leisure and tourism scene worldwide, ranging in complexity from the *Olympic Games* to a local neighbourhood fête. The definition of an event would include the fact that it is a 'one off', or at least occurs infrequently, and that it is an opportunity for the public to enjoy its leisure time, or business people to meet, while at the same time allowing the organisers to achieve their objectives. While it is true that events are not a new phenomenon (the Olympic Games originated in 776 BC), the scope of events held today goes well beyond celebrating a religious festival or recognising the cultural importance of a date in the calendar. Nowadays, events can be staged very quickly to meet ever-changing needs, tastes and fashions, and areas can develop *events-led strategies* to help towards economic and social development.

events-led strategy: a promotional programme that uses a series of events, either already existing or newly created, to raise the awareness of an area and attract visitors to it. An events-led strategy is seen as a way of contributing to the economic and social development of both rural and urban areas, e.g. the *Mid Wales Festival of the Countryside* and the *Castlefield Urban Heritage Park* in Manchester. Such a strategy is particularly attractive to an area that has few inherent *natural* or *man-made visitor attractions.*

Exchange Rate Mechanism (ERM): an important arrangement, part of the *European Monetary System (EMS),* which was established in 1978 to limit fluctuations in the currencies of the member states of the *European Union (EU).* Political and economic tensions between countries led in 1992 to the UK suspending its membership of the ERM.

exchange rates: see *rate of exchange*

excursion fare: see *APEX, PEX*

excursionist: a term which originated in North America to describe an individual who makes a visit which doesn't involve an overnight stay away from their normal place of residence. In Britain an excursionist would be called a day visitor. For statistical purposes, excursionists include travellers in transit and those on ocean cruises who do not use *accommodation* in the country visited.

executive director: a full-time employee of an organisation who will sit on its board of directors, thereby helping to determine *policy.* An executive director will normally be responsible for a department or group of departments within an organisation, and will have a number of managers working under his or her leadership. (See also *non-executive director.*)

expatriate: a person who chooses to live in a country other than that of which he or she is a citizen. The move is not necessarily permanent, but is usually relatively long term.

expenditure budget: a chart which shows the spending limits that must be adhered to so that a department or whole organisation achieves its financial targets. It will include all the *fixed* and *variable costs* that are attributable over a given period of time, which could be monthly or annually. Showing monthly expenditure will allow management to rectify swiftly any variances between the budgeted and actual expenditure by taking the appropriate action. The performance of the expenditure budget cannot be divorced from the figures contained in the *sales budget* and it is a matter of preference whether or not the two budgets are combined or kept separate. (See also *budgetary control.*)

exports are goods and services sent overseas from their country of origin. They may be either *'visible'* or *'invisible'* items and the flows of currency associated with exports are shown in a country's *balance of payments.* The earnings from *overseas visitors* coming to Britain is considered as an export, since they are bringing money into the country, in the same way that a British car manufacturer does when it earns money from exporting its vehicles.

external communication is liaison between an organisation and a range of outside bodies. In leisure and tourism, these will include *customers*, the Inland Revenue, trade associations such as *ABTA*, professional bodies such as the *Tourism Society*, the *Health and Safety Executive (HSE)*, the police, neighbours and other organisations in the many sectors of the industry.

external constraint: is something outside of an organisation's immediate control that limits its ability to achieve its full potential. Typical external constraints in the leisure and tourism industries are economic factors, such as changing exchange rates or *interest rate* rises, social factors, including the rise in one-parent families, political considerations, such as a change in the government, and technological developments, including the introduction of new global communications systems. (See also *internal constraint.*)

external cost: see *social cost*

external environment: see *macro environment*

external recruitment: the process of identifying and employing the most suitable person from outside an organisation to fill a job vacancy.

externalities are those costs or benefits of an organisation's operation that are borne by the wider community or society in general, rather than by the organisation itself, e.g. an external benefit of building a fifth terminal at Heathrow may be that the energy costs for the airport as a whole are reduced, but an *external cost* may be that local people will have to put up with more noise from aircraft. (See also *internal costs.*)

'extra product' is a common *sales promotion* technique in leisure and tourism, when a *customer* is given additional benefits when buying a product or service, at no extra cost, e.g. three weeks for the price of two on a holiday.

extrapolation: the technique of *forecasting* future events based on an analysis of past performance. Tour operators, for example, will plot their past sales figures for particular products and destinations on a graph and attempt to forecast future sales on the same graph. Extrapolation can only give a short-term guide to likely future trends.

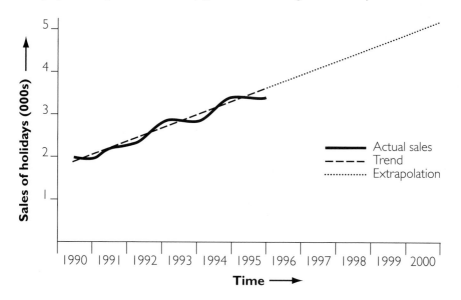

F

face-to-face communication is the most common way that individuals communicate with each other. For staff working in leisure and tourism, the number of occasions when they will be communicating face-to-face is very diverse, e.g. a travel agency clerk advising a client, a coach teaching children how to play tennis or a concierge directing hotel guests to the nearest railway station. Information and decisions within an organisation are often communicated on a face-to-face basis, although it does have the disadvantage of being an informal technique, i.e. there is no written confirmation of what was said. For this reason, decisions made in a face-to-face situation, e.g. a meeting or briefing event, will often be confirmed in writing. Face-to-face communication allows an individual to see how a person reacts to a situation and observe any *non-verbal communication* signals.

face-to-face interview: a survey that involves an *interviewer* asking questions of a member of the general public, known as the *respondent*, and recording his or her answers on a *questionnaire*. This type of survey is very common in all sectors of the leisure and tourism industries, from leisure centres to *seaside resorts*, and is a good way of obtaining both *qualitative* and *quantitative data*. Face-to-face interviews can be carried out in a number of different locations, such as at the respondent's home, in the street, at a leisure or tourism facility, en route to a *destination* or at work. They have a number of advantages over other *survey* techniques, for example:

- the interviewer can explain difficult questions
- visual aids can be used
- the interviewer can prompt the respondent for further detail
- initial interest on the part of the respondent is aroused

The principal disadvantages of face-to-face interviews are that they are expensive, since interviewers have to be recruited and fully trained, and that they are time-consuming when compared with other techniques, e.g. *telephone surveys*.

facsimile transmission: the sending of written documents nationally and internationally using fax machines connected by telephone lines. It combines the speed of the telephone with the accuracy of the printed word and is, therefore, particularly suited to the needs of *travel agents, tour operators* and airlines, who operate globally, often across different *time zones*.

factoring is the practice of selling off *bad debts* at a reduced rate to an agency which specialises in their collection. For the organisation selling off the debts it has the advantage of eliminating the time and effort needed to chase outstanding payments, plus any legal fees and interest payments associated with them, but the price at which the debts are passed on is considerably less than their face value.

factory tourism: a particular type of tourist activity where working factories open their doors to members of the public, either as individuals or in organised groups.

'fam' trip: see *familiarisation trip*

familiarisation trip: an educational visit which gives *travel agents, tour operators* and other members of the *travel trade* the opportunity of trying facilities and services first hand, so that they are in the best position to advise clients on their holiday choices. Also referred to as 'fam' trips or educational trips, they are an important part of both *sales promotion* and *public relations.*

Farm Holiday Bureau is a network whose primary function is to promote the concept of *farm tourism* in the UK. It represents the interests of more than 1 000 independent farmers who offer hospitality either in farmhouses, as bed, breakfast and evening meal, or in *self-catering accommodation.* Each member belongs to a local marketing group, of which there are now 92 in the UK affiliated to the Farm Holiday Bureau. The Bureau produces an annual guide, ensures high standards of accommodation in conjunction with the *National Tourist Boards* and acts as a forum for debate.

farm open day: an event held on a working farm to which the general public are invited as a way of educating them in the work of the farming community, as well as providing an extra source of revenue for the farmer. The open day is a type of *interpretation*, in that it is providing visitors with items such as demonstrations, self-guided trails and guided walks, that are designed to enhance their enjoyment and understanding.

farm tourism: a type of *rural tourism* centred on working farms. It takes many forms, but is most commonly associated with *accommodation*, including farmhouse bed and breakfast and self-catering accommodation in cottages and converted, redundant farm buildings. Farm tourism provides a welcome alternative source of income for farmers and their families and can help stop rural depopulation, particularly among young people. Farms also provide facilities for day visitors, including *farm open days* and rare breeds centres.

fast-food outlet: a limited-menu catering enterprise that offers food and drink for consumption on or off the premises. Fast-food outlets aim to serve a high volume of *customers* in as short a time as possible, thereby maximising revenue. Many are part of multinational chains, such as BurgerKing and McDonalds, and operate on uniform recipes, procedures and products.

fast-moving consumer goods (FMCGs) are products that sell in volume through a network of sales outlets. FMCGs include food, toiletries, clothes and cars. Much of the early work in *marketing* was focused on FMCGs, particularly in the USA. Techniques such as *market segmentation, niche marketing* and *target marketing* were applied first to the FMCG sector and have only recently been applied to *service sector* industries, including leisure, travel and tourism.

Fastrak: a *viewdata system* used in travel agencies to access *principal's computerised reservation systems (CRSs)* using a *VDU* plus either a telephone line or cable connection. Its main rival is *Istel.*

fax: see *facsimile transmission*

feasibility study: a systematic analysis of a possible project or development to determine whether it is sensible to go ahead, both financially and operationally. The study, whether carried out in-house or by external consultants, should include information on the *capital* and revenue costs of the proposal, the likely market, any environmental consequences, an assessment of the *competition* locally and any legal constraints that may cause a problem. After careful analysis of the facts, the feasibility study should include a recommendation on whether or not the proposal should be given the go-ahead. (See also *pre-feasibility study.*)

features statement: that part of the *sales process* in leisure and tourism, before the *customer* has made a decision whether or not to purchase, when a sales person highlights the features of a particular service or product. This could be the number of rooms in a hotel, the frequency of flights from a particular airport or the type of equipment available in a health and fitness club. Often a customer shows a degree of indifference at this stage, making it necessary to introduce an *advantages statement* or *benefits statement* in the hope of finally *closing the sale*.

Federation of Tour Operators (FTO): an independent membership body representing the interests of the leading British tour operating companies. Formerly the Tour Operators' Study Group (TOSG), the FTO is active in lobbying government for changes to *legislation* that affects its members' interests.

feedback: the process of inviting and collecting comments, suggestions and complaints from a variety of sources and using the information to influence future *policies* and *strategies*. Feedback is an essential aspect of any *communication* process in leisure and tourism, and is made available by customers, staff, volunteers, local people, politicians, pressure groups, councillors, etc. Feedback from customers can be either formal or informal, and can be obtained from surveys, customer comment forms, *customer satisfaction questionnaires (CSQs)*, suggestion boxes, *focus groups* and *'mystery shopper'* techniques. The feedback obtained will help determine future products, services and customer service standards.

feelgood factor: the notion that people have to feel confident in themselves before a nation's economy can prosper, irrespective of how positive any economic indicators show the economy to be.

ferry services: shipping that carries passengers, freight and vehicles on relatively short-duration trips, linking one land mass with another. The most popular ferry services in the UK are those concentrated on the English Channel, especially the Dover-Calais route. Other important services link the UK with Ireland and Scandinavia. Growth in the popularity of ferry travel in recent years has seen the introduction of longer crossings to Spain, with P&O operating to Bibao and Brittany Ferries to Santander.

Ferries operating on the Dover-Calais route are facing competition from the *Eurostar* and *le Shuttle* services using the *Channel Tunnel*. Ferry companies are responding to increased competition in a number of ways, e.g. the introduction of new, faster ferries, improvements to the quality of ship accommodation and price reductions.

Festival of Arts and Culture 1995: a year-long initiative devised and co-ordinated by the *British Tourist Authority (BTA)* with the support of all four *National Tourist Boards* in the UK and the *Regional Tourist Boards* in England. The Festival's aim is to provide a sharper focus for Britain's arts and culture, with a view to increasing earnings from tourism. The Festival has a number of themes, including literature, crafts and the performing arts. BTA has earmarked £10 million for the campaign, with promotion in more than 50 countries worldwide.

field research: see *primary research*

fifty/fifty marketing: see *co-operative marketing*

financial accounting is concerned with the preparation of the financial information an organisation is required by law to produce. In the private sector, these statutory accounts are:

- the *profit and loss account*
- the *balance sheet*
- the *cash-flow statement*

Financial accountants are bound by legislation contained in the various Companies' Acts concerning the method of presentation of financial data and the disclosure of certain information. Financial accounts are prepared to meet the needs of owners, managers, shareholders, the Inland Revenue, HM Customs and Excise (in the case of VAT), the Registrar of Companies and any providers of finance to the organisation. (See also management accounting.)

financial performance of a leisure or tourism organisation will be affected by a number of external and internal factors. External factors, outside the immediate control of the organisation, could include the general state of the economy, changes in tastes and fashions, government *legislation*, industrial disputes, competitor activity or *seasonality*. Internal factors might include low sales volume, high levels of *credit*, poor *stock control* or high *fixed* and *variable costs*.

financial ratios are a means by which managers can measure the financial *effectiveness* and *efficiency* of their organisation. Common ratios used in leisure and tourism include the *return on capital employed (ROCE)*, *gross profit/sales ratio* and the *net profit/sales ratio*. When combined with *performance indicators*, financial ratios will provide essential information for *planning* and *management* purposes.

Fire Certificate: a statutory document issued by local fire authorities to regulate the use of public premises and specify certain minimum standards of fire equipment and procedures that must be adhered to. A Fire Certificate will list a number of conditions that the owner or operator of the premises will need to comply with, including:

- keeping escape routes clear in case of emergency
- providing employees with fire safety training
- limits to the number of people allowed on the premises
- carrying out fire drills at specified times
- keeping records relating to fire safety matters

Fire Precautions Act 1971: legislation to regulate the use of premises and reduce risks to the public from fire-related incidents. Under the terms of the Act, the operator of any premises providing entertainment, *recreation* or use of a club or association, where there are more than twenty employees on the ground floor or more than ten above ground floor level, must apply for a *Fire Certificate* from the local fire authorities. *Hotels* and other *serviced accommodation* also fall within the scope of the Act, with a Fire Certificate necessary if the accommodation sleeps more than six guests at first floor level or just one guest at either second floor level or below ground.

first aid refers to treatment procedures that can be carried out immediately at the scene of an accident, prior to the emergency services arriving to take control of the situation. The *Health and Safety at Work, etc. Act* and its associated regulations, in particular the Health and Safety (First Aid) Regulations 1981, place a duty on employers to provide adequate first aid for both employees and non-employees, which in the case of leisure and tourism would include guests, visitors, spectators, customers and contractors.

fiscal: a term used to describe anything to do with *taxation*, e.g. fiscal legislation would be Acts of Parliament dealing with tax matters.

fixed assets are items of a monetary value that have a long-term function in an organisation and can be used repeatedly. Fixed assets, which include land, buildings, facilities, vehicles, equipment and machinery, are not primarily held for conversion into cash, but to further an organisation's trading activities in the long term. They not only provide the basis on which trading activity is carried out, but can also be used as security for additional *loans*. Fixed assets are shown in an organisation's *balance sheet*. (See also *current assets*.)

fixed costs: expenditure that remains constant despite an organisation's level of business activity. A museum, for example, will need to pay rates, rent and salaries, whether it has 2 000 or 20 000 visitors through its doors. Other examples of fixed costs in leisure and tourism include energy costs, fixtures and fittings, *depreciation*, interest charges, equipment *leasing* costs and *insurance*. The costs that fluctuate in line with the level of business activity are known as *variable costs*.

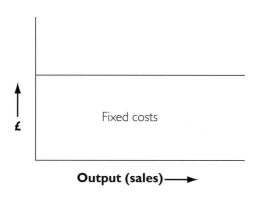

FLA: see *Football Licensing Authority*

flag of convenience: when shipowners register vessels in a country other than their own, so as to avoid, among other things, paying government taxes, paying agreed wage rates and meeting health and safety requirements. Ships flying under flags of convenience are often considered by the owners of legitimately registered fleets to be a threat to their livelihoods and a constant danger on the high seas.

flat hierarchy: see *'flat' pyramid*

'flat' pyramid: a type of *hierarchical* structure in which there is a wide span of control, i.e. decision making is delegated downwards within the organisation, rather than resting with a few senior managers, as is the case with *'steep' pyramid* structures. A 'flat' pyramid structure, sometimes called a flat hierarchy, is a form of *decentralisation*, often resulting in faster decision making, better *communication* and a positive effect on staff morale.

The flat pyramid structure

flexi-time is a working arrangement that enables staff to complete a set number of hours' work per week, but on a flexible rather than fixed basis. A *travel clerk*, for example, may be required to work 40 hours in a standard week. Whereas this would normally be made up of 5 days' work at 8 hours per day, a flexi-time arrangement would allow, for example, 4 days at 10 hours per day, thereby giving one day off. Flexi-time is particularly suitable for working parents who have young children to look after.

flight series charter: a type of *charter flight* arrangement used by tour operators where they will contract with an airline for a fixed number of flights to a particular *destination* on a specific time each day or week. The disadvantage of this arrangement over, for example, *time series charter*, is that there will be *'empty legs'* at the beginning and end of the season.

floppy disk: a device for storing and retrieving *data* files outside of a computer's hard disk. Many software packages and *computer* games are sold on floppy disks and loaded into the computer before use. Floppy disks are also a good way of storing data so as not to overload a computer's internal memory, thereby slowing it down. Back-up copies of files can also be stored on floppy disks to prevent data loss resulting from failure of the main memory.

flotilla: a collection of boats, often yachts, sailing as a fleet under the guidance of a lead boat. Flotilla sailing is a popular product in the Mediterranean, especially around the Greek Islands, offered by a number of specialist UK-based *tour operators*.

flume: the name given to a slide or chute found in many modern swimming pools and leisure centres.

fly-cruise: a holiday arrangement combining a *charter* or *scheduled flight* to and/or from a port with a sea cruise. It is possible, for example, to fly from London to New York on Concorde and sail back to the UK on a luxury cruise liner such as the Queen Elizabeth II (QE2).

fly-drive: a holiday arrangement combining a charter or *scheduled flight* with car hire. It is normally sold as a package with either *serviced* or *self-catering accommodation* included. Some fly-drive packages include a set itinerary for clients to follow, with pre-booked accommodation en route.

FMCG: see *fast-moving consumer goods*

focus group: a technique used to collect in-depth information on *customers'* habits and to explore the reasons why they choose one product or service instead of another. A focus group usually consists of up to ten consumers under the guidance of a skilled interviewer, who will use a number of techniques to delve into the innermost thoughts and values of the members of the group. The sessions are usually video-recorded for future analysis and will often cause an organisation to change its product range or promotional activities.

Food Hygiene Regulations: a set of regulations introduced under the Food Safety Act 1990 to regulate all aspects of food offered for sale. The Regulations lay great emphasis on cleanliness and sanitation, as well as the correct storage and preparation of food. *Local authorities* enforce the Food Hygiene Regulations through teams of inspectors, who have wide-ranging powers including the right to enter premises at any reasonable hour of the day to check whether the Regulations are being complied with. Penalties for breaching the Regulations are severe, including heavy fines for the original offence and additional daily fines for each day the breach continues. In exceptional circumstances, the establishment could be banned from serving food altogether until measures to rectify the situation are completed.

Food Safety Act 1990: see *Food Hygiene Regulations*

Football Licensing Authority (FLA): established under the Football Spectators Act of 1989, the FLA is concerned with ensuring the safety of football grounds. It operates a licensing scheme for football grounds, advises government on the introduction of all-seated accommodation in stadia and keeps under review the safety standards of football terracing. (See also *Taylor Report*.)

Football Trust: established in 1990, the Trust helps football at all levels, from national stadia and FA Premier League clubs to the grass roots of the sport. The grants it is able to give are funded by the reduction in pools betting duty and donations from 'spot the ball' competitions.

forecasting: the technique of estimating a future likely outcome, based on the best possible information available. This may be achieved by carrying out *market research*, *extrapolation* or by seeking expert opinion (*Delphi technique*).

foreign exchange: another word for *currency*.

Forestry Commission: a government department responsible to the Secretaries of State for Scotland and Wales, and the Minister for Agriculture, Fisheries and Food in England. Established in 1919 to help reduce timber shortage problems experienced during the First World War, the Commission has two main aims: the sustainable management of our existing woods and forests, and a steady expansion of tree cover. In 1992, the Commission underwent an extensive reorganisation, resulting in the creation of two new bodies, the Forest Authority, which administers felling licences, and Forest Enterprise, which is responsible for the management of the nation's forests, including providing opportunities for *recreation* and *leisure*.

formal communication is *communication* between two or more parties that is the result of a pre-planned course of action. This could be a letter to an aggrieved customer, a company *report* on financial performance, a staff appraisal, a memorandum or the minutes of a meeting. Formal communication methods may be either written, verbal or electronic, and are used to establish efficient working methods within organisations and between outside agencies. (See also *informal communication.*)

forming is the initial stages of team development, when the *objectives* and team roles are being clarified. Team members are likely to feel anxious at this stage and will be trying to establish their credentials and create an impression on both the *team leader* and other members of the group. (See also *storming, norming, performing.*)

Forte is one of the world's leading hotel and restaurant companies, with approximately 940 hotels and 600 restaurants in 60 countries worldwide. The Forte Group includes a number of well-known subsidiary companies, including Travelodge, Harvester and Welcome Break. Forte has the largest stock of hotels of any hotel group in the UK, with 344 British hotels giving a room availability of more than 30 000.

Fortres is the *Forte* Group's worldwide reservation system.

Foundation for Sport and the Arts (FSA): set up by the pools promoters after the 1991 Budget, FSA was created through a reduction in the pools betting levy. This released around £20 million, to which a contribution of £40 million was added by the Pools Promoters' Association. FSA donates approximately £60 million annually to a wide range of projects established by sports and arts organisations.

four Ps: refers to the four elements of the *marketing mix*, namely *price, product, place* and *promotion.*

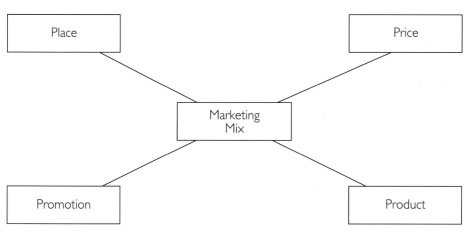

The four Ps of the marketing mix

franchising: an arrangement between two companies where the principal company (the franchisor) permits the other company (the franchisee) the right to use its trading name and methods in return for an agreed payment. Franchise operations in *leisure* and *tourism* include Wimpy, Budget Rent-a-Car and Kentucky Fried Chicken. The benefit for the franchisee is that the company name is already well established and he or she will have access to the advice, expertise and promotional activities of the franchisor. The franchisor gains financially, from an initial start-up payment and an annual fee, and can expand its operations relatively quickly and cheaply.

freedoms of the air: a set of five airline operating procedures that were agreed at the *Chicago Convention on Civil Aviation* in 1944. These so-called 'five freedoms of the air' are:

1 the right to fly across another country without landing
2 the right to land in a country, e.g. to refuel
3 the right to off-load freight, mail or passengers from an aircraft of the country from which they originated
4 the right to load freight, mail or passengers onto an aircraft of the country for which they are destined
5 the right to load or off-load freight, mail and passengers on aircraft other than those of the country of destination or origin

These principles provided a framework for agreements between countries and to ensure that the flights operating between one country and another would be restricted to the carriers of the two countries concerned.

freelance describes a person who is not employed full-time by any one organisation, but works on a number of different projects for different people on a contract basis. Self-employed freelancers work in many support services to the *leisure, travel* and *tourism* industries, e.g. *public relations*, design, photography, *marketing*, project feasibility and *training*. Employing freelance staff is sometimes seen by an organisation as a way of cutting costs, since there are less overhead costs involved.

freesale: an agreement that allows *tour operators* to sell an agreed number of rooms in a *hotel* without first checking availability with the hotelier. The tour operator simply confirms the sales by telephone, telex or fax, in return for which the hotel agrees to make the specified accommodation available. Freesale differs from an *allocation* of rooms, since the hotel is likely to 'block out' certain busy periods in the year and not offer rooms at these times.

frequent flyer programmes are *incentives* operated by most major airlines to reward *customers* who use their services regularly. They work by collecting points for journeys made, with more points for longer journeys. Once a certain number have been collected, the traveller can exchange them for free flights or other gift items. Frequent flyer programmes are a very good way of maintaining *brand loyalty*.

fringe benefit: see *'perks'*

front of house: see *front office*

front office is a term used to denote the point at which *customers* and the public in general come into contact with staff in a leisure or tourism facility, e.g. the reception area in a *leisure centre* or a *hotel*. Sometimes called the 'front of house', staff working in the front office carry out a range of clearly defined functions, including welcoming visitors, taking bookings, providing information, issuing equipment, controlling entry and promoting services. Unlike *back office* functions, which take place 'behind the scenes', the duties of front office staff bring them into direct contact with the public on a regular basis. It is important, therefore, that front office employees are chosen for their excellent *customer service* skills.

- Controlling entry
- Promoting services
- Answering enquiries
- Welcoming visitors
- Maintaining records

- Issuing equipment
- Providing information
- Selling services
- Taking bookings
- Giving directions

Typical 'front office' functions

FSA: see *Foundation for Sport and the Arts*

FTO: see *Federation of Tour Operators*

full board: an *accommodation* arrangement, sometimes known as *American Plan*, consisting of room and three meals per day. (See also *half board.*)

functional structures are *management* structures based around the main functions carried out by an organisation. A *National Tourism Organisation (NTO)*, for example, may operate a functional structure based on the following departments:

- *marketing*
- *development*
- research and corporate planning
- finance and administration

Although it is relatively easy to allocate job roles in these types of organisations, some critics point to a lack of flexibility with functional structures, which can sometimes be overcome with a *matrix organisation.*

funding of leisure and tourism is a complex issue, involving a host of *private, public* and *voluntary sector* organisations. Private sector operators receive the bulk of their start-up funding from commercial sources, principally the banks. They may apply for funding from central or local governments, or even European sources, in the form of grants or low-interest loans. Public sector organisations receive their funding from central government sources and from their local *Council Tax* payers. Voluntary bodies rely on donations, subscriptions and bequests, along with *sponsorship* from commercial companies and grants from central and local government organisations.

G

Galileo: a *computerised reservation system (CRS)* pioneered by *British Airways* and other major European airlines to compete directly with the American Airlines' *Sabre* CRS. Galileo has now merged with United Airlines' *Apollo* CRS.

gateway: an interactive computer facility allowing selected *travel agents* to access *computerised reservation systems (CRSs)* of major *principals*, including airlines, hotel companies and tour operators, in order to check product availability and make bookings. Access is gained via the travel agent's *visual display unit (VDU)* connected to a telephone line.

GATT: see *General Agreement on Tariffs and Trade*

GDP: see *gross domestic product*

GDS: see *global distribution systems*

gearing: a financial term used to describe the proportion of a company's *capital* that is supplied by long-term borrowing. Generally, the higher the gearing the higher the risk the company is taking, with a company that has a greater than 50 per cent proportion of its capital as borrowed funds being referred to as highly geared.

General Agreement on Tariffs and Trade (GATT) is a series of trade agreements which, since 1947, has established strict procedures for international trade. Some 96 countries are parties to the GATT discussions and agreements, which together account for more than 80 per cent of total world trade. The underlying principle of GATT is that its members should enjoy favourable trading terms between themselves, provided that home producers are not disadvantaged.

General Household Survey (GHS): a survey undertaken by the *Office of Population Censuses and Surveys (OPCS)* to discover factual information about the habits and possessions of households in Britain. The GHS collects data about, for example, the number of households that have televisions or dishwashers, as well as information about participation in *leisure* and sporting activities. (See also *Social Trends*.)

General National Vocational Qualifications (GNVQs) are knowledge-based, work-related qualifications designed to offer a choice of opportunities in employment or higher education. GNVQs are available in a number of occupational areas, including leisure and tourism, and are part of the *National Vocational Qualification* framework, endorsed by the government, *CBI* and *TUC*. GNVQs offer students a flexible qualification based around mandatory, optional, additional and core skill units. They are currently available from three awarding bodies: RSA, City & Guilds and *BTEC*. GNVQs are gradually replacing qualifications such as the BTEC National Diploma and City & Guilds awards.

general sales agent (GSA): an individual or organisation that is appointed by a travel company, usually an airline or tour operator, to represent them in a particular country. The company benefits by not having to set up a sales operation of its own, thereby saving costs. A GSA often represents more than one company and can handle a range of functions, including *marketing*, reservations, ticketing and enquiries. The GSA will usually operate on a *commission* basis plus an initial fee for start-up costs.

generating country: see *tourist generating country*

ghetto tourism: a term describing the policy of restricting *mass tourism* to a small number of selected resorts, so as to minimise its *socio-cultural impacts* on a wider area. Some people consider this approach to be more sustainable than allowing tourists free movement within a country. (See also *tourist enclave*.)

GHS: see *General Household Survey*

global distribution systems (GDS) is the name sometimes used to describe the major *computerised reservation systems (CRS)* that have been developed by the world's biggest airlines, e.g. *Sabre* and *Worldspan*. The main feature of a GDS is that it gives the user access to a wide range of related travel services, not just airline information.

global warming refers to long-term changes to the earth's climate brought about, in part, by increased carbon dioxide emissions from vehicles and aircraft. Scientists suggest that the earth's temperature is rising, with potentially damaging consequences for tourist *destinations* in the long term, e.g. the loss of marginal ski resorts, rise in water levels in low-lying countries and increased algal growth in warmer seas.

globalisation: the process of striving for world dominance in an industry sector, through company takeovers, strategic alliances, *vertical* and *horizontal integration*. *Multinational corporations* seek to achieve *economies of scale* by operating at a global level. Improved electronic communication methods, such as the *Internet* and *global distribution systems (GDS)* facilitate the move of airlines, hotel companies and travel companies towards globalisation.

GMT: see *Greenwich Mean Time*

GNP: see *gross national product*

GNVQ: see *General National Vocational Qualification*

goals: a term that originated in the USA and means the same as *objectives*. Goals are targets that an individual or organisation seeks to achieve by implementing a number of different strategies. The goal of *British Airways*, for example, is 'to be the best and most successful company in the airline industry'.

governing body of sport: each organised *sport* in Britain has a governing body whose job it is to represent the interests of that particular sport. Governing bodies draft and amend the rules and laws of the sport, organise local and national competitions and select teams for international competitions such as the *Olympic Games*. They also keep players and participants informed about their particular sport and maintain relations with the media. The national governing bodies are all members of the *CCPR* and are grouped into six main divisions: games and sports, interested organisations, major spectator sports, movement and dance, outdoor pursuits and water recreation.

Grand Tour: the name given to a circuit of the major cultural centres in Europe undertaken by young aristocrats from a number of countries from the seventeenth century onwards. The aim of the Grand Tour was to widen the young men's education and cultural awareness prior to seeking positions at court on their return home. Cities such as Paris, Venice, Florence, Rome and Geneva gave such gentlemen the opportunity to sample different cultures, societies and experiences. Most of those from Britain who took part in the Grand Tour were drawn from the ranks of the landed classes of peers and gentry.

grant aid: sums of money made available to *leisure* and *tourism* organisations from central and local government bodies, such as the *Sports Council* and *Arts Council*. The granting of the funding is usually tied to the achievement of certain *objectives* and subject to certain criteria, e.g. no one individual should be allowed to gain financially from the grant aid. Sometimes referred to as grant-in-aid, it is often given for *capital* projects only and not for *revenue* purposes.

grant-in-aid: see *grant aid*

gratuity: a payment made to a member of staff by a *customer* for services rendered. Gratuities, often called tips, are commonly paid to staff working in hotels, restaurants and for taxi firms. (See also *service charge.*)

Great Britain: see *Britain*

green belt is the name given to areas of land surrounding urban areas on which there is some degree of protection against further *development*, particularly house building. The idea of green belt policies, which incidentally have applied to London since 1938, is to restrict the size of towns and cities, by controlling the spread of built-up areas, while at the same time providing open spaces for *leisure* and *recreation*. In Britain, there are green belts around most major urban areas, including London, Birmingham, Manchester and Bristol. In many respects, green belt policies have failed to meet their aims, with new development 'leap frogging' the protected areas.

Green Flag International (GFI) is a non-profit making *conservation* company working with the *travel and tourism industry* to help improve its environmental performance and to establish conservation projects at tourism *destinations*. Members of GFI include a number of specialist tour operators, including Eurocamp, Saga Holidays, Cox & Kings, Sunvil Travel and Simply Crete. Services to members include an environmental advice service, training on environmental issues and *environmental audits*.

Green Globe: a worldwide *environmental management* and awareness programme for, and led by, the *travel and tourism industry*. Its prime *objective* is to provide a low-cost, practical means for all *travel* and *tourism companies* to undertake improvements in their environmental practice. Green Globe helps a company to develop an environmental programme and provides advice and information on a range of environmental issues to its members.

'green' tourism: a general term used to describe a type of tourist activity which aims to be respectful of the environment in which it takes place and the communities that live there. Variously described as alternative tourism, appropriate tourism, intelligent tourism, 'soft' tourism, responsible tourism and *ecotourism*, 'green' tourism is characterised as small-scale activities which make use of local labour and produce to provide a holiday experience that is an alternative to *mass tourism*. 'Green' tourism has developed from an environmental standpoint, whereas the evolving notion of *sustainable tourism* argues that both *environmental* and *socio-cultural* issues need to be addressed.

Greenwich Mean Time (GMT) is the local time at the *Greenwich Meridian*, from which standard times around the world are calculated, e.g. 0900 hours GMT will equate to 0400 hours New York time and 1000 hours Paris time.

Greenwich Meridian: the point on the globe representing 0° longitude and on which world *time zones* are based.

grievance procedures: the steps that an employee can take to raise objections to the treatment he or she is receiving at work. Details of the procedures are often set out in a staff handbook and should be included in an organisation's induction training. (See also *industrial tribunal.*)

gross domestic product (GDP) is a measure of the size and value of a nation's economy, usually expressed as the total value of all goods and services produced during a specified time period, usually one year. GDP is made up of a number of items, found in the manufacturing and *service sector* of an economy. Earnings from tourism contribute to a country's GDP, with those nations relying heavily on tourism revenue having the highest percentage contributions to GDP, e.g. tourism accounts for more than 20 per cent of Spain's GDP, while the figure for the UK is in the region of six per cent. (See also *gross national product.*)

gross margin: a calculation of the proportion of a company's *sales revenue* that is *gross profit.* It is calculated as follows:

$$\text{FORMULA: gross margin} = \frac{\text{gross profit}}{\text{sales revenue}} \times 100$$

gross misconduct: any action by an employee that is so serious as to warrant instant *dismissal.* Such actions would be detailed in a *contract of employment* and include being drunk on duty, theft, fraud, assault, causing damage to property, insubordination and the misuse of equipment.

gross national product (GNP) is a measure of a country's economic growth, calculated by adding the value of all goods and services produced to the net revenue from abroad. *Tourism* can play a significant role in contributing to a country's GNP through extra expenditure in the economy on goods and services, e.g. the contribution of tourism to Greece's GNP rose from 2.3 per cent in 1970 to 6.4 per cent in 1990. (See also *gross domestic product.*)

gross profit is the difference between a company's *sales revenue* and the cost of its sales.

gross profit/sales ratio is an important measure of an organisation's financial performance. Sometimes called the gross profit percentage, it shows how much *profit* an organisation is making as a percentage of sales. It is calcultated as follows:

$$\text{FORMULA:} \quad \frac{\text{gross profit}}{\text{sales}} \times 100$$

A fall in the gross profit/sales ratio may be the result of increased *competition*, forcing a reduction in the prices for facilities and services. (See also *net profit/sales ratio.*)

gross profit percentage: see *gross profit/sales ratio*

ground arrangements: the range of local services provided for *tourists* at *destinations*, such as transfers to and from their accommodation and airport, excursions and car hire arrangements. They are often provided by specialist companies, known as ground handling agents, working on behalf of tour operators and airlines.

group dynamics: the way in which individuals interrelate when in a group situation. Establishing a group of people to work on a project can bring benefits to an organisation, but it can also cause management some problems, such as conflict between team members and personality clashes. It takes an effective *team leader* to cope with such problems and to steer all group members to achieving their *objectives*.

Groundwork: an independent charitable organisation that helps people to improve their local environment and the prospects for their local economy through a sustainable approach to *development* and *management*. Local Groundwork Trusts have been set up across the country, working in partnership with private, public and voluntary sectors of communities, enabling them to take action for a better local environment.

group motivation is the way that team members inspire each other, and are inspired by their leader, to work together as an effective unit to achieve the group's goals. The leader should aim to maintain a cycle of motivation and success, since one feeds on the other. When appropriate, group members should be praised for their efforts and given tangible rewards for their hard work.

GSA: see *general sales agent*

guided walk: a type of *interpretation* where a guide leads an individual or group of people around an area pointing out and explaining points of interest en route. Guided walks can greatly enhance a person's understanding and enjoyment of the place they are visiting.

Guild of Business Travel Agents (GBTA): When it was formed in 1967, GBTA's six original members sought special attention for the needs of business *travel agents*, which it considered were not properly represented by the existing national organisation. Today, the Guild is called upon as an adviser in every sphere of travel, technical, commercial or political, and, with the help of a parliamentary consultant, it maintains a continual pressure on the legislators to make special provision for business travellers. With around 40 members, including large multiples like *Thomas Cook* and *American Express,* medium-sized multi-branch agencies and small independents, who collectively have 75 per cent agents' business house air traffic in the UK, the Guild has a turnover of £4.34 billion and employs over 15 000 people in more than 1 670 outlets.

Gulf Stream: see *climate*

Gulf War broke out in the winter of 1991 and was to have long-lasting and far-reaching effects on world *travel and tourism.* By the time it ended in the spring of 1991, many prospective holidaymakers had decided to cancel their trips, particularly those travelling from North America. The majority of US corporations withdrew their staff from world travel for fear of terrorist attacks and unrest, leaving many *business tourism* companies at an all-time low, with airlines and hotel companies bearing the brunt of the problem. Although worldwide leisure travel has all but returned to its former pre-Gulf War state, business travel has yet to recover fully.

H

half board: an *accommodation* and meal arrangement consisting of room, breakfast plus either a midday or evening meal. It is sometimes referred to as *Modified American Plan*.

hard currency: the term used to denote a *currency* in high *demand* and with a stable or rising rate of exchange. The opening up of the former Eastern Bloc countries since the late 1980s has led to a high demand for hard currencies, particularly US dollars, in hotels and shops there.

hard disk: the permanent, high capacity memory installed inside a *computer*. Computer programs that are used frequently, such as *word processing, database* and *spreadsheet* packages, will be installed on the hard disk for speed and convenience, rather than stored on *floppy disks* and loaded each time the computer is used. Documents created on the computer can also be stored on the hard disk. The storage capacity of the hard disk is measured in megabytes (Mb); a memory of 270 Mb means it can hold 270 million bytes of data, one byte being equivalent to a single character.

hard sell refers to an aggressive sales technique used by sales people who will try to *'close the sale'* at all costs. In leisure and tourism, selling *timeshare* and other leisure products, particularly by telephone, are examples of hard sell.

hardware refers to the *computer* equipment which houses and operates a range of computer programs (the *software*). *Personal computers (PCs)* are the most common type of hardware available, for business, home and leisure uses.

haute cuisine: a French term to describe food of the highest culinary quality served in elegant surroundings.

hazards: identifiable health and safety problems in the workplace that could lead to accidents to staff and visitors. Hazards should be identified by means of health and safety inspections and *risk assessments*. Once identified, remedial actions need to be carried out to reduce the risks of personal injury.

HCIMA: see *Hotel, Catering and Institutional Management Association*

HCTC: see *Hotel and Catering Training Company*

headhunter: an individual or organisation that specialises in identifying suitable applicants for jobs, rather than waiting for those individuals to make applications themselves. Headhunters are often recruited by large organisations who are looking to fill senior positions. The advantage of using the services of a headhunter is that he or she takes the initiative in making contact with suitable applicants, who may not necessarily be looking for another position and would, therefore, not see the job advertised.

health and fitness is an important element of leisure and tourism, since it can have a bearing on how people choose to use their *leisure time* and the type of *holidays* they buy. There has been a general increase in people's concern for their health in recent years, evidenced by the growth in health and fitness clubs, aerobics classes and activity holidays.

Health and Safety at Work, etc. Act 1974 was introduced to promote and encourage high standards of health and safety in the workplace. Part 1 of the Act, the part that concerns *leisure* and *tourism* organisations the most, aims to:

- secure the health, safety and welfare of people at work
- protect other people against risks to health and safety
- control the storage and use of dangerous substances, e.g. chemicals
- control the emission of noxious or offensive substances from premises

The Act places duties on both employers and employees. Employers must safeguard, so far as is reasonably practicable, the health, safety and welfare of all those in their employment. In practice, this will include such matters as providing information and *training* to all staff in health and safety matters, providing plant and equipment that is not a risk to health and providing a written safety policy (applies only to those employing five or more staff). Employees must take reasonable care to avoid injury to themselves and others in the workplace, co-operate with their employers to make sure that the Act is enforced and not interfere with or misuse anything provided to protect their health, safety and welfare.

The Act is enforced by inspectors appointed by the *Health and Safety Executive (HSE)*, who have wide-ranging powers to enter premises and inspect records. If an inspector discovers that the Act is not being fully implemented, he or she can, as a last resort, close down the premises until such time as action to rectify the situation is completed.

Many of the requirements of the Health and Safety at Work, etc. Act have been clarified and updated by the *EU Directives on health and safety* which came into operation on 1 January 1993.

Health and Safety Commission (HSC) is a government-funded body responsible to the Secretary of State for Employment for taking the necessary steps to secure the health, welfare and safety of people at work and also to protect the public against those risks to health and safety arising out of a work situation. The HSC was established in 1974 under the *Health and Safety at Work, etc. Act* and its membership is made up of employers, *trade unions* and *local authority* representatives.

Health and Safety Executive (HSE) is the operating arm of the *Health and Safety Commission (HSC)* and is responsible for enforcing the legislation under the *Health and Safety at Work, etc. Act*. HSE appoints teams of inspectors who have wide powers to enter premises and examine records and staff to check that the Act is being complied with. Inspectors can also investigate accidents that take place on premises, not only to employees but also visitors. This could include, for example, accidents at sports centres, *theme parks* and other leisure and tourism facilities.

health and safety management: the Management of Health and Safety at Work Regulations 1992 were developed as a direct result of the *EU Directives on health and safety*. The regulations are aimed at encouraging employers to take a more systematic approach to health and safety by, among others things, drawing up a *risk assessment*. Once risks have been identified, measures must be put in place to rectify the situation. The regulations also require employers to appoint competent people to devise and apply the health and safety measures, provide training in health and safety matters, set up emergency procedures and co-operate with other employers who may share the same work site.

Heart of England Tourist Board is the official *Regional Tourist Board* covering the counties of Gloucestershire, Hereford and Worcester, Warwickshire, West Midlands, Staffordshire and Shropshire.

heritage is an all-embracing term that is used increasingly to describe anything that has some kind of link, however tenuous, with past events. The more traditional uses of the word relate to the natural and man-made world in which we live, e.g. our 'natural heritage', to include mountains, moors, lakes and rivers, and the 'built heritage', relating to monuments, buildings and artefacts. People also talk of 'cultural heritage', referring to customs and traditions of the past, including the arts and music.

In present day leisure and tourism, we are all familiar with heritage centres and heritage museums, but some people are concerned that the term 'heritage' is being exploited for commercial advantage, thereby losing its authenticity. We even have a *Department of National Heritage*, concerned with everything from the Royal Palaces to the *National Lottery*. The use of the term 'heritage' is closely allied to the ways in which *museums* and other attractions are redefining their roles so as to offer the visitor an 'experience' rather than merely an educational or pleasurable trip.

Heritage Coasts are among the most precious assets for wildlife and landscape, as well as for *leisure* and *tourism*. Concern over the harmful effects of increasing numbers of visitors has led to the designation of 44 Heritage Coasts in England and Wales. A programme of work, partly funded by the *Countryside Commission*, to ensure that the Coasts remain in good heart, includes creating and repairing footpaths, cleaning up beaches and stabilising sand dunes. Stretches of coastline are also protected by the *National Trust* under its *Enterprise Neptune* project.

Heritage Lottery Fund is administered by the National Heritage Memorial Fund and has been set up to distribute funds from the *National Lottery* to projects which safeguard land, buildings, objects and collections of outstanding interest to the nation's heritage. Projects eligible for financial help could include work on ancient monuments, special library collections, manuscripts, archives and collections held by *museums* and galleries.

Herzberg: an American psychologist who is best known for his two-factor theory of *staff motivation* in the workplace. Herzberg identified a series of positive motivational factors, which he called 'satisfiers', and negative motivational factors termed 'dissatisfiers'. 'Satisfiers' included recognition, sense of achievement, responsibility and personal development. Negative factors were salary, job security, working conditions, level and quality of supervision and interpersonal relations. Herzberg's theory has been implemented in many large corporations, but is sometimes criticised for taking little account of the benefits of *group motivation*.

HETB: see *Heart of England Tourist Board*

HHA: see *Historic Houses Association*

hierarchical organisation: a type of *organisational structure* that is characterised by a small number of senior decision makers at the top of the organisation who control its activities and resources. Sometimes called pyramid structures, hierarchical organisations are often very *centralised structures*, with power and responsibility resting with a very small number of senior staff. Decisions flow downwards from the top, affecting a succession of layers of employees lower down. Hierarchical organisations are often criticised for being too bureaucratic. Depending on the degree of centralisation, they are sometimes referred to as *'steep' pyramids* or *'flat' pyramids.*

hierarchy of needs: see *Maslow's hierarchy of needs*

high season: see *peak season*

Highlands and Islands Enterprise (HIE): the government-funded *quango* that promotes inward investment to the north of Scotland and carries out measures to help the social and economic well-being of those living there. HIE works with the *Scottish Tourist Board* to improve the quality of tourism in their area and its *promotion* to as wide an audience as possible. Highlands and Islands Enterprise used to be known as the Highlands and Islands Development Board.

hire purchase is a method of providing medium-term finance for a business or an individual. Hire purchase is commonly used by organisations to buy *fixed assets* such as equipment, vehicles and machinery, allowing repayments to be spread over an extended period of time, rather than a large cash payment having to be made at the outset. Ownership of the property being bought on hire purchase remains with the finance house until all payments, including interest, have been made.

histogram: a diagram used to gain a quick visual impression of data. Unlike a *bar chart*, the bars used in a histogram are usually connected.

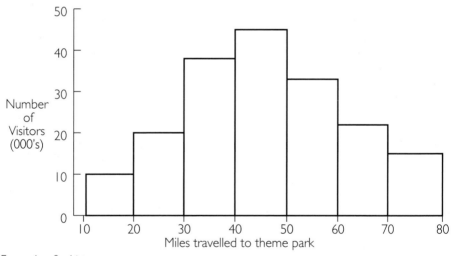

Example of a histogram

Historic Houses Association (HHA): an independent body representing the interests of private owners of historic houses and gardens in the UK. It advises members on the commercial, legal and financial aspects of running a *tourism* and *leisure* business, and plays an active role in lobbying national and local government on matters of concern to private owners, e.g. inheritance tax legislation.

Historic Royal Palaces Agency is a directorate within the *Department of National Heritage* responsible for the management of a number of Britain's ancestral buildings and their promotion as tourist attractions. Buildings within their remit include the Tower of London and Buckingham Palace.

historic monuments play an important role in leisure and tourism in the UK. Most are in public ownership, with many London monuments under the management of the *Historic Royal Palaces Agency*, a division of the *Department of National Heritage*. Together with castles and stately homes, they attract both UK and *overseas visitors*.

holiday: a period of time when work is officially suspended. For statistical purposes, UK *tourist boards* define a holiday as a stay of four nights or more away from home, although this is sometimes relaxed for overseas holidays. Holidays are sometimes divided into *package holidays* and independent holidays. (See also *Bank Holidays, independent travel.*)

holiday camp: a purpose-built complex providing family *accommodation* and a range of entertainment facilities on one site for a low, all-inclusive price. Now more commonly referred to as holiday centres, the concept of the holiday camp was pioneered in the 1930s by Billy *Butlin*, who opened his first camp at Skegness in 1936. Holiday camps worked on the principle that if the children were happy on holiday, then the parents would be as well. To this end, today's camps still offer a child-minding service to allow parents to enjoy themselves. Butlin's, Pontin's and Warner's became market leaders in this type of holiday which is still popular today, albeit in a modified form.

Holiday Care Service: a registered charity, set up in 1981 with *sponsorship* from the English Tourist Board and the full support of the UK *travel industry*. It is a free service to those who are elderly, disabled or with special family circumstances who are looking for budget holidays or holidays suitable for single parents or unaccompanied children. The Holiday Care Service provides information and advice to individuals, their families or friends, or those who care for them.

holiday centre: see *holiday camp*

Holiday Which?: a magazine produced by the *Consumers' Association* that includes features on *destinations* and resorts, as well as articles on issues of concern to the travelling public, e.g. ferry safety and *overbooking*. The magazine claims to provide unbiased opinions and independent research to help readers choose their holidays and travel arrangements with confidence.

Holidays with Pay Act 1938: government *legislation* that encouraged voluntary agreements on paid holidays for employees and began the notion of a two-week paid holiday for all staff in British companies.

home-based leisure is any leisure activity that takes place in the home and includes such activities as watching television, listening to the radio, reading books, gardening, DIY, dressmaking and visiting or entertaining friends and relatives. Industry analysts predict that home-based leisure will grow significantly up to and beyond the year 2000. In particular, the development of new technology equipment based on CD-roms, multimedia and *virtual reality*, will open up a huge array of home entertainment possibilities.

horizontal integration: unlike *vertical integration*, which links companies at different levels in the distribution chain, horizontal integration refers to mergers between organisations at the same level in the distribution chain, e.g. a large hotel company such as *Forte* taking over a small independent hotel or the takeover of Dan Air by *British Airways*. Firms integrate horizontally to gain *competitive advantage*.

hospitality: a general term to describe the *hotel* and *catering* sectors of the leisure and tourism industries. Hospitality is a major source of *employment in leisure and tourism*.

host community: a term used in the debate on *sustainable tourism* to denote a place where people go for holidays and the people who live there. There is a growing acceptance that the wishes of host communities in relation to tourist *development* need to be given a higher priority, to allow minimum disruption to their lives, while at the same time providing economic benefits.

hotel: defined by the *English Hotel Occupancy Survey (EHOS)* as 'an establishment having five or more letting bedrooms, not calling itself a guesthouse or boarding house, and not being listed as providing bed and breakfast accommodation'. On the basis of this definition, the *BTA* estimates that there are in the region of 27 000 hotels in England, Wales, Scotland and Northern Ireland. The majority are operated by owner-proprietors who usually live on the premises. Many of the larger establishments are run by hotel groups, such as *Forte* and Queens Moat Houses, which benefit from *economies of scale* in terms of purchasing, recruitment and marketing. Forte is currently the top hotel group in the UK with approximately 30 000 rooms available. In order to ensure consistency of standards, there are a number of voluntary *accommodation grading schemes* in operation in Britain.

Hotel and Catering Training Company (HCTC) is an independent *company* that specialises in all aspects of craft, supervisory and management *training* for the hotel and catering sector. It produces *distance learning* materials, runs its own training courses and is actively involved in the development of *National Vocational Qualifications (NVQs)* in hotel and catering, as the *Industry Lead Body (ILB)* for the industry.

Hotel, Catering and Institutional Management Association (HCIMA) is a *professional body* set up to represent the interests of managers in the *hospitality* industry. Established in 1971 with the aim of identifying, promoting and maintaining the highest professional and ethical standards for management, education and training in the international hotel and catering industry, HCIMA has some 23 000 members in more than 90 countries. It undertakes a wide-ranging programme of activities, including running professional qualification courses, assisting with management development, keeping members informed of developments in the industry, *lobbying* government and organising conferences.

hotel grading: see *accommodation grading schemes*

HRM: see *human resource management*

HSC: see *Health and Safety Commission*

HSE: see *Health and Safety Executive*

hub and spoke system: a *transportation* arrangement, most often associated with air transport, where a central airport acts as a 'hub' for feeder services from other outlying destinations (the 'spokes'). Birmingham Airport, for example, acts as a hub for many of *British Airway's* European flights. Operating a hub and spoke system leads to increased airline efficiency and reduced operating costs.

human resource management (HRM) is the activity that deals with all aspects of an organisation's staff, their deployment, *training*, development, support and relationships with their employer. More than merely the mechanistic approach of personnel management, HRM is a more all-embracing concept to signal that an organisation is taking a more long-term view of all aspects of employing, empowering, supporting and rewarding its employees. HRM is concerned with achieving a balance between the ambitions of the individual and the returns to the organisation. It is crucial that the right balanace is achieved, particularly since staff costs typically make up more than three-quarters of all costs for many leisure and tourism businesses.

hypothesis: a theory that can be tested analytically using a range of statistical techniques.

REVISION: There is a set of revision lists at the back of this book to help you prepare for GNVQ unit tests. See pages 246–250 for unit tests in GNVQ Advanced Leisure and Tourism.

I

IATA: see *International Air Transport Association*

IATA agent: a *travel agent* who has been accepted into membership of the *International Air Transport Association (IATA)* and, as such, can sell tickets of IATA member airlines and offer a full service of worldwide air travel. To gain acceptance as an IATA agent, the organisation must first meet a number of strict criteria, including staff *training* requirements, security of premises and financial security of the business. The majority of multiple travel agencies and larger independent agents hold IATA licences.

IBRM: see *Institute of Sport and Recreation Management (ISRM)*

ICAO: see *International Civil Aviation Organisation*

IFTO: see *International Federation of Tour Operators*

IIP: see *Investors in People*

ILAM: see *Institute of Leisure and Amenity Management*

ILB: see *Industry Lead Body*

ILG: see *International Leisure Group*

image: the impression that a *product*, organisation or destination shows to the outside world. Image is very important in leisure and tourism, particularly in relation to *destination marketing*. The good or bad image portrayed by a holiday destination will materially affect its popularity. Images that people have of destinations and products are built up from a number of information sources, including *brochures*, television and radio programmes, newspaper articles, first-hand experience and 'word of mouth'. Organisations try to portray a consistent, positive image to the outside world, by means of a clear *corporate identity* and effective *advertising* and *public relations* campaigns.

impacts of leisure and tourism: these are generally categorised into:

- *environmental impacts,* e.g. pollution, erosion, etc.
- *socio-cultural impacts,* e.g. loss of traditional crafts, overcrowding, etc.
- *economic impacts,* e.g. job creation, income generation

Impacts may be positive or negative, with environmental and socio-cultural impacts generally being seen to be negative, while economic impacts are invariably portrayed as being positive. *Planning* can help to reduce the negative impacts on a nation or local community.

improvement notice: one of the options open to a health and safety inspector if he or she discovers that an organisation is contravening the *Health and Safety at Work, etc. Act,* the other being the issuing of a *prohibition notice.* The improvement notice is, in effect, a written warning to the organisation, indicating what must be done to comply with the requirements of the Act and the time limit within which the action must be completed.

imports are goods and services brought into a country from overseas. They may be either *'visible'* or *'invisible'* items and the flows of currency associated with imports is shown in a country's *balance of payments*. The expenditure by British people on holidays and travel abroad is considered to be an import, since money is flowing out of the country, in the same way that it does when a manufacturing company pays an overseas company for imported goods.

inbound tourism: see *incoming tourism*

incentives are payments and other inducements made to:

- employees – to encourage them to work harder, or
- customers – to persuade them to buy a particular product or service

Examples of incentives include free gifts, special offers, discounts, store vouchers, *bonuses* (for staff) and free use of facilities.

incentive travel is a type of *business tourism* concerned with offering *holidays* and *leisure* products as incentives for staff. These sort of incentives are not only on offer to employees in leisure and tourism, but are a common reward system in many industry sectors, e.g. banking, insurance, financial services, retail, etc. An example would be a weekend break at Gleneagles for achieving top monthly sales for a company or a two-week holiday in Florida for clinching a new multi-million pound deal.

inclusive tour (IT): another name for a *package holiday*

inclusive tour by charter (ITC) is a package holiday where the travel component is made up of a *charter flight* as opposed to a *scheduled flight*. The vast majority of package holidays sold in the UK use this arrangement. (See also *inclusive tour by excursion*.)

inclusive tour by excursion (ITX) is a package holiday where the travel component consists of a *scheduled flight* rather than a *charter flight*. In the UK this arrangement is less common and more expensive than an *inclusive tour by charter*.

income multiplier: see *multiplier effect*

income tax: a *direct tax* paid by individuals on their earnings and investments. The basic rate of income tax is currently 24 pence in the pound, and the higher rate 40 pence in the pound. Income tax is payable on a person's taxable income, i.e. that which is left after certain tax allowances are taken into account, such as the personal allowance and married person's allowance. The Conservative government is committed to reducing income tax when it is prudent to do so.

incoming tour operator: a company that specialises in meeting the needs of visitors from overseas who wish to stay in its country. In the case of Britain, incoming tour operators develop products and market themselves to the increasing numbers of *overseas visitors* who visit this country. There are some 300 such operators based in the UK who fall into this category. Some are little more than handling agents offering a transfer or 'meet and greet' service on behalf of an agent or operator. Others, such as Frames Rickards and British Heritage Tours, offer complete *package tours* of the UK, including visits based on gardens, castles or theatres. Many UK incoming tour operators are members of *BITOA*.

incoming tourism is a form of international tourism which deals with people entering another country from their own country of origin or another country which is not their home. For example, an Italian couple flying from Rome to Heathrow Airport and a Spanish family arriving by ferry at Newcastle from Scandinavia are both types of incoming tourism to the UK. The *British Tourist Authority* estimates that there were 19.2 million overseas visits to Britain in 1993 with total spending by *overseas visitors* exceeding £9 billion. Incoming tourism is sometimes referred to as inbound tourism. (See also *outbound tourism*.)

independent travel is generally considered to be any form of travel which is not part of a *package holiday*. Independent travellers prefer to put their own itinerary together by purchasing *accommodation* and *transportation* directly from suppliers or via *travel agents*. Independent travel from the UK to overseas destinations has grown at a faster rate than the sales of package holidays since the mid-1970s, indicating that tourists like the flexibility that this travel arrangement can offer. (See also *'new tourist'*.)

Year	Visits (000s)	Percentage change on previous date
1976	3153	—
1981	6297	+100
1986	7235	+15
1991	9984	+38

(Source: IPS)

The growth in independent travel for overseas holidays

independent travel agent: a travel retailer who is not part of a *travel agency* chain. Independent agents offer as wide a range of holiday and travel products as the multiple travel agents (some would say more!), and may be members of the *National Association of Independent Travel Agents (NAITA)*.

indexing: the practice of linking a value to a defined index of numbers, such as the *retail price index (RPI)*, in order to preserve its real value. In the UK, rises in *pensions* and wages are sometimes linked to the RPI.

indirect costs: see *overheads*

indirect tax is one which is levied by central government on goods and services that people buy, as opposed to *direct taxes*, which are paid on income and profits. Examples of indirect taxes are *value added tax (VAT)* and duty on alcohol and petrol. The Conservative government has, since 1979, attempted to shift the burden of taxation away from direct to indirect taxation, on the grounds that taxes on income are a disincentive to hard work and enterprise.

induction is an important part of the *recruitment and selection* process in leisure and tourism, concerned with providing a new member of staff with a structured introduction to their new organisation and its employees. An induction programme should be designed to help new members of staff familiarise themselves with their new work environment, to settle easily into their new jobs and to establish good working relationships with other members of staff. Some organisations ask a member of the existing workforce to take care of a new employee until he or she is settled; this member of staff is known as a *mentor*.

INDUCTION CHECKLIST

Your Manager will tick the tasks that have been completed during your induction.

1 Show the Starter:
a) Main areas of the Club
b) Position of the clocking-in machine / signing in book
c) Position of Fire-fighting equipment
d) Staff room
e) Emergency exits
f) Video "Welcome to Top Rank Ltd"
g) Pensions Video

2 Introduce Starter to:
a) Management Team
b) Appropriate Supervisor
c) Staff Representative
d) Departmental Colleagues

3 Issue to all new Starters:
a) Conditions of Employment Agreement
b) Statement of Hours
c) Uniform Receipt
d) Wishes Letter (all employees)
e) Disciplinary Rules & Procedures booklet
f) Health and safety at Work Policy booklet
g) Fire Information & Procedures booklet
h) Legal requirements form
   (to be signed on engagement and thereafter every 12 months)
i) Cinema Discount Card (after 6 months)
j) Pensions
   * Gatefold leaflet "Your Pension Choice"
   * RO Pension Plan application card
   * RO Money Purchase Scheme application card
   * Disclaimer card
   * Pension booklet (as appropriate)

4 Explain to all Starters:
a) Conditions of Employment (show "Employees Guide")
b) Job Description
c) Fire Drill & Evacuation Procedure
d) Benefits
e) Legal Requirements
   - Main provisions of the Gaming Act
   - Health & Safety Policy
   - Hygiene Regulations
f) Function of the SRC
g) Company Pension Arrangements

An example of an induction checklist (courtesy of Top Rank Ltd)

induction booklet: a document given to all new members of staff outlining the structure of their new organisation and including a number of important points of information, including health and safety, *first aid* and *disciplinary procedures,* as well as details about social clubs, *pension* arrangements and *trade union* membership.

industrial heritage: the term used to describe *visitor attractions* which depict the workings of a bygone age. Parts of Britain that were once dependent on primary and secondary industries, e.g. coal mining in South Wales, shipbuilding on Tyneside and textile manufacturing in Lancashire, have developed industrial museums and centres to attract *tourists,* thereby contributing to their local economies. Various industrial processes are explained to visitors with the help of guides, audio-visual aids and other types of *interpretation.* (See also *factory tourism.*)

industrial relations is a broad term covering all aspects of the relationship between employers and employees and their representatives, including works councils and *trade unions.* The government also has an influence on industrial relations through its employment *legislation.* In the 1980s, a series of Acts of Parliament were aimed at reducing the perceived power of trade unions. In the workplace, harmonious industrial relations makes for a contented workforce and an efficient organisation. If things go wrong, it may be necessary to call on the services of arbitrators, who may be attached to the *Advisory Conciliation and Arbitration Service (ACAS).*

Industrial Revolution: a period in eighteenth and nineteenth century Britain characterised by rapid urbanisation in response to greater mechanisation and mass production techniques. The often overcrowded housing conditions, with long working hours and low wages, gave few opportunities for travel and leisure activities to the majority of the population. The privileged 'middle classes', however, had the means to indulge in a variety of recreational pursuits, ranging from horse racing to prize fighting.

As the Industrial Revolution progressed, working people began to demand greater freedom from work and time for leisure. Many of the sporting associations still surviving today were formed during the Industrial Revolution, including the Football Association and the Rugby Union. The development of the railways from 1830 onwards was to give working people greater access to the countryside and coast. Today, we have entered the realms of the *post-industrial society,* with a shift from a manufacturing economy to one based on service industries.

Industry Lead Body (ILB): an organisation, working under the direction of the *National Council for Vocational Qualifications (NCVQ),* given the responsibility of developing *occupational standards* for its own industry. Within leisure and tourism, there are a large number of ILBs representing different industry sectors, e.g. the Travel Services Lead Body, the Museum Training Institute and the Arts and Entertainment Training Council. Each ILB is made up of specialists from the public, private and voluntary sectors, who have direct experience of the work requirements needed by staff.

industrial tribunal: a court at which cases arising out of employment *legislation* are dealt with. Industrial tribunals were set up by the government in 1964 and commonly deal with cases of *unfair dismissal* and discrimination in the workplace. They aim to try and obtain an agreement between the employer and the aggrieved employee and have the power to demand reinstatement of the employee or to award financial compensation if the former is not practicable.

inflation: the process of sustained rises in the price of goods and services in an economy. Rising inflation in an economy is considered to be undesirable because it leads to an overall reduction in buying power and increases the price of unfinished capital projects, such as major *leisure* developments and *hotel* construction. Travel to countries with spiralling inflation and generally unstable economies will be discouraged, leading to reductions in revenue from *incoming tourism.*

in-flight catering: food and drink provided as part of a flight on an aircraft, sometimes free of charge. The service is often provided on a contract basis by large catering firms such as Gardner Merchant.

in-flight entertainment: services such as videos and magazines provided as part of a flight on an aircraft. Increasing competition between major airlines has led to the provision of in-flight entertainment services becoming an important factor in sales.

informal communication: unlike *formal communication,* which takes place as a result of a pre-planned course of action, informal communication is a more spontaneous activity, e.g. a chance conversation with a colleague in another department or a favourable comment by a client to a travel agency manager. Although informal communication can sometimes lead to problems at work, e.g. gossip and the spreading of rumours, it is nonetheless an important and common way of passing information and instructions between staff.

information overload occurs when a person is given so much information from a variety of sources that he or she cannot cope and, to relieve the stress of the situation, chooses to ignore much of what is received.

information processing is the collection, storage, retrieval, distribution and analysis of information, and its presentation in a form that is readily usable for *management* purposes. Systems for processing information have existed since the beginning of human enterprise, but the advent of the *computer* has revolutionised information processing, with many mundane tasks previously carried out manually being transferred to automated systems. Information processing is sometimes divided into word processing and data processing, each with its own dedicated computer software.

'information superhighway': see *Internet*

information technology (IT): a term used to describe the systems that collect, interpret, store, analyse and distribute data, using *computers* and telecommunications equipment. IT is giving all leisure, travel and tourism enterprises, regardless of their size, the opportunity of communicating and conducting business on a global scale, using *global distribution systems (GDS)* and access to the *Internet.* In domestic tourism, IT is increasingly being used by *tourist information centres (TICs)* to offer booking and information services. In the home, IT forms the basis of much *home-based leisure* and entertainment, with computer games and CD technology becoming commonplace.

infrastructure refers to items such as airports, communications, roads, railways, water supply and sewage services, i.e. all those services that need to be in place before *development* of any kind, including *leisure* and *tourism* projects, can go ahead. A country's infrastructure is generally financed and built by the public sector, with private sector operators developing the *'superstructure'.* There are, however, an increasing number of private/public sector *partnerships* to provide infrastructure improvements.

injection: an economics term used to describe payments into a national or local economy. In the case of tourism, injections would include payments for *accommodation* and other services, *tourist taxes* and duty on goods sold in retail outlets. (See also *multiplier effect.*)

Institute of Groundsmanship (IoG) aims to promote the profession of groundsmanship and the *management*, maintenance and improvement of playing surfaces, sports stadia, recreation grounds, golf courses, playing fields and amenity areas. It is Europe's largest association of turf care professionals, with around 4 000 members, who benefit from a range of IoG services, including lectures and exhibitions, Institute examinations and proficiency tests, legal advice and information booklets.

Institute of Leisure and Amenity Management (ILAM) is a *professional body* formed in1983 to represent the interests of leisure professionals involved in the management of parks and open spaces, *recreation, tourism,* the arts and *sport.* With a membership of over 6 000, ILAM recognises the need for all leisure managers to develop a wide range of professional expertise in order to fulfil their personal potential and that of the industry. ILAM has its own professional qualification scheme and liaises with educational establishments in the development of courses in leisure management. ILAM is headed by a National Council which oversees the work of its 13 regions. The Institute has specialist panels, covering interests such as arts and entertainments, leisure education, sports development and tourism.

Institute of Sport and Recreation Management (ISRM): a voluntary membership organisation that aims to improve the management of swimming pools and other indoor leisure and recreation facilities. Known until recently as the Institute of Baths and Recreation Management, ISRM organises a programme of regional seminars, lectures and short courses for its members, as well as an annual conference.

Institute of Travel and Tourism (ITT): a *professional body* established in 1956 with the aim of developing the professionalism of its members within the industry. Unlike the *Tourism Society*, which attracts its membership mainly from public sector tourism, the ITT was originally set up to promote the interests of *travel agents* and *tour operators*, and today still draws its membership primarily from these sectors. The ITT aims to help practising and potential members to develop and maintain their industry knowledge and skills, by offering its own professional qualifications. The Institute also accredits college courses throughout the UK and organises a series of seminars on subjects as diverse as travel law, technology, brochure production and selling skills.

insurance represents a payment to cover the consequences of a specific eventuality, which may be an illness while on holiday abroad, an injury while playing sport or the loss of business income as a result of a fire on the premises. *Travel agents* can earn substantial *commission* payments from selling holiday and travel insurance alongside their more conventional products.

intangibility is a characteristic of leisure and tourism *products*, in that a customer cannot actually touch and examine many products before they agree to a sale, e.g. a 30-minute session on a golf driving range or an airline flight to Dublin. We are all accustomed to examining, for example, sports goods or luggage, before we buy, but with many leisure and tourism products we are buying the expectation of an experience.

integrated services digital network (ISDN): a sophisticated electronic system, developed by British Telecom, that makes use of cable technology to transfer signals, allowing services such as *video conferencing, desktop conferencing* and data transfer to take place.

integration: see *horizontal integration* and *vertical integration*

intelligent tourism: see *'green' tourism*

interest rate: the cost of borrowing money, paid by both individuals and organisations. Interest rates in the economy are set by the government in consultation with the Bank of England. From these figures, banks and other lending institutions set their own interest rates for the *overdrafts* and *loans* to their own *customers*. If government interest rates are increased, there is a general 'knock-on' effect, with banks increasing their rates in similar proportions. This has the result of reducing the general level of spending in the economy, and at the same time making it more expensive for businesses to finance their operations and expansion plans. When interest rates rise, leisure and tourism tend to suffer, given that they are discretionary purchases.

interlining: the reciprocal facility offered by airlines of issuing tickets and accepting bookings for airlines other than their own.

intermediary: a person or organisation that comes between two parties, perhaps providing a service or offering *conciliation* and advice. In the travel industry, the best known intermediaries are travel agents, who provide the link between customers and principals, such as airlines, tour operators and hotel companies. For their services, agents earn a commission, usually a percentage of the value of what they sell. In industrial relations, intermediaries are sometimes needed to resolve conflicts between workers and their employers. In such circumstances, officers of the *Advisory Conciliation and Arbitration Service (ACAS)* are sometimes called upon to mediate.

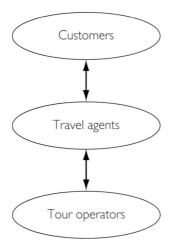

The travel agent acts as an intermediary between customers and the tour operators

internal communication is liaison within an organisation, perhaps between staff in different departments or in different branches of the same company. Organisations use a range of different *communication systems* to distribute information throughout their organisation. (See also *external communication*.)

internal constraint is something within an organisation that limits its ability to achieve its full potential. Internal constraints are usually factors over which the organisation has some degree of control, e.g. staff, *management style, suppliers,* finance, *marketing strategy,* buildings and facilities. A common internal constraint in leisure and tourism organisations is that there is insufficient investment in *staff training,* either through lack of funds or poor management. (See also *external constraint*.)

internal costs: expenditure that affects an organisation's own accounts directly, as opposed to *external costs,* which are outside of its immediate sphere of activity and are borne by the community and society in general.

internal customer is a colleague working in the same organisation who you come across in the course of normal day-to-day work activities and on whom you rely for services and support. Examples of internal customers are maintenance staff, receptionists, clerical and administrative staff, canteen staff and computer support staff. Good customer service requires a team approach within an organisation and a recognition that it is not just the customers 'on the other side of the counter' who need respect and consideration, but colleagues working in the same organisation as well.

internal environment: see *micro environment*

internal recruitment: the process of identifying and employing the most suitable person to fill a job vacancy from an organisation's existing staff members.

International Air Transport Association (IATA): a voluntary international trade body representing the interests of more than 80 per cent of the world's major airlines. IATA's principal aim is to promote safe, regular and economic air travel. It offers a clearing house system, which organises financial settlements between members, and promotes standardised procedures for the issuing of tickets and appointment of *IATA agents* worldwide. It is influential in determining price structures for some airline routes, although the final approval lies with national governments, operating through its three *Traffic Conference Areas (TCAs)* of the world.

International Bank for Reconstruction and Development: see *World Bank*

International Civil Aviation Organisation (ICAO): established in 1944 under the Chicago Convention on Civil Aviation, ICAO is a specialist agency of the *United Nations (UN),* which works with national aviation authorities, including the *Civil Aviation Authority (CAA),* to ensure safe and efficient practices in air travel around the world.

International Date Line: an artificial time boundary broadly corresponding to 180° from the *Greenwich Meridian.* The Date Line represents the point at which calendar days change, so that countries on the western side of the Line are one day ahead of those on the eastern side, resulting in travellers across the Date Line either 'gaining' or 'losing' a day depending on their direction of travel. (See also *time zones*.)

International Federation of Tour Operators (IFTO) is a European network of leading, mass market *tour operators.* Established as an independent membership organisation, IFTO lobbies on behalf of its members at European level in the same way that the *Federation of Tour Operators (FTO)* does for UK operators at national level.

International Leisure Group (ILG): a major leisure and tourism company which expanded rapidly in the 1980s, only to collapse dramatically in 1991. Perhaps best known for its Intasun holidays brand, the majority of ILG's holiday clients were transferred to its rivals, principally *Thomson* and Airtours.

International Olympic Committee (IOC) was founded in 1894, in advance of the first Modern *Olympic Games* held in 1896 in Athens. The IOC enlisted the help of sports organisations and individuals to draw up a policy for the Modern Games. The aims of the IOC are the promotion of those physical and moral qualities which are the basis of sport, education through sport towards understanding and friendship, the spread of the Olympic principles, creating goodwill and the bringing together of athletes from all over the world in a festival of sport. With its headquarters in Switzerland, the IOC currently recognises the work of 186 national Olympic committees, including the *British Olympic Association (BOA)*. Members of the IOC are responsible for choosing the sites for the winter and summer Olympic Games.

International Passenger Survey (IPS) is carried out by *BTA/ETB* on behalf of the Employment Department (now *Department for Education and Employment*), the Central Statistical Office (CSO) and the Home Office. The survey collects information on both UK incoming and outbound tourism and makes estimates for the UK *balance of payments* and for migration. The IPS estimates are based on interviews with some 165 000 travellers every year. Data provided by the survey includes the number of visitors in a given time period, the purpose of their visit, the region visited, their expenditure and duration of stay. Results from the IPS are published quarterly in the Business Monitor MQ6 – Overseas Travel and Tourism and the annual results are similarly produced in an annual version of the Business Monitor.

International Standards Organisation (ISO): an independent body that lays down minimum *quality* standards across a wide range of industry sectors and production processes. Of particular interest to leisure and tourism organisations is *ISO 9000*, the standard incorporating *BS 5750* and focusing on consistent levels of service delivery.

international tourism: travel by residents of one country to another country, as distinct from *domestic tourism.*

international visitor: see *visitor*

Internet: sometimes called 'the information superhighway' or simply 'the net', the Internet is a non-centralised, interactive system of networked computer databases, which offers households and businesses a wide range of services. Already, it is possible for the 30 million users of the Internet to access information on countries and travel services via the Internet, and to communicate globally. Many people regard 'the information superhighway' as the biggest development in global electronic technology, since the introduction of the *personal computer*. (See also *World Wide Web*.)

interpersonal skills: a variety of skills that are useful not only in the workplace, but throughout life in general. They include negotiation, *communication*, listening, decision making, problem solving, working collaboratively and many more. Training in these skills can be carried out 'in-house' or with the help of a specialist training consultancy. A popular way of developing interpersonal skills is for members of staff to spend time at *outdoor activity* centres, where they are given practical and mental challenges in group situations.

interpretation is defined by the *Centre for Environmental Interpretation (CEI)* as 'the art of explaining the meaning of sites visited by the public'. It is concerned with offering visitors more than just an enjoyable experience, but one that will help them better understand the place they are visiting. Sites as varied as farms, ancient buildings, archaeological excavations, coasts, wildlife reserves, landscape features and urban areas can all be interpreted using a range of different techniques, including leaflets, signposting, self-guided trails, audio-visual aids, *guided walks* and demonstrations. Interpretation is also an important tool in the *management* of sites, helping to reduce conflict and physical erosion.

interview survey: see *face-to-face interview*

interviewer: the name given to an individual who asks questions of another person, either as part of a *face-to-face interview* survey, a *staff appraisal* or as part of the recruitment process for a job. To be a good interviewer takes a great deal of *training* and commitment. (See also *respondent.*)

interviewing has a number of meanings in leisure and tourism, including that part of the *recruitment and selection process* at which a candidate is asked to attend a formal meeting, where he or she is asked questions and given the opportunity of learning about the post on offer. Another meaning of interviewing is carrying out a *face-to-face interview* survey or *telephone survey* as part of a *market research* exercise.

investment appraisal: an in-depth financial analysis of a potential capital project to investigate if there are sufficient grounds for it to go ahead. A range of techniques can facilitate the appraisal, such as *discounted cash-flow (DCF)*. Investment appraisal is common for large leisure and tourism projects such as airports and *tourist attractions.*

Investors in People (IIP) is the national quality standard in the UK for effective investment in the training and development of people to achieve organisational objectives. Administered by the *Training and Enterprise Councils (TECs)*, IIP provides a framework for improving business performance, through a planned approach to offering employees training and development opportunities to help the organisation survive and flourish. In other words, what people can do and are motivated to do in

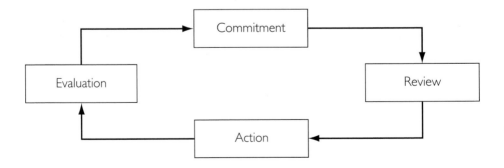

The key principles of IIP

an organisation, matches what the organisation needs them to do to be successful. Leisure and tourism organisations, large and small, have achieved or are working towards achieving IIP.

'invisibles' are services whose value is shown on a country's balance of payments, i.e. those items that cannot be seen or touched, e.g. banking, financial services, shipping and *tourism*. Such services brought into a country are known as imports, while those sent abroad are exports. Historically, Britain's balance of payments has enjoyed a surplus on 'invisible' items, which has helped to offset the deficits on *'visible'* items.

invoice: a document which is provided by a supplier to a customer as a request for payment. The invoice will show details of the goods or services supplied, their costs, any credit period offered and the total cost payable by the purchaser.

IOC: see *International Olympic Committee*

IPS: see *International Passenger Survey*

Iron Curtain: a phrase first coined by Winston Churchill to denote the divide between East and West in Europe. The momentous events that began in 1989 with the fall of the Berlin Wall have opened up the former Eastern Bloc countries to the West, allowing people to move freely and enjoy each others' cultures and scenery. To all intents and purposes, the term 'Iron Curtain' is now obsolete, although much still needs to be accomplished to raise living standards in many of the former Eastern Bloc countries.

ISDN: see *integrated services digital network*

ISO: see *International Standards Organisation*

ISO 9000: see *BS EN ISO 9000*

ISRM: see *Institute of Sport and Recreation Management*

Istel: a *viewdata system* used in travel agencies to access *principal's' computerised reservation systems (CRSs)* using a *VDU* plus either a telephone line or cable connection. Istel, now part of the AT & T Corporation, is fast becoming the number one choice for UK travel agencies. Its main rival is *Fastrak*.

IT: see *information technology, inclusive tour*

ITC: see *inclusive tour by charter*

ITT: see *Institute of Travel and Tourism*

ITX: see *inclusive tour by excursion*

J

JES: see *job evaluation study*

jet aircraft: a method of *transportation* that was instrumental in developing *mass tourism* in the latter half of the twentieth century. Technological advances in jet aircraft design resulting from the Second World War led to air travel becoming a reality for the masses of the population from the 1950s onwards. The Boeing 707 was introduced in 1958 and led to a surge in *scheduled* and *charter flights*, the latter becoming the basis for the *package holidays* so familiar to us all in the 1990s.

JICNARS: see *socio-economic classification*

job analysis: the starting point in the *recruitment and selection process*, concerned with identifying what a particular post entails, before setting about finding a suitable person for the job. Information to be included in a job analysis can be obtained from the existing postholder, previous records, other members of staff and by direct observation. The job analysis will form the basis for writing a *job description*.

job description: a document outlining the nature of a particular job and the duties and responsibilities involved. A typical job description will include details such as the title of the job, the key objectives of the post, to whom responsible and for whom responsible, detailed duties and general *conditions of employment*, which are likely to form part of an employee's *contract of employment*.

job enlargement: the practice of increasing the scope and variety of a job and the range of tasks that a person is responsible for carrying out. A public relations assistant for a large tour operator, for example, whose job usually consists of writing *press releases*, may be given the responsibility of organising a *familiarisation visit* for a group of journalists. While job enlargement can be useful for a person's career development, it must not be seen as a form of 'cheap labour', i.e. getting junior staff to carry out jobs that are usually done by more senior, and higher paid, employees. If managed as part of an individual's personal development, however, job enlargement can give added *job satisfaction*.

job enrichment is a human resources process that aims to give a person greater responsibility in their work, more opportunities for achievement and recognition, and a greater involvement in their own personal development, so as to achieve more *job satisfaction* and become a more motivated individual. Job enrichment can be achieved in many different ways, e.g. by giving workers greater freedom in the scheduling of their work tasks, reducing the level of direct supervision over employees and providing opportunities for more direct contact with customers.

job evaluation study (JES): an exercise that compares the relative demands of different jobs, so as to help with the setting of pay scales and gradings of employees. Under the terms of the *Equal Pay Acts*, a JES may need to be undertaken before similar jobs can be said to be of equal value, thereby resulting in equal pay for all workers. The study will look at factors such as skills needed, degrees of responsibility, levels of decision making and effort required to carry out the job.

job role: the expected pattern of behaviour of an employee occupying a specific position in an organisation. The particular roles associated with a post are normally set out in a *job description.*

job rotation is a type of *job enlargement,* with an employee's work tasks being alternated over a period of time, so as to relieve the monotony of mundane tasks and to expose employees to the work of other departments or individuals in their organisation. Job rotation should be seen as a form of staff training and development, allowing employees to gain useful transferable skills. It needs to be well planned and managed in order to give staff sufficient time to master the changed *job roles* that they are expected to undertake.

job satisfaction reflects the degree to which a person feels fulfilled and motivated in his or her work environment. Time and money spent by an organisation on measures to increase employees' job satisfaction can pay dividends in the long run, with reduced absenteeism and staff turnover, enhanced customer service standards and greater staff productivity. Introducing *job enrichment* schemes, such as *job rotation* and *job enlargement,* can lead to greater job satisfaction for employees.

job specification: a written document, often used in conjunction with a *job description,* listing the skills and characteristics needed to do a particular job successfully. Sometimes called a person specification, it acts as a blueprint of the 'ideal' person for the job, in terms of qualifications, experience, skills, character and achievements, and is a helpful tool in an organisation's selection and recruitment processes. Some job specifications divide the qualities, experience and skills sought into those that are essential and those which are desirable.

joint use is the shared use of a facility so as to maximise revenue or use. Sometimes referred to as dual use, it is common for *local authority* leisure facilities to be operated on a joint use basis, e.g. a school having exclusive use of a sports centre between 9 am and 4 pm, with the local community able to use it at all other times.

joint marketing: see *co-operative marketing*

K

k: a shorthand way of writing thousand, e.g. a salary of £13 k would mean £13 000 or a computer with 120 k bytes of memory would mean 120 000 bytes.

Key Classification Scheme: a voluntary grading scheme for *self-catering accommodation* in Britain. Operated on similar lines to the *Crown Classification Scheme* for serviced accommodation, the Key Scheme has been designed to help people choose the type of self-catering accommodation which best suits their requirements and expectations. It covers both the level of facilities provided and an objective measure of quality, from 'approved' to 'de luxe'. Self-catering establishments are awarded from one to five Keys, depending on the level of facilities provided.

'kitemark': a seal of approval awarded by the *British Standards Institution (BSI)* to organisations whose products and services meet certain minimum *quality* or safety standards.

REVISION: There is a set of revision lists at the back of this book to help you prepare for GNVQ unit tests. See pages 246–250 for unit tests in GNVQ Advanced Leisure and Tourism.

L

LAI: see *Local Area Initiative*

LAN: see *local area network*

Landmark Trust: a charitable trust that preserves unusual historic buildings in the UK and lets them out for holidays. Included in their directory are castles, folleys, cottages and lighthouses. Most Landmark properties are let on a *self-catering* basis.

laptop computer: a portable *personal computer (PC)* that allows its user to carry out a range of computing functions while 'on the move'. Laptops do not need a fixed power supply, so can be used in aircraft, trains, cars and even in the great outdoors! The latest laptop computers are as powerful as many PCs found in offices, with the ability to run sophisticated word processing, database and *spreadsheet software*.

latent demand: see *deferred demand*

leadership style: see *management style*

leading question: a question that invites a positive response, e.g. 'don't you agree that the accommodation is comfortable?' suggests that the person being asked the question should agree with the questioner. This question would be better if written as follows: 'what are your views on the level of comfort in the accommodation?'. When designing *questionnaires*, it is important not to introduce bias by including leading questions.

leakage: the loss of money from a local or national economy as a result of, for example, fluctuations in exchange rates, payments to *shareholders, taxation* and purchases of goods and services from national distributors. (See also *multiplier effect*.)

leaseback: see *sale and leaseback*

leasing is the practice of acquiring specific *fixed assets* from a leasing company in return for the payment of an agreed, regular sum. Leasing is a common method of providing vehicles, office equipment and fixtures and fittings. The main advantage of leasing is that an organisation avoids the need for a large initial payment. It is particularly suitable for equipment that quickly goes out of date, such as *computers* and telephone systems. At the end of the leasing period, the equipment or vehicle is returned to the leasing company, or it may be purchased on favourable terms.

legislation: refers to Acts of Parliament passed by central government, e.g. *Health and Safety at Work, etc. Act 1974* and *Development of Tourism Act 1969*.

leisure: a complex phenomenon which most people associate with *leisure time* or *leisure activities*, choosing to spend their spare time in ways which give them the most satisfaction. Some people regard leisure as time when they are not at work, while others think of leisure in terms of the recreational activities they carry out in their leisure time, such as gardening, watching television, reading books or knitting.

Treating leisure as time away from paid employment does not give a complete picture of the nature of leisure, since it fails to take into account the many necessary duties and functions that we all have to perform in our daily lives, such as eating, sleeping and carrying out domestic chores. Unemployed people don't fit into such a notion of leisure either, with most agreeing that they have more leisure time than they want.

Given that it is a difficult concept to fully understand, any definition of leisure would necessarily include that it is:

- time outside of a formal employment situation
- time over and above that devoted to household chores
- time outside sleeping, eating and personal hygiene functions
- time at the disposal of the individual
- time when a person has the freedom to do as they please

The last two points concerning an individual's freedom of choice are perhaps getting closer to the true meaning of leisure, in that it is a creative period during which a person can strive to reach his or her potential as a human being and productive member of society.

leisure activities are normally divided into those that are *home-based*, including reading books, listening to the radio and hi-fi, gardening, dressmaking, needlework, watching television and DIY (do-it-yourself), and those that take place away from the home, such as going to the cinema, visiting tourist attractions, taking part in sports, *sports spectating*, taking holidays and day trips. Figures from Leisure Consultants forecast that spending on leisure activities is set to increase from £100 billion to more than £130 billion before the end of this century. Activities predicted to grow over this time period include home-based electronic entertainment, creative and productive leisure, active leisure pursuits, purposeful travel and community leisure. Of declining interest are likely to be established 'mass' leisure (cheap package holidays, network TV, etc.), socially discouraged activities (heavy drinking, etc.), activities with health or environmental hazards and young adult leisure (going to pubs, discos, etc.).

leisure and recreation industry: a diverse part of the UK economy, spanning the public, private and voluntary sectors, and made up of a number of interrelated components, including:

- *sport* and *physical recreation*
- *arts and entertainment*
- *countryside recreation*
- *community recreation*
- *outdoor activities*
- *home-based leisure*
- *play*
- *heritage*
- *leisure shopping*

According to figures produced by Leisure Consultants, consumer spending on leisure and recreation in 1993 was over £100 billion, representing almost a quarter of all consumer spending by British people.

leisure centre: a purpose-built facility providing a variety of indoor and outdoor sport and *recreation* activities. The introduction of *compulsory competitive tendering (CCT)* has changed the management of local leisure centres dramatically, aimed at making them compete more effectively with commercial facilities.

leisure participation is affected by many factors, some within the control of individuals, some not, including:

- availability of leisure time – no leisure time equals no leisure activity!
- income level – people with higher disposable incomes are more likely to take part in leisure activities
- personal mobility – access to a car greatly increases the opportunities for leisure activities
- culture and demography (age, gender, cultural background, etc.) – studies have shown that leisure participation is lower among certain minority groups in society
- level of provision of facilities – if there are few facilities available, participation rates will be lower
- long-term changes in society – factors such as ageing of the population, increasing rates of divorce, technological advances and changing patterns of employment, all affect participation rates for leisure activities.

leisure shopping refers to the growing trend for shopping centres, particularly those in out-of-town locations, to become the focus of a new type of leisure activity, often combining a number of elements, e.g. shopping plus a visit to the cinema or shopping plus a meal out. The growth in out-of-town retail centres, such as Meadowhall near Sheffield and Lakeside in Essex, coupled with the relaxation of Sunday trading legislation, has given a boost to trading and further developed the concept of leisure shopping, particularly with families.

Leisure Studies Association was established in 1975, in response to the (then) little-known and little-researched concept of leisure. Today, the Association represents researchers, planners, policy makers, administrators and practitioners in a wide range of leisure areas. LSA's objectives include stimulating an exchange of ideas on contemporary leisure issues, disseminating knowledge of leisure studies to create the conditions for informed decision making, encouraging leisure research and promoting discussion through its publications and conferences.

leisure time is time outside of paid employment, at the disposal of the individual and during which he or she has the freedom to choose what to do. Not surprisingly, statistics in *Social Trends* show that retired people have the most leisure time in a typical week in the UK, retired men enjoying 90 hours and retired women 71 hours of leisure time. Women in full-time employment also have less leisure time than their male counterparts, the result of spending more time on household chores and child care.

leisure tourism is the category of the *travel and tourism industry* concerned with travel for leisure purposes, rather than travel for business purposes (*business tourism*). Leisure tourism includes taking holidays at home and abroad, *visiting friends and relatives (VFR)* and travel for a variety of reasons, such as for health and fitness, sport, education, culture, religious and spiritual.

le Shuttle is the vehicle-carrying rail shuttle system that operates through the *Channel Tunnel* (the passenger train service is known as *Eurostar*). At peak times in the summer months, le Shuttle will be operating four services per hour, on a turn-up-and-go basis, linking Folkestone and Calais. Freight and passenger vehicles are driven onto specially constructed shuttle carriages for the 30 minute journey through the Channel Tunnel. The introduction of the service has led to fierce competition with the Channel ferry operators, particularly those on the Dover-Calais route, and has led to speculation that one or more operators will be unable to survive as the Tunnel grows in popularity.

lessee: the party in a *leasing* agreement to whom equipment is provided by the leasing company in return for regular payments.

lessor is another name for the *leasing* company in a leasing agreement, which provides equipment to the *lessee* in return for regular payments. The lessor generally retains ownership of the property when the leasing agreement expires.

liabilities are what an organisation or individual owes to another party. Liabilities may be either *current*, i.e. those that will be converted into cash within a short period of time, such as taxation and short-term bank loans, or long-term, i.e. those that are due to be repaid in a period of longer than one year, such as *commercial mortgages* and *debentures*.

licensing: the regulation of certain activities by central and local government, and other regulatory authorities. In leisure and tourism, this would include the regulation of those providing public facilities in order to ensure the moral and physical protection of the general public. The main licences that a leisure or tourism operator would need to consider include the *Public Entertainments' Licence (PEL)*, Indoor Sports' Licence, Cinema Licence, *Liquor Licence* and Theatre Licence.

life cycle: see *product life cycle*

life cycle classification: a way that marketers classify people according to where they are in their life cycle, rather than according to their social status or occupation as with the *socio-economic classification*. The stages are as follows:

- bachelor stage
- newly-wed/living together
- full nest (couples with children)
- empty nest (children have left home)
- solitary survivor

By placing people in one of the categories, marketers are able to determine their likes and dislikes, even down to what newspaper they are likely to read and what type of *holidays* and *leisure* products will appeal to them.

life style classification: a technique used in *marketing* to classify people according to their life style, rather than their social status or occupation as with the *socio-economic classification*. Life style classifications are increasingly being seen as the most effective way of classifying people and thereby segmenting the market. One such classification is the 4Cs, developed by advertising agency Young and Rubicam, which labels people as either mainstreamers, aspirers, succeeders or reformers, each with quite distinct work and leisure habits.

limited company: a commercial organisation whose owners enjoy the benefit of *limited liability*, thereby limiting their risk to the amount they have invested in the company. A limited company, denoted by the words 'limited' or 'ltd.' after its name, is a separate entity in law, capable of suing and being sued in its own right. Limited companies fall into one of two categories:

- company limited by shares – by far the most common and is divided into *public limited company* and *private limited company*
- company limited by guarantee – when company documents show that an individual (known as a guarantor) will contribute a specified sum of money in the event of the company being wound up

All limited companies are regulated by the *Companies Acts* of 1985 and 1989, which states that they must produce a *Memorandum of Association* and *Articles of Association*.

limited liability: a benefit enjoyed by investors in *limited companies*, meaning that they are only liable, in the event of company failure, to the amount they have actually invested in the business, rather than their personal wealth and possessions.

line manager: an individual who is given the *authority* to make executive decisions and is responsible for the performance of one or more members of staff. Line managers have an agreed place in a *hierarchical organisation*, where they report to a senior manager and employees report to them.

linear park: a recreational space that follows a number of linear features, such as railway lines, bridleways, footpaths, cycle tracks and canal towpaths. Often developed in urban areas, they provide opportunities for passive *recreation* and nature *conservation*.

liquidity is a measure of whether an organisation has sufficient funds to pay its debts when they fall due. Comparisons can be made between years to see whether liquidity is improving or declining or whether the organisation is remaining in a solvent state when comparing actual with forecast results. Liquidity can be estimated from a company's published accounts using the *liquidity ratio*.

liquidity ratio tells us the ratio between a company's readily available cash or near-cash assets and its *current liabilities*. It is calculated by dividing a company's current liabilities into its liquid assets (current assets less stock). It is sometimes called the acid-test ratio or current ratio.

Liquor Licence: a licence needed by the operators of all establishments where alcohol is sold or consumed. Liquor Licences range from a full on-licence, where the licence holder can sell alcohol for consumption on the premises, to a seasonal licence, which allows the establishment to sell alcohol only at certain times of the year, normally the main holiday periods. In deciding whether or not to grant a liquor licence, a magistrates' court will consider a number of factors, including the character of the applicant, the suitability of the premises, previous applications for licences and the views of official agencies, including the police and council officers.

load factor: the number of airline seats sold as a percentage of the total number available, i.e. if 125 seats are sold for a flight on an aircraft that holds 250 passengers, the load factor would be 50 per cent. Load factor, like the *occupancy rate* in hotels, is a performance measure that companies use to determine their profitability and plan their operations. *British Airways* achieved an overall load factor on scheduled services of 67.8 per cent in the 1994–95 operating year. (See also *break-even load factor*.)

loan: a source of medium- or long-term *capital* for a business to allow expansion and *development*. Most leisure and tourism organisations will approach banks to obtain a loan. The bank will usually require some form of *security* before it agrees to a loan, in case the lender should default on repayments. Interest will be charged, the rate depending on the term of the loan, the amount being borrowed, the degree of risk involved and the track record of the applicant. In leisure and tourism, medium-term loans are typically used to finance new plant and equipment, while long-term loans are used for new building work or for extending premises.

loan capital: that part of a company's *capital* made available from *loans*.

lobbying is the practice of informing key decision makers about specific concerns, opinions and issues, in the hope of gaining their support for change. Lobbying takes place at a variety of levels, e.g. *pressure groups* letting local councillors know their views on an issue or large commercial organisations informing central government of their concerns over proposed legislation at home or in Europe. Lobbying is seen as a legitimate part of any country's democratic processes, but is sometimes misused by those in positions of power and influence.

Local Agenda 21: see *Earth Summit*

Local Area Initiative (LAI): see *Tourism Development Action Programmes (TDAPs)*

local area network (LAN): see *network*

local authority is the name given to the elected body responsible for providing a range of facilities and services in a locality. The particular services will vary depending on whether the authority is a *county council, district council* or *community council.* The policies of a local authority are determined by elected representatives of the local people (councillors) and put into operation by council employees and officers. For example, spending and priorities on *leisure* facilities will be agreed by a committee of the council, who will expect the staff in the leisure services department to carry out the day-to-day operation of facilities. Local authorities play an important role in the local provision of leisure and tourism facilities, both for residents and visitors.

Local Plan: a document produced by a district or borough council indicating its priorities for future development. A Local Plan will implement many of the recommendations of a county council's *Structure Plan*, giving detailed plans for housing, leisure services, refuse collection and environmental improvements. Local authorities are obliged to consult local residents as part of the process of drawing up Local Plans.

logo: a symbol used by an organisation as part of its *corporate identity.* Effective logos in leisure and tourism include the crown symbol on Sovereign Holidays brochures and the *ABTA* logo.

London Marathon: an annual race in the streets of London, with around 35 000 competitors, most running to raise money for charity. One of the main objectives of the event is to generate funds which can be used to improve recreation and leisure facilities in the London boroughs. The marathon also aims to help British marathon running in general. The field is made up of club runners, members of the general public and a small number of elite runners. The event relies heavily on the *sponsorship* of large and small organisations; past race sponsors include Gillette, Mars, ADT and NutraSweet. Event organisers have signed a sponsorship contract with Flora for the 1996 London Marathon.

London Tourist Board is the official *Regional Tourist Board* serving the Greater London area.

London Transport (LT) is a statutory corporation reporting to, and funded by, the *Department of Transport*. It was established in its present form in 1984, with a remit to plan, provide or procure services to meet the present and future public transport needs of London. In so doing, LT has a responsibility to ensure that the operation of its services are safe, efficient, economic and make provision for all passengers, including those with disabilities. In 1994/95, it sold its ten remaining bus-operating companies into the private sector, but retains responsibility for running the London Underground.

long haul destinations are generally considered to be those beyond Europe, e.g. Australia, the Far East, USA and India. Advances in aircraft technology, coupled with low prices offered by some mass market *tour operators*, have opened up many new long haul destinations for package holidays, e.g. Goa, the Gambia and the Caribbean. While this trend has provided much-needed foreign currency in the short term for the destinations concerned, there are fears for the long-term *socio-cultural impacts* of such developments.

loss leader: see *penetration pricing*

Lottery Sports Fund is the body set up by the *Sports Council* to make decisions on which sporting projects should receive funds from the *National Lottery*. The range of projects eligible to apply for finance from the Fund is very wide, but they must be projects of a capital nature, i.e. construction, buying land, upgrading facilities, etc. Typical examples could include the building or refurbishment of sports pitches, sports halls, swimming pools, jetties, etc.

low season: the period when there is least *demand* for a product or service, e.g. the winter months for summer package holidays. Many tourism businesses will close down altogether in the low season, making many resort areas feel rather 'dead' out of season. The low season, on the other hand, can be a good time to pick up a bargain holiday, since those establishments that do remain open will offer discounted rates for *accommodation* and other facilities in order to attract some custom.

LSA: see *Leisure Studies Association*

LTB: see *London Tourist Board*

M

macro environment: a term used to denote certain factors 'in the wider world' which may have an effect on an organisation and its operation and *profitability*. Sometimes referred to as the external environment, they are often factors over which the organisation will have little control, such as the state of the national economy, the level of unemployment, changes in the social structure, government *legislation* and technological advances. The acronym *PEST* is sometimes used to classify these factors, standing for political, economic, social and technological. (See also *micro environment*.)

MAFF: see *Ministry of Agriculture, Fisheries and Food*

mail merge: a facility available on many *word processing* packages that allows the creation of personalised documents from the merging of a standard letter and a list of names and addresses. A mail merge facility is very useful for producing promotional letters as part of a *direct mail* campaign.

mailing house: a specialist firm that handles all aspects of the distribution of items that form part of *direct mail* campaigns. A large tour operator, for example, will use the services of a mailing house to co-ordinate the distribution of its *brochures*, either to travel agents or direct to the public. The services offered by the mailing house will include folding items, filling and closing envelopes, franking and onward distribution.

mailing list: a list of names and addresses used as part of a *direct mail* campaign. Lists can be assembled from internal records or bought from specialist suppliers, grouped according to interests, geographical location, gender, etc.

maintenance is any work undertaken to keep an asset at an acceptably safe standard; by assets, we mean buildings, machinery, plant, accommodation, equipment, vehicles, communication systems, etc. Failure on the part of a leisure or tourism organisation to maintain its assets effectively may have serious repercussions, including:

- poor safety standards
- poor *image* to the outside world
- customer dissatisfaction
- loss of service as a result of breakdowns and closures
- loss of *revenue* and possible legal proceedings

Maintenance can be either *planned* or *corrective*; planned maintenance is programmed and scheduled in advance, whereas corrective maintenance is work carried out in response to an emergency or failure of equipment. It is good *management* practice to adopt a policy of planned maintenance in order to reduce the probability of the failure of systems or equipment and hence the need for expensive corrective maintenance.

management is a structured process involving *planning*, organising, directing, co-ordinating and controlling a range of *resources*, in order to achieve pre-determined *objectives*. (See also *management style, management by objectives*.)

management accounting: whereas *financial accounting* focuses on the preparation of statutory accounts, management accounting is concerned with the provision of financial information to help with business decision making and for control purposes. Management accounts are used purely within an organisation and there is no statutory requirement for them to be published. Management accounts will provide an organisation with information on such matters as the costs of the operation, total sales, performance of individual *profit centres* and the profit for the organisation as a whole.

management buy-out: the process of former employees, directors or senior managers of an organisation taking over its *management* and operation by acquiring a substantial *equity* stake in the business. Examples of management buy-outs in leisure and tourism include the acquisition of *National Express* by its former managers in 1988 and the purchase of Wookey Hole Caves in Somerset from its former owners the Tussauds Group. The winning of a contract by the management of a former local authority leisure centre is also a form of management buy-out. (See also *direct services organisation.*)

management by objectives (MBO) is a formal approach to the management of an organisation, which has four identifiable steps:

1 the establishment of clear *objectives*
2 the agreement of targets and time limits for action
3 monitoring to see that action is taken
4 review of the process and amendment of objectives as necessary

MBO operates best within a clearly identified management structure, where each manager and member of staff is aware of his or her responsibilities and duties. Advocates of MBO argue that it offers many benefits to an organisation, such as clear lines of communication and the encouragement of *motivation*. Others believe that it is too rigid a structure, not allowing individual managers the flexibility needed to operate effectively in a dynamic environment.

Management Charter Initiative (MCI): a government-and industry-sponsored attempt to introduce a range of competence-based qualifications for working managers in all industries. The Initiative is linked to the *National Vocational Qualifications (NVQ)* system, and offers three levels of achievement at Certificate, Diploma and Masters level. The aim of the MCI is to identify the core skills and competences needed by managers in industry and the public sector, and to help organisations fill any skills gaps they detect, through a programme of *staff training* and development.

management information system (MIS): a mixture of manual and automated resources, concerned with the collection, collation, storage, retrieval, communication and use of data for purposes of an organisation's sound *management* and forward *planning*. A MIS used in a leisure or tourism facility will focus on three distinct types of information, namely financial data, operational information and customer details.

management style: the manner that a senior member of an organisation deals with his or her subordinates in the workplace. Management styles vary enormously, but can be categorised as follows:

- motivational management – a leader who is supportive and who consults widely with staff
- aggressive management – a manager who is generally not a good listener

and prefers not to enter into discussion on decisions

- administrative management – a manager who 'does everything by the book', but lacks a motivational spark
- committee management – a manager who always steers a middle course and is afraid to make decisions
- passive management – a leader who does the bare minimum and will resist change

A motivational manager is one who will have the best chance of achieving success in an organisation. Displaying a management style that is 'open' rather than defensive, is assertive rather than aggressive and praises rather than undermines staff achievement, is far more likely to achieve results.

manager: a person who takes responsibility for *planning*, organising, directing and controlling specified elements of an organisation's business, to help achieve its *objectives*. Managers have to marshall their *resources*, be they staff, plant, finance, machinery or facilities, determine priorities and work within *budgets* to achieve their aims. Managers often have leadership roles and must be able to communicate with their employees and motivate them to achieve overall success.

managing director: an individual responsible for executing an organisation's *strategy* and running its day-to-day affairs, in conjunction with other directors and staff. The managing director is the most senior of the board of directors and, in some cases, he or she may also be its chairman. The managing director is chosen by the other board members, who will be looking for an individual who has the ability to work under pressure, is a good delegator and leader, has wide experience of business and excellent management skills.

manifest: an official list of the names of the passengers carried on an airline, a vessel or a vehicle.

man-made attractions are purpose-built tourist facilities designed to give enjoyment, education and entertainment. Popular man-made attractions in the UK include *theme parks* such as Alton Towers and Chessington World of Adventures, historic sites including Stonehenge and Windsor Castle, and *museums* such as the British Museum and the Museum of Science and Industry in Manchester. (See also *natural attractions.*)

manpower planning gives an organisation the opportunity to look at its existing staffing levels and to forecast the mix of *human resources* it will need to meet its future objectives. The stages in developing an organisation's manpower plan will include:

- an examination of its strategic plan
- analysis of the existing staff resources in the context of the strategic plan
- an estimate of any likely future changes in the supply of staff
- the likely demand for staff in the future
- development of the future human resource 'mix'

The dynamic nature of the *leisure* and *tourism* industries makes manpower planning an essential *management* exercise in order to keep costs to a minimum, thereby maintaining *profitability*. At a national level, governments undertake manpower planning as a way of determining future training and employment needs.

manual handling of loads: the Manual Handling Operations Regulations came into force on 1 January 1993 as a direct result of the *EU Directives on health and safety*. They apply to any manual handling operations that may cause injury at work, e.g. loading bulk supplies of brochures into a travel agency or moving sports equipment in a *leisure centre*. Under the regulations, employers must avoid hazardous manual handling operations whenever possible, assess any operations that cannot be avoided and reduce the risk of any injury as far as is reasonably practicable.

MAP: see *Modified American Plan*

marginal costing is another name for *contribution pricing*.

market: the total number of people who buy (existing market), or may buy (potential market), a *product* or service. It is generally expressed in monetary terms, e.g. the total market for spending on leisure products in the UK is estimated to be more than £100 billion. Organisations need to have reliable data on the characteristics of the market for their products and services, most often obtained by undertaking a *market research* exercise. The size of the market for overseas *package holidays* bought by British people is currently in the region of 11 million holidays per year. Tour operators compete to get as big a share of this market as possible, by constant product development and market analysis.

market-led pricing is a pricing *policy* that takes market factors and conditions, rather than costs of production, as the basis on which prices are determined. A market-led approach to pricing is common in leisure and tourism, given the highly competitive nature of the industries. Two of the most widely used market-led methods are *competitive pricing* and *penetration pricing*. (See also *cost-based pricing*.)

Market Opinion and Research International (MORI): a commercial organisation that specialises in commissioning and conducting *market research*. Perhaps best known for the polls that it carries out on behalf of political parties, MORI undertakes surveys of a wide range of national and international topics, including attitudes to new technology, use of *leisure time* and holiday-taking.

market orientation is concerned with spending time and money on researching the *needs* of the *market* and providing products and services that *customers* will want to buy. It is a *management* practice that is more concerned with giving customers complete satisfaction than purely concentrating on the products and services that are supplied (*product orientation*).

market penetration: the technique of attempting to increase *market share* by offering customers a range of promotional incentives, such as discounts, free gifts and 'extra product'.

market research is the process of gathering information on existing and potential *customers* and its use for *management* purposes. It is an essential first step in an organisation's *marketing* activity, since without reliable data on customers' attitudes and desires, any leisure or tourism organisation will have difficulty in providing appropriate products and services. Research may be needed at any stage in the marketing process and can help an organisation plan for the future, identify new market opportunities or sales outlets, identify problems and suggest solutions, monitor the reaction of customers, reduce costs and monitor general trends in the leisure and tourism industries. Market research involves the collection of both *secondary data*, i.e. information that is already published, and *primary data*, which is new data collected for a specific purpose, often involving *observation*, a *focus group* or a *survey*.

Market Research Society (MRS): an independent membership organisation that oversees the work of the major *market research* companies operating in the UK. It has introduced a strict *code of practice* for its members, in order to increase the professionalism of the industry and improve the image of market research generally.

market segmentation is the process of sub-dividing the total *market* for a product or service into different groups, each with similar characteristics. Market segmentation enables an organisation to target a particular group, whose members become the focus of all its marketing efforts, with the introduction and *promotion* of products and services designed to meet the individual's needs. Markets can be segmented in a number of ways, including:

- by region, e.g. all the people living in a particular postcode area of a city
- by age, e.g. designing products for senior citizens
- by social class, e.g. targeting all the people in a town in the C2 socio-economic group
- by gender, e.g. developing courses for women
- by life style, e.g. introducing new holidays for young people who live adventurous life styles

Mass market *tour operators* are constantly looking to develop new products to meet the needs of particular market segments, as a way of maintaining their *market share* and improving profitability.

market share is the proportion of a *market* that is held by an organisation, in relation to its main competitors, e.g. *Thomson's* share of the *package holiday* market in the UK is approximately 30 per cent. In leisure and tourism, market share is usually measured either by volume, e.g. the number of holidays sold to a particular destination, or by value, e.g. the revenue generated by sales of sports goods. Organisations are constantly monitoring and refining their range of products and services in order to maintain or increase market share.

market size: the total sales of all the producers in a particular market, e.g. the total market for overseas *package holidays* in the UK is around 11 million each year. It is important for an organisation to know the precise volume or value of the market in which it operates, or hopes to operate, in order to identify whether it is an expanding or contracting market. Knowing the total market size will also enable an organisation to calculate its own *market share*, and if that too is growing or shrinking.

market trends: the way in which the *demand* for, and supply of, particular goods and services fluctuates over time. The market for UK holidays, for example, has remained fairly static since the beginning of the 1990s, while the demand for overseas package holidays taken by British people has increased sharply. The study of market trends, and the analysis of the reasons for their fluctuations, is a key factor in helping organisations survive and grow, giving them the opportunity to forecast the likely demand for their products and services. Analysing market trends requires an organisation to have access to comprehensive *market research* data.

marketing is the process concerned with identifying customers' *needs* and supplying products and services in the right place, at the right time and at the right price. It is defined by the *Chartered Institute of Marketing* as 'the management process for identifying and satisfying customer needs profitably'. Being a management process means that marketing ranks alongside personnel, finance and other management functions in terms of the structure of an organisation. The importance given to marketing will depend in part on the nature of the business and the attitude of management.

Market research plays a fundamental role in any marketing process, in helping to discover customer likes and dislikes. Satisfying customer needs is all about developing products and services that customers will want to use or buy, as well as the various techniques that can be used to promote their sale or use, e.g. *advertising, direct mail, public relations, direct marketing* and *personal selling*. Marketing must be undertaken with the aims of the organisation in mind, since not all leisure and tourism organisations put profit as their main *objective*.

marketing budget: the sum of money that a leisure or tourism organisation has at its disposal to carry out its *marketing* plans. It is important to remember that the marketing budget will not only be spent on advertising (*above-the-line promotion*), but also on *below-the-line* activities such as direct marketing, sales promotion, merchandising and public relations work. The cost of producing brochures and other promotional items will also fall within this budget. An organisation's marketing budget will change from year to year, in response to factors in both the *internal* and *external environment*.

marketing communications: the term used to identify the techniques and channels that an organisation uses to inform and influence its *customers*. In leisure and tourism, the most important marketing communications techniques are *advertising, public relations* activity, *sales promotion, direct marketing* and *personal selling*. The range of techniques used will be chosen to help the organisation best achieve its *marketing objectives*. Whichever techniques are chosen, each is likely to follow the *AIDA* principle (attention, interest, desire, action).

marketing environment: see *business environment*

marketing mix: commonly referred to as the four Ps (*product, price, place* and *promotion*), the marketing mix is one of the most important concepts in *marketing* today. In attempting to achieve its *marketing objectives*, an organisation must decide what emphasis to put on each element of the mix; a newly opened leisure centre, for example, will spend more on promotion in order to attract new customers; a major tour operator may be forced to change its pricing structures when it discovers that a competitor has undercut its prices; a *visitor attraction* will need to review its product from time to time in response to changing market expectations; and a major travel company may decide to close down its regional sales offices, thereby altering the 'place' component of the marketing mix. These examples show that the emphasis on the different components of the marketing mix will vary over time, as well as between the different sectors of the industry.

marketing objectives: the specific aims or goals that an organisation has in mind when devising its *marketing* activity. Examples of marketing objectives could be:

- to maximise income
- to manage the effects of change
- to expand the customer base

- to analyse competitor activity
- to identify customer needs

Marketing objectives, which must be clear, measurable and realistic, will vary between the different sectors of the leisure and tourism industries. Private sector operators, for example, will gear their marketing towards achieving maximum sales, while the public and voluntary sectors will be seeking to fulfil their wider community and social aims, perhaps by targeting under-represented and disadvantaged groups in society.

marketing plan: a written document giving details of what action an organisation will take to achieve its overall *marketing strategy* and thereby fulfil its *marketing objectives.* The plan will consider what the organisation wants to achieve, where it sees itself now (*situation analysis*), where it wants to be in the future and how it reaches that point, by careful attention to the different elements in the *marketing mix.* The plan should give a timescale and include details of *budgets.*

marketing principles: the underlying practices and processes that guide all marketing activity, e.g. the *marketing mix, market segmentation, customer needs, target marketing,* etc. It is the job of the marketer to apply these principles to best effect, given the nature of the *business environment.*

marketing research is the term used to describe the process of gathering and analysing data that affects a wide range of factors that influence the marketing process of an organisation. Unlike *market research,* which is concerned specifically with customers and their attitudes to products and services, marketing research is a more all-embracing activity, involving, for example, product research, promotion research and price research.

marketing strategy refers to the overall means by which an organisation hopes to meet its *marketing objectives.* In deciding on its marketing strategy, an organisation has a number of different options, including:

- undifferentiated marketing – when a single marketing mix is offered to the total market. This is unlikely to succeed, since markets are made up of many types of buyers, all with different characteristics
- differentiated marketing – when different marketing approaches are tailored to different sectors of the market. A leisure centre, for example, will have different ideas for promoting to families and senior citizens
- concentrated marketing – when an organisation chooses to compete in only one sector of the market, developing the most effective marketing mix for that sector. Eurocamp is a good example of a company that concentrates on one sector of the market, i.e. those wanting camping holidays.

In addition to deciding which type of strategy to adopt, any *leisure* or *tourism* organisation can implement the strategy in a different way. It may, for example, adopt a defensive strategy, which is designed to hold onto its existing customers. It could opt for a developing strategy, designed to offer existing customers a wider range of products or services. Another option would be to implement an attacking strategy, with the aim of generating extra business through new customers. Having decided on its overall marketing strategy, its next step is to draw up a *marketing plan.*

mark-up is the amount by which a retailer increases the price of an article, in order to cover his or her *costs* and produce a profit margin.

Maslow's hierarchy of needs: a theory of individual development and *motivation*, based on the principle that all human beings have *needs*, and that these needs vary between people and over time. Maslow developed different needs into a hierarchy as follows:

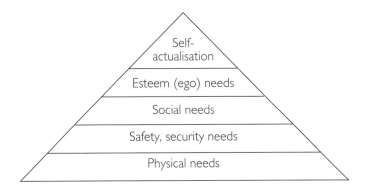

Maslow's hierarchy of needs

Maslow's concept can be related to the demand for leisure and tourism products and services, in terms of demand *motivators*. Taking the example of a holiday:

- physical needs, e.g. food, sleep and drink, etc.
- safety and security needs, e.g. safe means of transportation, safe destination, etc.
- social needs, e.g. meeting new people, socialising, etc.
- esteem/ego needs, e.g. going to a fashionable resort, travelling in style on Concorde, etc.
- self-actualisation, e.g. learning a new skill on holiday, becoming spiritually enlightened, etc.

It should be remembered that Maslow's model relates to individual development and motivation in life and not just to motivation in the workplace.

mass media are channels of *communication* that are available to the majority of the population, such as television and daily newspapers. The mass media can exert a great influence over people's lives, by promoting particular ideas, beliefs and fashions. Advertisers regard the mass media as their most powerful promotional channels, especially television, which is why the mass media are able to command the highest prices for advertising.

mass tourism: the term used to describe the movement of people in large numbers for leisure and business purposes, a characteristic of the latter half of the twentieth century in Western developed countries. Mass tourism became a reality as a result of developments in *jet aircraft* technology, increased personal mobility, higher disposable incomes and the development of package holidays. Although it has brought economic and political benefits to many countries, mass tourism does have its disadvantages, including harmful *environmental* and *socio-cultural impacts*. These problems have given rise to pressure for tourism that is more *sustainable*.

matrix organisation: a type of organisational structure combining the roles of *line managers* with a range of *'staff' functions*, including personnel, administration and finance. Matrix organisations evolved to try and create more effective work teams, who could cross divisional boundaries and benefit from decentralisation. There may, however, be difficulties with this type of structure, since the lines of *responsibility* and *accountability* can become blurred leading to lengthy decision-making processes.

MBO: see *management by objectives*

McGregor: an American psychologist who is credited with extending *Maslow's hierarchy of needs* and applying it to the real world. McGregor devised the two opposing styles of management, which he called Theory X and Theory Y. In Theory X, managers believed that human beings were born lazy and would do as little as possible at work, shunning responsibility and showing no ambition. Theory Y, on the other hand, proposed that employees were more than willing to work hard, accept responsibility and be involved in making decisions. McGregor's work has encouraged managers to take a more positive view of their workforce and adopt a more open management style.

MCI: see *Management Charter Initiative*

MCO: see *miscellaneous charges order*

mean: the most common way of calculating the arithmetic average of a set of data. It is found by adding all the values together and dividing by the total number of values, e.g. the results of a visitor survey conducted at a zoo concerning how far people had travelled were as follows:

20 30 30 25 15 20 40 25 20 25

In this example the mean is 25 (250 divided by 10). One disadvantage of using the mean is that extreme results can distort the situation, giving misleading results. (See also *mode, median*.)

media: the term used to denote the various channels of communication an organisation can use to advertise its *products* and services (a single channel is known as a medium). Types of advertising media include:

- *consumer press*
- *trade press*
- television
- cinema advertising
- commercial radio
- outdoor advertising
- transport advertising

The types of media selected will depend on the size of advertising budget and target market. *Advertising agencies* specialise in helping organisations plan and execute advertising campaigns in a variety of media. Details of the costs of advertising in the various media can be found in *BRAD*.

media buyer: a specialist working in an *advertising agency* whose role is to liaise with the various *printed media* (newspapers, magazines, journals, etc.) and *broadcast media* (TV, cinema, cable TV, commercial radio, etc.) to place advertisements on behalf of the agency's clients. The agency will earn a *commission* from the media company, which may be passed on to the client in the form of a reduced fee for services provided.

media planner: usually one of a team of people working in an *advertising agency*, responsible for deciding when and where particular *advertisements* will be placed for a particular client's advertising campaign. The media planner will often decide on a mixture of *above-the-line* and *below-the-line* promotional activities, e.g. a newspaper advertising campaign linked to a discount coupon promotion on breakfast cereal packets. Once the schedules have been agreed, a *media buyer* will liaise with the chosen media to confirm arrangements.

median: an arithmetic term used to find the average of a set of data. The median is simply the middle number of a group of numbers, e.g. the results of a visitor survey show the following ages of respondents:

45 37 29 25 47 46 26 25 14 36 26

In this example the median is 46, since it appears in the middle with 5 numbers either side of it. The median is mathematically less precise than the *mean*, but is less influenced by extreme values. (See also *mode*.)

mediation: another name for *arbitration*.

Meetings Industry Association (MIA) is a professional trade organisation for the conference industry in the UK. Founded in 1990, MIA encourages the maintenance of the highest professional standards within the meetings industry. It maintains a regular dialogue with government, the *media*, buyers and industry colleagues in order to strengthen the position of its members' businesses and raise the profile of the UK as an international conference destination.

memorandum: a type of *written communication* commonly used in organisations in place of a formal letter or *report*. Usually shortened to memo, it can be used for a number of reasons, such as to confirm a verbal agreement or message, to ask for information, to remind a colleague of something or to pass on information or instructions. In organisations that use *electronic communications*, *E-mail* is often used in place of written memos.

Memorandum of Association: one of two formal documents that must be produced by limited companies, under the terms of the *Companies Acts* of 1985 and 1989, the other being the *Articles of Association*. The Memorandum of Association is concerned with a company's relationship with the outside world and contains the company name, its address, the purpose for which the company is formed, the liability and voting rights of the *shareholders*, and the amount of share capital.

mentor: an individual who volunteers, or is chosen, to look after a new member of staff in an organisation and make him or her settle into the new surroundings as easily as possible. The mentor will be able to advise the new recruit on *organisational structures* and operational practices. In the wider world, the term 'mentor' is often used to describe an individual who provides support to, and commands the respect of, his or her *peer group*.

MEP stands for Member of the *European Parliament*, a person directly elected to represent their country's interests in the Parliament.

merchandising: a range of methods adopted by retailers to stimulate customers to purchase at the *point-of-sale (POS)*. This may include brochure racks, posters, hanging cards, displays and signs. Merchandising opportunities are often linked to a popular media personality or current fashion, e.g. T-shirts, mugs, calendars, books, etc. with the name and photograph of a pop group or *Disney* cartoon hero.

MIA: see *Meetings Industry Association*

micro environment: a term used to denote those influences and factors that are close to an organisation and over which it has some degree of control. Sometimes called the internal environment, these include *customers*, staff, facilities and *suppliers*. Prudent control within an organisation should ensure that these internal elements are managed effectively, but an organisation will be affected by a number of factors in the *macro (external) environment* over which it has little control.

microcomputer: see *personal computer*

mid-centric: one of a number of types of tourist behaviour developed by Plog in 1977 as part of a research study for airline companies. Mid-centrics made up the bulk of tourists to a particular destination, i.e. the mass market. They tend to move in after resorts have been discovered by the more adventurous *allocentrics*, who are then forced to move on to discover another area. (See also *psychocentric*.)

Mid Wales Festival of the Countryside: a series of events which take place in the towns, countryside and villages of Mid Wales each year from June to December. Its aim is to show that informed concern and respect for the environment can go hand-in-hand with economic development. Launched in 1985 as a contribution to the World Conservation Strategy, the Festival of the Countryside has grown into a pioneering model of *sustainable tourism* in a rural environment.

'milk run': the name given to the network of UK regions and cities most frequented by *overseas visitors* to Britain. It is made up of London, Oxford, Bath, Cardiff, Chester, the Lake District, Edinburgh, York, Cambridge and returning to London. The round trip is most commonly undertaken by visitors on their first visit to Britain.

Millenium Fund: administered by the *Millenium Commission* under the direction of the *Department of National Heritage*, this is the proceeds from the *National Lottery* that will be used to fund projects celebrating the start of the twenty-first century. The Fund will be used to support around a dozen large-scale projects throughout the UK, a larger number of smaller projects of local significance, the Millenium Festival and a bursary scheme. *Camelot*, the operator of the Lottery, estimates that the Fund may approach £1.6 billion by the end of the year 2000.

Millenium Commission: this is one of the five 'good causes', supported by the *National Lottery*, set up to help communities to mark the start of the next millenium after the year 2000. It will use money raised by the National Lottery to encourage projects throughout the UK which will be lasting monuments to the achievements of the nation. Financial support will be given to a range of projects to appeal to all ages and interests, which will contribute to the local, regional and national *heritage*. The Commission will also support a Millenium Festival to become the focus of celebrations in the year 2000. The Commission made its first allocation of funds in August 1995, granting £66.5 million to 27 projects, with £42.5 million going to *Sustrans*, to help set up a national network of cycleways by the year 2000.

miniple travel agent: a travel company that has a number of branches located in a particular part of the country, meeting a regional demand, e.g. Woodcock Travel, with branches mainly in Yorkshire and Humberside. Miniples do not benefit from 'economies of scale' to the same extent as *multiple travel agents*, but they are able to build close ties with business and leisure travellers in their region and operate very successful businesses. Their success, however, often makes them prime targets for takeovers or mergers.

Ministry of Agriculture, Fisheries and Food (MAFF): a government department responsible for the nation's agricultural policy, but with interests and responsibilities in other countryside matters, such as *Set-Aside, Environmentally Sensitive Areas (ESAs)* and rural business advisory services through its agency *ADAS*.

minority groups: see *disadvantaged groups*

minutes: a written record of a meeting, usually written down by the secretary, including details of who was in attendance and what was decided. The minutes of a meeting are often agreed to be an accurate record of what happened before the start of a future meeting.

MIS: see *management information system*

miscellaneous charges order (MCO): a voucher issued by an airline and exchangeable for a specified service in connection with the *transportation* covered by the airline ticket, e.g. car hire, accommodation, excursions or meals.

mission statement: a brief explanation of an organisation's fundamental purpose. Its aim is to convey to all those with an interest in the organisation, be they staff, shareholders or the public in general, what business it is in, where it sees itself going and how it will relate to its environment and other organisations. Some mission statements also introduce an element of an organisation's philosophy and values. Some individuals are very sceptical about the value of mission statements, considering them nothing more than a *public relations* exercise. What a mission statement can do is set out the general direction in which an organisation is hoping to progess and provide a framework for the development of more specific *objectives*.

MMC: see *Monopolies and Mergers Commission*

mode: an arithmetic term which denotes the number that occurs most frequently in a given set of data, e.g. a visitor survey gives the following results for the amount spent by children at a theme park:

3 5 6 2 5 3 7 4 2 5

The mode in this example is 5, since it appears more frequently than any other number. It is a rather crude method of calculating an average, so statisticians prefer to use the *mean* or *median*.

models are representations of reality that are used to give an understanding of past developments and/or a forecast of future occurrences. Often constructed in graphical form, a model can be used to help management decision making and the wise use of an organisation's *resources*. The *destination life cycle* is a common model used in leisure and tourism *development*.

modem: an electronic device that connects a *personal computer* to a telephone line, allowing the transmission of *data* and the establishment of a communications network. A modem is necessary for gaining access to the *Internet* and other on-line databases.

Modified American Plan: an *accommodation* arrangement based on half board, with a room and breakfast plus one other meal per day, either at midday or in the evening. (See also *American Plan, Continental Plan, European Plan.*)

Monopolies and Mergers Commission (MMC): a government-funded body set up to monitor trading activity to make sure that the public's interest is safeguarded. The Secretary of State for Industry may refer intended large-scale company takeovers to the Commission for advice and comment, where it is thought that the public interest may be affected and, for example, consumer choice may be limited. The merger of Horizon Holidays with *Thomson* in the late 1980s was investigated by the MMC, although it was considered not to be against the public interest. The Commission itself cannot take legal action when necessary, but relies on the *Office of Fair Trading* to act on its behalf.

monopoly: an economics term to denote many purchasers but only one supplier of a product or service. In reality, monopoly suppliers rarely exist, since there are many competing suppliers of the vast majority of goods and services. Even the former state-controlled monopolies supplying the nation's utilities and energy resources, e.g. water, electricity and gas, are subject to competitive pressures. Monopoly situations generally act against the public interest, since it is thought that the single supplier will exploit customers by charging higher prices. It is for this reason that the government established the *Monopolies and Mergers Commission (MMC)*. In leisure and tourism, *British Rail* operates in a monopoly situation, although it is soon to be opened up to private competition.

MORI: see *Market Opinion and Research International*

Mosaic: a *database marketing* system that allows potential *customers* to be targeted according to their life styles and residential neighbourhoods. Mosaic is a computer-based system that works in a similar way to *ACORN* and allows leisure and tourism organisations to market their products and services effectively.

motel: an *accommodation* establishment providing rooms and eating facilities for passing motorists, who often stay for just one night. The concept originated in the USA, but has now spread to all parts of the world, although the term 'lodge' is preferred in some European countries.

motivation: see *staff motivation, group motivation*

motivational management: a supportive leadership style that seeks to cement a *partnership* between a manager and his or her staff, thereby empowering individuals and inspiring them to work effectively. A manager adopting this style will agree goals with members of staff, let them know clearly what is expected of them and monitor their progress regularly. Motivational management contrasts starkly with an aggressive management style, where there is little consultation between a manager and his or her staff.

motivators are factors within the psychological make-up of an individual that help influence his or her patterns of behaviour. In leisure and tourism, motivators are an important consideration when it comes to examining the present and future *demand* for products and services. Typical motivators of concern to the leisure and tourism professional include:

- status, social and ego needs (as shown in *Maslow's hierarchy of needs*)
- education levels
- income levels
- employment status
- state of health
- amount of *leisure time*

A study of motivators will help to show why, for example, one person's ideal holiday is sailing in the Mediterranean, while another's is bird-watching in Suffolk. Motivators are usually studied alongside *determinants*, to give marketers a full picture of the pattern of demand and, as a result, a guide as to which products and services to develop.

In a work situation, motivators are those factors that will give a person a degree of job satisfaction, e.g. tangible recognition for good work, *staff training* and development opportunities, and a supportive environment.

MRS: see *Market Research Society*

MTI: see *Museum Training Institute*

multinational corporation: a *company* that operates across international frontiers, with its headquarters in one country and operating interests in a number of others. In leisure and tourism, multinationals (sometimes called transnationals) are involved in the production of both goods and services. Many household names are multinationals, including Dunlop, Reebok, Nike, Avis, Sheraton, *Forte*, Granada and *British Airways*. *Developing countries* are often happy to welcome multinational corporations who may wish to build hotels and leisure resorts, but they are sometimes criticised for exploiting virgin areas, providing only poorly paid jobs and taking their profits away from the developing nations.

multiple travel agency: a travel *company* that has many branches located throughout the UK. Many are household names in the travel industry, such as Thomas Cook, Lunn Poly and Going Places, and are sometimes part of large parent organisations. Lunn Poly, for example, is owned by *Thomson*, while Going Places is owned by Airtours PLC. Multiple travel agents benefit from *'economies of scale'* and can negotiate the best prices on holidays that they sell. They are not always able, however, to match the level of personal service and range of products offered by independent agents. (See also *miniple travel agent*.)

multiplex: a cinema complex offering the choice of a number of screens and films, often coupled with other leisure facilities, such as fast-food outlets, bowling and roller skating.

multiplier effect: an economic concept which, when applied to tourism, shows that the money spent by visitors to an area is re-spent in the local economy and is actually worth more than its face value. The factor by which the final sum is greater than the original spent is known as the multiplier, or income multiplier. For example, £200 spent by a family on a short break in a guesthouse could be worth, say, £200 × 1.5 (the multiplier), i.e. a total of £300 to the local economy. The actual value of the multiplier will vary, depending on which area of the country is concerned and the type of accommodation used. A farm guesthouse, for example, will have a higher multiplier than a city-centre hotel that is part of a *multinational* chain. This is because the guesthouse is more likely to buy its goods and services locally, thereby retaining money in the local economy, whereas the city-centre hotel will have bulk purchasing contracts with national distributors, with payments being made outside of the local economy. This loss to the local economy is known as a *leakage*.

Museum Training Institute (MTI) was set up in 1969 with the support of the Department of Employment and the *Department of National Heritage*. MTI is the *Industry Lead Body* for the museum, gallery and heritage sector and, as such, is responsible for identifying the key skill needs and training requirements of the sector and promoting the use of *occupational standards* and *National Vocational Qualifications*. MTI's overall aim is to support the development of better museums through promotion, training and information.

museums have long been an important part of the *tourism* industry, with some 2 300 in the UK alone, according to the *Museums and Galleries Commission (MGC)*. Museums are popular with UK and overseas visitors, for both their entertainment and educational value. Museums of national significance in Britain are not only located in London, but are also to be found in places as diverse as Bradford (the National Museum of Photography, Film and Television), St Ives in Cornwall (the Tate Gallery) and Cardiff (the National Museum of Wales). Local museums and galleries also play an important role in meeting the needs of visitors to both town and country, helping to sustain local economies and services. In recent years there have been moves to try and change the sometimes 'stuffy' image of museums with the introduction of more 'hands-on' exhibits, e.g. Eureka! the Museum for Children in Halifax.

Museums and Galleries Commission (MGC): originally formed in 1931, the MGC took on a range of new functions in 1982 on all matters relating to museums. It is funded by the *Department of National Heritage* with the objective of encouraging better standards in museums, providing advice to the government and working directly with museums. To date, it has established a museums' registration scheme, created a series of standards and guidelines for the profession, provided grant aid for a number of museums and galleries, and developed a conservation unit to support the highest standards of work in maintaining the nation's *heritage*.

Museums Association is an independent national organisation established in 1889 to campaign on behalf of *museums* and galleries. It aims to maintain and improve professional standards through information and advice, and to raise awareness of the key issues affecting museums. One of its main functions is to promote and protect the development of museum services and to advance the cause of museums at all levels of government through *lobbying* and consultation. The association has a membership of over 3 500 drawn from all sections of the museum community.

'mystery shopper' is the term given to somebody who anonymously visits a *leisure* or *tourism* facility, or uses a product or service, and reports back to the management on his or her experiences. The technique can be used to gain valuable information on, for example, the performance and attitude of staff to customers, or even the level of service offered by competitor organisations. 'Mystery shoppers' are widely used in the commercial sectors of leisure, travel and tourism, especially in airlines and travel agencies, to help gain a *competitive advantage*.

N

NAITA: see *National Association of Independent Travel Agents*

National Association of Independent Travel Agents (NAITA): a grouping of independent *travel agents* in the UK, set up to act in a similar way to *ABTA (Association of British Travel Agents)*. Representing more than 800 branch outlets, NAITA has been able to negotiate favourable trading terms for its members with a number of *principals* and has established a free legal advisory service. NAITA membership criteria include the holding of an *IATA* licence and membership of ABTA.

National Coaching Foundation (NCF) was established in 1983 and is an independent organisation funded primarily by the *Sports Council*. The overall aim of NCF is to work with partners to develop more and better coaches in as wide a range of sports as possible, for people of all levels of experience. The NCF provides a comprehensive range of services, available regionally via a network of Coaching Development Officers, including:

- a general enquiry service for coaches, including a selection of basic fact-sheets
- an in-depth information search service for coaches
- a current awareness service for coaches to help keep them up to date with current issues

NCF's in-house database on coaching and performance contains over 5 000 records of books and articles. (See also *Champion Coaching*.)

National Council for Vocational Qualifications (NCVQ): a government-funded body established in 1986 to develop a new system of *vocational qualifications* for all occupations. Working with *Industry Lead Bodies*, NCVQ is overseeing the development of occupational standards and subsequent qualifications at levels 1 to 5. The diverse nature of the leisure and tourism industries has led to delay in fully devising occupational standards and *NVQs* in certain sectors. NCVQ is also responsible for the introduction of *General National Vocational Qualifications (GNVQs)* in conjunction with a number of awarding bodies.

National Council for Voluntary Organisations (NCVO): established in 1919, NCVO seeks to be the voice of voluntary organisations in all sectors, including *leisure* and *tourism*. It aims to extend the involvement of voluntary bodies in responding to social issues of the day, to be a resource centre and to protect the interests and independence of voluntary organisations.

National Cycle Network: a proposed 5 000-mile network of traffic-free paths through urban and country areas, protected on-road sections and minor roads, which together will make a safe route for cyclists throughout Britain. Launched by *Sustrans* in 1994, the Network will stretch from Inverness to Penzance, passing through the centre of each town and city along its way, linking schools, houses, shops and workplaces with each other and with the countryside. Sustrans has received a grant of £42.5 million from the *Millenium Commission* to help fund the building of 2 000 miles of the network by the year 2000.

National Exhibition Centre (NEC): a purpose-built facility located close to the motorway network near to the city of Birmingham and its international airport. The NEC stages business events, such as conferences and exhibitions, as well as a wide range of sporting and entertainment events, including concerts by world-famous artists.

National Express is Britain's only national, scheduled coach service, serving more than 1 200 destinations every day, from Penzance to Inverness in the north of Scotland (see map opposite). National Express tickets are available through over 2 000 agents nationwide, ranging from newsagents to large coach stations such as London Victoria. The former state-run enterprise, which was bought by its management in 1988, offers a range of concessionary fares via a number of discount offers, targeted particularly at students, young people and the over 50's. National Express's sister company, Eurolines, offers European coach travel to more than 270 destinations, while Scottish Citylink provides Scotland with a networked coach service.

National Liaison Group for Higher Education in Tourism in the UK (NLG) is an independent membership organisation established in 1993 to provide a focus for the development of *tourism* in higher education. Initially developed under the auspices of the *Tourism Society*, NLG encourages high standards in course provision, develops and promotes links between education and industry, communicates 'good practice' and liaises with other bodies concerned with higher education in tourism. Membership is open to organisations that are employers and educators in the tourism industry, as well as representatives of awarding bodies.

National Lottery: launched in the UK in November 1994, with the principal aim of providing extra funds for a range of 'good causes', the National Lottery has come as a welcome boost to the *leisure* and *tourism* industries. Five specific areas were identified in the National Lottery Act 1993 to receive Lottery funding, namely:

- *sport*
- the arts
- *heritage*
- charities
- projects to mark the new millenium

At least a quarter of the income from the Lottery is paid into a fund called the National Lottery Distribution Fund. The Fund, and any interest or dividends it earns, is divided equally between the five areas listed above. *Camelot*, the company chosen to operate the Lottery, estimates that, in its first year, ticket sales for the Lottery will total £2.7 billion, £750 million of which will be divided equally among the five good causes, with each receiving £150 million. In the case of sport, the £150 million will be divided according to the population of the four home countries, with England receiving the most at £125 million.

The Lottery was set up to benefit projects both large and small, from the refurbishment of a local cricket pavillion to the financing of facilities of national significance. (See also *OFLOT, Millenium Commission, Lottery Sports Fund* and *Heritage Lottery Fund.*)

National Nature Reserve (NNR): there are some 130 of these reserves in England, covering around 43 000 hectares. They represent the best examples of different kinds of countryside or contain unusual communities of plants or animals, or important natural features such as rock exposures or gorges. Most NNRs are either

The National Express network (courtesy of National Express)

owned or controlled by *English Nature* and all of them are managed specifically for nature *conservation*.

National Parks: the 1949 National Parks and Access to the Countryside Act led to the formation of ten National Parks in England and Wales, each administered by a National Park Authority. Following on from the American idea, with the establishment of the first US National Park at Yellowstone in 1872, the National Parks in England and Wales were established with two prime objectives in mind: the preservation and enhancement of their natural beauty and amenity, and their promotion for *leisure* and *recreation*. Today, the *Countryside Commission*, as the body charged with overseeing the *management* of the Parks, is faced with trying to maintain a delicate balance between the recreational needs of the visitors and the *conservation* of the natural environment. Concern is also expressed about potential conflicts between those visiting for enjoyment and the needs of the people who live and work in the National Parks all year round. Increasing *car ownership* has opened up the countryside to urban dwellers and poses a particular threat to the National Parks, with more than 70 million visitors in a typical year.

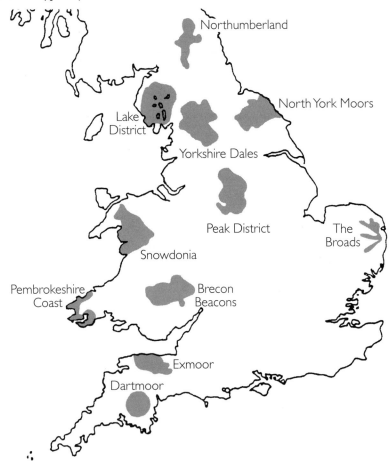

The National Parks in England and Wales. Note that The Broads is not a National Park, but has equal status

National Play Information Centre was set up in 1988 with the aim of developing a national library on children's *play*, available in a variety of different *media*. It provides an extensive collection of information for people in a wide range of professions. Researchers and historians are able to use its archives and there is up-to-date information for all those interested in play issues. The Centre's library material now amounts to the largest specialist collection on play in the world.

National Playing Fields Association (NPFA) was established in 1925 to mount a *campaign* to ensure that everyone had *access* to recreational and play space within easy reach of their homes. It is the only national organisation which has specific responsibility for acquiring, protecting and improving playing fields, playgrounds and other *public open spaces*. It does not generally receive funding from central or local government, but raises funds through membership, public subscription, fund-raising, the sale of its expertise and publications. In recent years, the role of the NPFA has changed significantly, with more emphasis being placed on the provision of *play* space for disabled people.

National Rivers Authority (NRA): a government agency established under the Water Act 1989. The NRA operates in ten regions based upon the river catchment areas of England and Wales. As well as responsibilities for pollution control, environmental protection, water resources and flood defence, it is also responsible for the *promotion* of *leisure* and *recreation*, such as fishing and boating. NRA officials sample the bathing water around our coasts in accordance with the *EU Bathing Water Directive*.

National Sports Centres are purpose-built facilities aimed at raising the standards of performance of *sport* in England and Wales. Funded primarily from *Sports Council* resources, the six 'centres of excellence' currently operating are at Crystal Palace, Bisham Abbey, Lilleshall, Holme Pierrepont (water-based activities), Plas y Brenin (mountain activities) and the National Cycling Centre near Manchester.

National Tourism Organisation (NTO): an official body concerned with the *planning, development* and *promotion* of *tourism* within its own country, e.g. the Spanish National Tourism Organisation, United States Travel and Tourism Administration and French Government Tourist Office. NTOs may be full departments of government or independent agencies financed wholly or partly from government funds. Sometimes also known as National Tourist Offices, NTOs establish information offices in the main countries from which their visitors originate, e.g. the *British Tourist Authority* has a network of offices in major cities around the world, including New York, Paris, Tokyo and Rome.

National Tourist Board: see *National Tourism Organisation (NTO)*

National Tourist Office: see *National Tourism Organisation (NTO)*

National Trust is one of Europe's leading *conservation* charities, which celebrated its centenary in 1995. It is independent of government and relies on its voluntary supporters, including 2 million members, for most of its income. The Trust is the largest private landowner in the country, protecting more than 600 000 acres of land in England, Wales and Northern Ireland (there is a separate National Trust for Scotland) as well as over 200 houses and parks. Each year, some 11 million people visit its 400 buildings and gardens for which there is a charge, while untold millions freely enjoy the coastline, hills and woodlands that the Trust preserves. The Trust is at present running several special appeals including *Enterprise Neptune*, launched in 1965.

National Vocational Qualifications (NVQs): a range of qualifications introduced by the government to raise standards in the workplace by creating a highly skilled, flexible and qualified workforce. NVQs (Scottish Vocational Qualifications/SVQs in Scotland) are designed to test skills and competence in the workplace, rather than knowledge, in a particular industry sector. NVQs/SVQs are based on *occupational standards* developed by *Industry Lead Bodies (ILBs)*, who have documented appropriate tasks and skills for employees at different levels of experience. NVQs/SVQs are available in specific sectors of the leisure and tourism industries, including travel services, sport and recreation, hotel and catering, and management. They are offered at five levels, from basic skills at level 1 to professional skills at level 5. (See also *GNVQs, Tourism and Leisure Consortium.*)

natural attractions are an important element of the *attractions* sector of the *tourism* industry. Unlike *man-made attractions*, which are purpose-built facilities, natural attractions include the *National Parks, Areas of Outstanding Natural Beauty* and *Heritage Coasts* in England and Wales. Britain has an abundance of natural attractions, in its fine landscapes, rugged mountains, beautiful coastline, inland waterways and picturesque dales. They are a magnet for UK residents and *overseas visitors.*

NCF: see *National Coaching Foundation*

NCVO: see *National Council for Voluntary Organisations*

NCVQ: see *National Council for Vocational Qualifications*

NEC: see *National Exhibition Centre*

needs are an important consideration for all producers of leisure and tourism facilities and services, since they have a direct bearing on *demand. Maslow's hierarchy of needs* shows us that all human beings have needs in their lives, e.g. self-expression, ego and security. *Leisure* can help an individual fulfil his or her needs and contribute to a sense of well-being. A person's needs will vary with age and family circumstances and will affect demand for leisure and tourism *products.*

net current assets: see *working capital*

net profit is the difference between a company's *sales revenue* and all its *costs.* Sometimes called operating profit, it can be expressed either before or after deducting items such as taxation, *depreciation* and finance charges.

net profit/sales ratio is a measure of an organisation's financial performance, giving a figure for profit (or loss) made per £ of income. It is calculated as follows:

$$\text{FORMULA:} \quad \frac{\text{net profit (before tax)}}{\text{sales}} \times 100$$

The percentage profit on sales varies between different sectors, so it is essential to compare the ratio with similar businesses and also to make allowance for prevailing economic conditions.

network: a group of computers each with a cable connecting it to a central computer (the file server), allowing the simultaneous use of computer applications on a number of different machines. The file server is able to send and receive signals over these cables and store information on its large fixed disk. Computers linked in this way in a single facility are sometimes said to be part of a local area network (LAN).

networking is liaising with business contacts in order to create new opportunities for business activities. On a worldwide basis, networking can be carried out electronically using *E-mail* and *video conferencing*, but it is most often associated with face-to-face meetings at, for example, conferences, exhibitions and seminars.

'new tourist': a recent term used to identify a particular type of tourist who displays a number of emerging characteristics, including:

- a wish to be more independent in their holiday habits
- greater travel experience
- more environmental awareness
- greater flexibility in travel arrangements
- more health conscious
- more conscious of *quality*

Travel companies have identified these 'new tourists' as a *niche market* that is looking for more than a conventional two-week *package holiday* in the sun. Analysts believe that this segment of the market will grow in size in years to come.

news release: see *press release*

NGO: see *non-governmental organisation*

niche marketing is the process of targeting small, readily identifiable sections of a market, each with clearly defined characteristics, rather than trying to cover it all. By their very nature, specialist *tour operators* develop products for niche markets, whether they are wine lovers, collectors of antiques or white water rafters. In leisure and tourism, niche marketing can be a very effective *strategy*, since consumers are often willing to pay a premium for a more exclusive product, e.g. a flight on Concorde or a trip on the Venice-Simplon Orient Express.

NITB: see *Northern Ireland Tourist Board*

NLG: see *National Liaison Group for Higher Education in Tourism in the UK*

NNR: see *National Nature Reserve*

no show: the term used to denote a hotel guest or traveller with a reservation who fails to turn up without any prior notification. In some circumstances, a deposit may be forfeited or the individual may be liable for the full value of the reservation. Operators sometimes *overbook* in order to compensate for anticipated no shows.

Noise at Work Regulations 1989: a set of very technical regulations, which came into force on 1 January 1990, requiring managers and operators of facilities to monitor noise levels and take appropriate action to control any adverse effects. This may result in the wearing of ear defenders by staff or the reduction in the volume of music at *events*.

non-executive director: a part-time employee of a *company* appointed to its board of directors because of their broad knowledge of industry or because they have political influence. Their knowledge and contacts may prove useful in determining *policy* or securing funding or contracts. Non-executive directors may be the representatives of large *shareholders* who are keen to see that their interests are safeguarded.

non-governmental organisation (NGO): an independent international body, free from government influence, established by individuals, companies or other organisations, to pursue a specific aim. The NGO creates its own organisational structure and is normally subject to the law of the nation in which its headquarters are located. NGOs often assume the role of *pressure groups*, e.g. Greenpeace, *World Wide Fund for Nature (WWF)* or *Tourism Concern*.

non-verbal communication (NVC) is the process by which we send and receive messages without the use of spoken or written words. We all use our eyes, hands and facial expressions to emphasise points and to confirm information we have received. These are all examples of *body language*, the most common type of NVC. In the leisure and tourism industries, it is important to develop listening and observation skills, so as to be able to operate as an effective individual or member of a team.

norming: the stage of team development that is concerned with setting guidelines and standards of acceptable behaviour under which the team will operate. The *storming* stage should have united the group, while the norming stage sets the parameters within which all *team* members will seek to achieve their *objectives*. (See also *forming, performing*.)

North West Tourist Board is the official *Regional Tourist Board* covering the counties of Cheshire, Merseyside, Greater Manchester, Lancashire and the High Peak District of Derbyshire.

Northern Ireland Tourist Board (NITB) is the official *tourist board* responsible for tourism *promotion* and *development* in Northern Ireland. Established under the Development of Tourist Traffic Act (N Ireland) in 1948, the NITB is funded primarily by grant-in-aid from the Northern Ireland Office. The aims of the NITB are to encourage UK residents and *overseas visitors* to visit the province, by providing advice to tourism businesses, funding tourism projects, co-ordinating the *tourist information centre network* in Northern Ireland, running *marketing campaigns* and advising central and local governments. With the moves towards permanent peace in Northern Ireland, the NITB has embarked on a major national and international promotional campaign to attract tourists to the province.

Northumbria Tourist Board is the official *Regional Tourist Board* covering the counties of Northumberland, Tyne and Wear, Durham and Cleveland.

not-for-profit: a term which is being used increasingly to denote an organisation whose prime *objective* is not profit maximisation. Examples include voluntary societies, local clubs and national organisations such as the *National Trust*. Although not primarily concerned with making a profit, these organisations must, nevertheless, be seen to be making the best use of their resources at all times.

NPFA: see *National Playing Fields Association*

NRA: see *National Rivers Authority*

NTB: see *Northumbria Tourist Board*

NTO: see *National Tourism Organisation*

NVC: see *non-verbal communication*

NVQs: see *National Vocational Qualifications*

NWTB: see *North West Tourist Board*

objectives are aims or *goals* that individuals and organisations set themselves, and which determine the *strategies* they undertake and the best use of their *resources*. Objectives may be short term, e.g. an airline achieving a *load factor* of 95 per cent for its coming winter flight programme, or long term, e.g. to be the number one *tour operator* from the UK to South America. Long-term objectives are usually contained in an organisation's *policy* and may be reflected in its *mission statement*.

To be useful for management purposes, objectives must be clear, realistic, achievable and set within a stated timescale. The principal objective of a commercial organisation will be profit maximisation, whereas non-commercial bodies will have wider *social objectives*, such as promoting *community recreation*. An organisation's objectives will be determined by those who have an interest in its affairs, sometimes referred to as *stakeholders*.

observation is the process of gathering *market research* information by direct observation of *customers* and their movements. Often carried out with the help of sophisticated electronic techniques such as *closed-circuit television (CCTV)* and *tally counters*, observation is used by management as a way of making alterations to systems and equipment, e.g. observation of the traffic flow at a major *theme park* may highlight the need for the separation of people from vehicles for safety reasons. On occasions, staff may be asked to 'mingle' anonymously with visitors and to eavesdrop on their conversations; people are often far more honest about their true feelings when talking in private than they may be when asked questions as part of a *survey*.

occupational standards are standards of performance recognised by an industry sector as being necessary for the satisfactory completion of work tasks. A travel clerk, for example, is likely to need skills and competence in selling, using *IT* systems, fare calculations, knowledge of overseas resorts and *customer care*, to name but a few. As part of the government initiative to introduce *National Vocational Qualifications (NVQs)*, *Industry Lead Bodies* have been given the task of identifying occupational standards for their particular sector. The standards, sometimes called workplace standards, are ultimately endorsed by the *National Council for Vocational Qualifications (NCVQ)* and form the basis for the development of the NVQs.

occupancy rate: a measure of how successful a *hotel* or other *accommodation* provider is at filling available bedspaces over a given period of time. It is a calculation of the number of rooms occupied as a proportion of total rooms available, expressed on a percentage basis. Sometimes referred to as room occupancy, it is a similar performance measure to the *load factors* used by airlines.

Occupiers' Liability Act 1984: *legislation* stating that, amongst others, the operator of a leisure and tourism facility owes a legal duty to all the people who use it, including visitors and spectators, to ensure that it is reasonably safe for its intended purpose. This would include, for example, making sure that seating for spectators is safe. As well as a duty to those on the premises, occupiers also have a duty to their neighbours and others living nearby. For example, a golf ball striking a pedestrian walking on a *public right of way* alongside the 18th fairway of a golf course is likely to result in a successful claim for negligence against the golf course owner, if the incident could reasonably have been foreseen.

OECD: see *Organisation for Economic Co-operation and Development*

off-the-job training is *training* that takes place away from a person's normal place of work. Some leisure and tourism organisations make use of 'day release' courses at local colleges, sometimes leading to *National Vocational Qualifications (NVQs)*. Evening classes are also popular in sectors such as travel and leisure centre management, while *distance learning* is increasingly used for *management* and supervisory training. Many organisations have found that *customer care* and foreign language training are particularly beneficial for staff working in leisure and tourism. (See also *on-the-job training.*)

Office of Fair Trading (OFT): established under the Fair Trading Act 1973, the OFT is the main government body responsible for monitoring and controlling trading activities in the interests of the general public. The increasing trend in the *travel industry* of tour operators owning travel agency chains and even their own airlines (*vertical integration*), has led the OFT to consider if such activity is against the public interest. The OFT also considers whether takeover bids should be investigated by the *Monopolies and Mergers Commission (MMC)*. The OFT also advises industry bodies on the content and wording of *codes of conduct.*

Office of the National Lottery (OFLOT) is the government agency responsible, through the *Department of National Heritage*, for the smooth running of the *National Lottery.* Established under the 1993 National Lottery Act, OFLOT has a duty to ensure that the Lottery is run with 'due propriety', the interests of all participants in the Lottery are protected and that the maximum amount possible is raised for the five 'good causes'. The Office is headed by the Director General of the National Lottery.

Office of Population Censuses and Surveys (OPCS): a government department that commissions and co-ordinates a number of important statistical surveys, including the *General Household Survey* and the Census of population, carried out every ten years.

off-line: a term used to show that a *computer* is being operated without a cable or telephone connection to another computer or central *database*. Although a computer may well have such a connection, it saves money if it can be used for some of the time 'off-line', thereby saving on telephone rental or cable usage charges.

off-peak refers to the time outside of the most popular dates and times for holidays. For overseas *package holidays* from the UK, this tends to be any time outside of the school holidays, the periods of peak demand. Tourists gain by travelling off-peak, with reduced prices and other *incentives* and offers. The operators of leisure and tourism facilities are keen to extend the peak season into off-peak periods so as to increase their *revenue*, while tourist boards promote off-peak travel as a way of providing year-round employment in the industry and reducing the harmful impacts of tourism. (See also *shoulder period.*)

OFLOT: see *Office of the National Lottery*

OFT: see *Office of Fair Trading*

Olympic Games: an international athletic event held every four years in a different host city and attracting competitors from the majority of countries of the world;

there were 172 participating nations at the 1992 Barcelona Olympic Games. Divided into summer and winter events, the first modern Olympic Games was held in 1896 in Athens, based on the original Games first held in 776 BC. The Games have come to signify the pinnacle of human sporting achievement. The number of medal sports at the 1992 Olympics totalled 28, including aquatics (swimming, diving, water polo, etc.), wrestling, track and field athletics, basketball and cycling. Atlanta in the USA hosts the 1996 Olympic Games.

OMR: see *optical mark reading*

on-line: a term used to show that a *computer* is linked in some way to another terminal or a central *database*, either by a fixed cable or via a telephone line. A number of global communications companies offer a range of 'on-line' services to computer users, such as access to financial *data* and travel information.

on-the-job training is any form of *training* that occurs in the workplace. Many jobs in *leisure* and *tourism* are ideally suited to this type of 'hands-on' training, e.g. learning to operate a *VDU* in a travel agency, working in a plant room at a *leisure centre* or training to be a chef in a restaurant or hotel. On-the-job training often gives employees the opportunity of gaining *National Vocational Qualifications (NVQs)*, giving staff credit for competence-based training related to the world of work. (See also *off-the-job training*.)

one-way communication: the process of passing a message or conveying information without receiving a response from the recipient. Examples of one-way communication methods in leisure, travel and tourism include notices, newsletters, signs, memoranda, reports and letters. One-way communication is an effective medium if no *feedback* is required from individuals or groups, but is ineffective if a response is needed. In such circumstances, *two-way communication* is preferable.

OPCS: see *Office of Population Censuses and Surveys*

open-jaw is a travel arrangement consisting of a different departure and arrival point for a return journey, e.g. a flight from Manchester to Malaga, returning to Gatwick.

open question: one that allows a *respondent* to give an expanded reply to a question, rather than inviting a specific response from within a small selection of replies, as is the case with a *closed question*. Examples of open questions are 'which company have you travelled with in the past?' and 'which country are you thinking of visiting?'. Open questions allow sales staff to quickly establish a rapport with a *customer*. They are also useful for survey work, when in-depth analysis is required, e.g. in a *focus group*.

operating profit: see *net profit*

operations management is concerned with the *planning* and use of an organisation's *resources* in order to meet its customers' needs. It is both a strategic process, focusing on the overall allocation of human, financial and physical resources to meet an organisation's *objectives*, and the operation of a company or facility on a day-to-day basis. It is the job of the operations manager to link the resources of an organisation to actual *demand* for its products and services, ensuring satisfied customers and an acceptable rate of return on investment.

opportunities: see *SWOT analysis*

opportunity cost is a term used by economists to indicate the monetary cost or other advantage that is lost when a particular course of action is taken. For example, a *local authority* which decides to use its capital resources to build an ice rink rather than a swimming pool could evaluate the opportunity cost of its decision, including the fact that local swimmers are denied a *leisure* opportunity.

optical mark reading (OMR) is a technique used in the analysis of *questionnaires* and other survey documents, to speed up the process and reduce error. OMR equipment automatically 'reads' the written responses marked on a questionnaire by an interviewer or respondent and transmits the data to an automated system, usually linked to appropriate computer software. OMR is particularly useful when a large number of responses is being analysed.

option is a term used in the travel business to describe a booking for a holiday or flight that has been reserved for a client pending his or her final confirmation. The option will be held for a specific period of time, in order to give the customer time to consider the purchase and pay the deposit.

ordinary shares are certificates which give their owners (*shareholders*) the right to a share of the profits of a *company*. The annual payment that an ordinary shareholder receives is known as a *dividend*, which will vary from one year to another depending on the profits earned by the company. Dividends are only paid to ordinary shareholders once all other calls on a company's profits have been met. (See also *preference shares, debentures.*)

organisation chart: a diagram showing, at a given moment in time, patterns of *authority*, lines of *communication*, division of *responsibilities* and work relationships within an organisation. Organisation charts vary greatly, some being very rigid, others more fluid and responsive to change. It is important to remember that leisure and tourism organisations operate in a very dynamic and competitive environment and that any organisation chart should be seen as temporary and liable to change in response to *opportunities* and *threats*. (See also *organisational structures.*)

Organisation for Economic Co-operation and Development (OECD): an alliance of countries drawn from the developed world, which was established in 1961 to act as a forum for discussion on global economic and trade issues. In the field of *tourism*, OECD has an input into *tourism planning* in individual countries, particularly in developing countries, and regularly produces statistical data and reports on global travel and tourism *development*.

organisational structures: the systems for allocating tasks and responsibilities within an organisation to aid decision making and the ultimate achievement of its goals. All but the smallest of leisure or tourism enterprises will need a clearly defined organisational structure, so that day-to-day operations and longer term *planning* are effective. A clear organisational structure will help to:

- define lines of communication
- identify sources of authority and responsibility
- clarify relationships between individual workers or departments
- identify the pattern of control for external and internal parties

In small enterprises the organisational structure is likely to be simple, with relationships between staff roles developing on an informal basis. Larger organisations will require a more complex *hierarchical* organisational structure, with more formal lines of *communication* and interaction between staff and departments. The nature of organisational structures varies greatly between one enterprise and another, depending on a range of external and internal factors. Some will be *centralised*, bureaucratic structures, while others will opt for *decentralisation*, where decision making is devolved down from senior management. (See also *'steep' pyramid, 'flat' pyramid*.)

outbound tourism is a form of *international tourism* which concerns people travelling away from their main country of residence for leisure or business purposes. Examples of outbound tourism would be a couple travelling from London to Brussels on the *Eurostar* train service and a business woman flying from Birmingham to Paris for a sales conference. The number of holidays abroad taken by British people has risen steadily in recent years, from 15.5 million in 1984 to 26.25 million in 1994, at the expense of holidays taken at home which have fallen over the same period of time.

outdoor activities: a wide-ranging term that can include any physical activity carried out in the open air, but which is most often associated with organised group activities held in outdoor facilities, e.g. canoeing, camping, orienteering, abseiling and rock climbing. Outdoor activity centres in the UK are operated in the public, private and voluntary sectors of the *leisure and recreation industry*, with many urban local authorities owning centres in the countryside for schoolchildren to use. The safety of outdoor centres is the subject of much debate, following the Lyme Bay canoeing tragedy in 1993, when four teenagers died.

outreach is the name given to work undertaken away from a leisure facility to help determine local needs and particularly to encourage participation by under-represented groups and individuals. *Local authorities* can sometimes secure funding to appoint officers to undertake specific projects in their local communities with, for example, *ethnic minorities* and disabled people.

Outward Bound is the trading name of the Outward Bound Trust Limited, an organisation that organises courses for anybody between the ages of 14 and 50 plus. As well as outdoor activity programmes, Outward Bound runs a series of personal development events, specialist training courses and events that contribute towards gaining the *Duke of Edinburgh's Award*, at its centres in Wales, the Lake District and Scotland.

overbooking is the practice of selling more seats on an aircraft, or other form of transport, or rooms in *accommodation*, than are actually available. This is sometimes merely a mistake on the part of the transport or accommodation provider, but more often than not it is deliberate, in order to compensate for the failure of people to turn up (*no shows*). It is common practice for airlines to overbook, offering generous compensation or *upgrades* if the plane becomes full.

overdraft: a type of borrowing available to both individuals and organisations used primarily to finance short-term cash deficiencies. Overdrafts are provided by banks and building societies for a fixed period of time and up to an agreed maximum limit. Overdrafts are usually offered to a borrower at a lower rate of interest than a *loan*, and may not require *security*. They are a very flexible way of meeting temporary *cash-flow* problems, often important given the peaks and troughs of activity experienced by many *leisure* and *tourism* operators.

overheads are *costs* associated with a business that tend to be *fixed* and which are not readily allocated to a particular activity. Typical overheads, sometimes referred to as indirect costs, in leisure and tourism include energy costs, rent, *Uniform Business Rates*, insurance, salaries and equipment *leasing* costs. (See also *fixed costs, direct costs.*)

override commission is a payment made over and above any existing *commission* earned by an agent. This may be as an incentive to boost sales or where a travel agent acts on a sole agency basis in a town for, say, the sale of *British Rail* tickets, offering other agents in the same town the opportunity to order their tickets through the sole agent.

overseas representative: see *courier*

Overseas Visitor Survey (OVS) is an annual *survey* of the behavioural patterns and opinions of visitors to Britain, conducted on behalf of the *British Tourist Authority (BTA)*. The purpose of the survey is to collect overseas visitors' information, which is either beyond the scope of or not currently available from the *International Passenger Survey (IPS)*, the UK's main source of statistical data on tourism. The OVS is carried out among a representative sample of 2,500 overseas visitors over the age of sixteen. The results of the OVS are presented to *ETB* operating departments and the BTA *marketing* department.

overseas visitors are a very important part of any country's *tourism* industry, helping to create and sustain jobs, provide income to businesses, improve local environments, contribute to tax revenues, and support music and the arts. Spending by the 19.2 million overseas visitors to Britain in 1993 amounted to more than £9 billion. Tourists are attracted to Britain's culture, heritage and history, as well as its countryside, cities and coastline.

OVS: see *Overseas Visitor Survey*

P

PA: see *public address, personal assistant*

Pacific Asia Travel Association (PATA): a *marketing* body, responsible for the Pacific Asia region, whose aim is to foster co-operation between the various private and public *tourism* concerns in the area and to promote its destinations direct to tourists and through the *travel trade*. PATA fulfils a similar role to the *European Travel Commission* in Europe.

package holiday: an all-inclusive holiday, sometimes referred to as an inclusive tour (IT), which normally consists of three components:

- *accommodation*
- *transportation*
- other services, e.g. *courier* support, excursions, etc.

Package holidays are put together by *tour operators* and offered for sale by *travel agents*, although it is possible to book direct with some package holiday companies. The popularity of package holidays has grown dramatically since they were first introduced in the UK in the early 1960s. In 1991 10.6 million overseas package holidays were sold in the UK, to destinations such as Majorca, mainland Spain, Greece, Turkey and Cyprus. The economic well-being of many Mediterranean countries rests heavily on their tourism industries and, in particular, the package tourists from the UK and other Western European countries. There is some evidence to suggest that the growth in package holidays has reached its peak and that what will change in the future is not the total number of packages sold, but the countries on offer, with long haul destinations set for continued growth.

Package Travel Directive: this *EU Directive* (full title the Package Travel, Package Holidays and Package Tours Directive) came into operation on 1 January 1993 in the then 12 member states of the *European Union*. Its main aim is to give people buying package holidays greater protection in law and access to compensation when things go wrong. The Directive places a number of duties on the organisers of package holidays, including providing clear contract terms, giving emergency telephone numbers, providing a variety of compensation options if the agreed services are not supplied, producing accurate promotional materials including brochures and providing proof of the organiser's security against insolvency.

The Package Travel Directive has come as something of a shock to the UK tourist industry, since the Directive covers *domestic tourism* as well as holidays taken abroad. This means that hotels, tourist information centres, resort offices, conference organisers, coach operators and even school trip organisers have discovered that they may well fall within the scope of the Directive. There has been much debate about what exactly constitutes a 'package', with *Trading Standards Officers*, the people given the job of policing the Directive in the UK, having differing views in different parts of the country.

parador: a type of *serviced accommodation* available in Spain, often using converted buildings of historic interest, such as castles and abbeys. Paradors are controlled by the Spanish National Tourist Office and can be found all over Spain, particularly in country districts 'off the beaten track'. Tour operators use paradors as the basis for *fly-drive* and other touring packages. (See also *pousada*.)

Pareto principle: the rule stating that 80 per cent of the benefits in a *company* tend to come from 20 per cent of the items sold. Conversely, 80 per cent of breakdowns will come from 20 per cent of the machines. In *travel and tourism*, it is a well-known fact that around 80 per cent of *package holidays* are sold through 20 per cent of the retail agents. The clear message from the Pareto principle, also known as the eighty/twenty rule, is that managers should concentrate their efforts on the key 20 per cent rather than spread their *resources* too thinly.

parish council: see *community council*

park and ride: a scheme to help ease traffic congestion in city centres and other popular tourist resorts. *Visitors* are encouraged to leave their cars at a point outside the town and travel instead by public transport, which may be a bus, tram or train. Popular tourist cities, including Cambridge and Oxford, operate such schemes in order to provide a more pleasant experience for visitors.

participation in sport: see *sports participation*

partnership: a form of business unit composed of between 2 and 20 people working in common with a view to making a profit. Partnerships are common in the *accommodation* sector of leisure and tourism, e.g. hotels and guesthouses. Although partnerships have some advantages over *sole traders*, such as shared risks and access to extra funds for expansion, each partner is still liable for all trading debts; in other words, they do not enjoy the benefit of *'limited liability'* as is the case with a limited company. Also, the decision of any one partner is binding on the others, which may cause problems if an individual proves to be unreliable or untrustworthy. Not all those involved in a partnership will necessarily be concerned with the day-to-day management of the enterprise; firms sometimes have 'sleeping partners' who merely invest money in the partnership in the hope of a healthy return.

Passenger Shipping Association (PSA) is an independent body representing the interests of UK-based ferry companies and cruise ship operators. Originally established in 1958 as the Ocean Travel Development, the PSA liaises with government and the *travel trade* to raise the profile of shipping and lobbies on behalf of its members on such matters as *duty-free* sales and safety issues. During the 1980s, the PSA initiated an extensive educational campaign, known as *PSARA*, aimed at *travel agency* staff to encourage the sales of shipping products to the public.

passport: an official document which confirms the nationality of an individual when travelling between countries. The move towards greater integration in the *European Union* has resulted in an easing of border controls and less inspection of passports by some member states.

PATA: see *Pacific Asia Travel Association*

payroll is the department within an organisation that deals with all matters relating to the payment of wages and salaries, including tax deductions, superannuation payments, *trade union* subscriptions, National Insurance payments and other regular deductions. The term is also used to indicate the total salary and wages bill of an organisation and the number of people it employs.

PC: see *personal computer*

peak season refers to the time of greatest *demand* for holidays and other travel products, e.g. the winter months for skiing holidays and the summer months for overseas *package holidays* to the Mediterranean. Holidaymakers will pay the highest prices in peak season, so it makes sense for those people who can travel *off-peak* to do so. The times either side of the peak season are known as *shoulder periods*.

peer appraisal involves the evaluation of the performance of members of staff by the other people in their *peer group*, i.e. their work colleagues. Formal rather than informal peer appraisal is more constructive, since it can prevent the exercise becoming too personalised. If managed effectively, however, peer appraisal can be very enlightening and help to identify any strengths and weaknesses present in members of staff, who can use the outcomes to identify any remedial measures that may be necessary.

peer group: the people that an individual works or socialises with on a regular basis, whose opinions and attitudes may be highly influential, e.g. the peer group of a recreation assistant at a *leisure centre* will be the other staff that he or she works with on a day-to-day basis.

peer pressure: the influence that others from within the same *peer group* can have on an individual and his or her actions and experiences. In a work situation, this pressure can be both beneficial, in that it may motivate an individual to work harder, and harmful, in creating undue stress and anxiety, thereby affecting work performance.

PEL: see *Public Entertainments' Licence*

penetration pricing: a pricing method that is used by organisations wanting to break into a new *market*, where suppliers of the same product or service already exist. Prices are set sufficiently low in order to persuade *customers* to switch their allegiance. A new health and fitness club, for example, opening in a city where other clubs already exist may offer reduced membership fees to entice people away from their current clubs. Sometimes referred to as a 'loss leader', it is important that penetration pricing is seen as a medium to long-term *strategy*, since customers will resent an early increase in prices. (See also *contribution pricing*.)

pension: a payment, which may be a lump sum or an amount paid regularly, made to an individual once he or she has retired from work. All UK citizens are entitled to receive a state pension when they reach retirement age, which will vary depending on the number of years during which a person was in employment.

Nowadays many people are part of company pension schemes or take out personal pensions in order to supplement their state pension. Company schemes are either contributory, where a member of staff pays a certain amount towards the pension, or non-contributory, where all pension payments are made by the employer. It is usual for both employers and employees to pay into a pension fund. Some people make extra payments, known as *additional voluntary contributions (AVCs)*, to top up a pension and give themselves a bigger pension on retirement.

perceptual capacity: see *carrying capacity*

performance indicator (PI) is a management device used to evaluate the *efficiency* and *effectiveness* of an organisation or individual. At senior *management* level, the most important PIs are those that help with the evaluation of financial and operational performance, e.g. the income per visitor to a theme park or the number of staff employed per 1 000 seats sold in an arena. The *hospitality* sector of leisure and tourism has long used PIs to evaluate performance and, as such, there is a wealth of information available that can facilitate performance evaluation both within a particular hotel and even between hotels with similar characteristics. In the leisure and recreation sector, the *Chartered Institute of Public Finance and Accountancy (CIPFA)* publishes comprehensive data on the finances and operation of *leisure centres*, which is useful for comparative purposes. (See also *financial ratios*.)

performance-related pay (PRP): remuneration that is linked to an employee's performance in the workplace, e.g. a *travel agent* being paid a bonus for every ten holidays sold to a particular *destination*. PRP can act as an incentive for staff to work harder and thereby increase an organisation's *profitability*.

performance standards are targets against which the performance of an individual or organisation can be measured. These could be concerned with financial performance, *market share*, levels of *customer service*, operational efficiency, etc. In leisure and tourism, much work is currently in progress to devise *occupational standards* in particular sectors of the industries, as a way of establishing minimum criteria for particular tasks and to act as a starting point for the development of *National Vocational Qualifications (NVQs)*.

performing is the final stage in team development, when its members have moved through the *forming*, *storming* and *norming* stages and are in a position to perform their roles and achieve the team's *objectives*, under the direction of the *team leader*.

perishability is a feature of leisure and tourism *products*, since an airline seat, theatre ticket or coach seat for use today cannot be resold tomorrow. Perishability makes leisure and tourism operators introduce techniques to maximise current sales, such as *standby* fares and late-availability discounts.

'perks' is shorthand for perquisites, meaning any benefit that an employee receives over and above his or her salary or wages. 'Perks', also called fringe benefits, are common in leisure and tourism, and are seen as a way of supplementing sometimes low basic pay. One of the most widespread 'perks' is the right to buy or use facilities and services either free or at discounted prices, e.g. discounted flights for *travel agents*, free use of leisure facilities for *recreation* workers and discounted rates at hotels for employees and their friends. 'Perks' are an important way of rewarding loyalty and helping reduce staff turnover.

person specification: see *job specification*

personal assistant (PA): an employee who works closely with a senior member of staff and assumes a high degree of *responsibility*, particularly in his or her absence. PAs perform a range of secretarial and administrative functions, and are chosen for their integrity, responsibility, reliability and ability to work under pressure.

personal computer (PC): a powerful machine which, since its introduction, has revolutionised the way that individuals and organisations manage their affairs, offering greater speed and capacity than many manual systems. PCs, sometimes called microcomputers, are found extensively in the *leisure* and *tourism* industries, from travel agencies to the desks of managers in *multinational corporations*. PCs are able to run a wide range of *software*, including *word processing, spreadsheets, databases* and communications packages, allowing access to global information systems such as the *Internet*. PCs can be 'stand-alone' or 'networked', i.e. joined to other computers and/or a central processor.

personal identification number (PIN): a unique number issued to an individual, often associated with *credit* and *debit cards*, or security codes for gaining entry to restricted areas in a building. PIN numbers, once memorised, should not be divulged to a third party for fear of improper use.

personal protective equipment (PPE): the Personal Protective Equipment at Work Regulations 1992 were developed as a direct result of the *EU Directives on health and safety*, replacing parts of more than 20 pieces of old law. PPE includes most types of protective clothing and equipment such as eye, foot and head protection, safety harnesses, life jackets and high visibility clothing. Employers must supply PPE free of charge to their employees and have a duty to ensure that it is properly used, stored and maintained.

personal selling: see *selling*

personnel records: see *staff records*

PERT: see *programme evaluation and review technique*

PEST analysis: a technique used by an organisation to investigate the *business environment* in which it operates, with a view to helping determine its future strategies. PEST stands for political, economic, social and technological, which are the main factors that influence organisations. The PEST (or STEP – social, technological, economic and political) analysis will vary between different leisure and tourism organisations, but is likely to include reference to:

- political – taxation, government policy, *EU policy*, local government policies
- economic – levels of *disposable income*, exchange rates, unemployment, *inflation*
- social – demographic trends, life style changes, education, changing work practices
- technological – global communications, home leisure, reservation systems, transport developments

The carrying out of a PEST analysis will involve an organisation in an extensive *data* collection exercise, from both internal and external sources.

PEX: see *public excursion fare*

physical recreation: a *leisure* activity that involves some degree of physical effort, as opposed to passive recreational activities such as sewing, knitting and reading. Participation in *sport* is one of the most common types of physical recreation, with over half of the adult population in the UK taking part in sport of some kind on a regular basis. (See also *sports participation*.)

PI: see *performance indicator*

pictogram: a *bar chart* in which the bars are presented in pictorial form. A chart showing levels of *car ownership*, for example, may use symbols of cars to represent the bars, the greater the number of cars the higher the value.

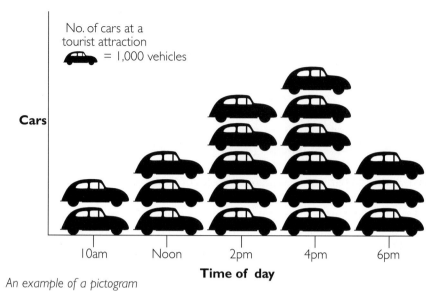

An example of a pictogram

pie chart: a way of presenting data in which a circle is divided into segments, with each segment representing a share of the total value. Pie charts are particularly useful for giving an approximate idea of different proportions or values, e.g. the number of *overseas visitors* to Britain from a range of different countries.

pilot survey: a preliminary *survey* involving a small number of *interviews*, carried out in advance of a main survey, to test whether the *questionnaire* is understood by the *respondents* and the whole of the survey process runs smoothly. The results of the pilot survey will be integrated into the main survey to improve the *data* collection process.

PIN: see *personal identification number*

place is one of the four key elements of the *marketing mix* in leisure and tourism, along with *price, promotion* and *product*. Place is concerned with both the location of facilities and the way in which products and services are made available to customers (*distribution channels*). Location can be crucial to the success of an organisation; a farm guesthouse, for example, which is deep in the countryside and well off the beaten track is unlikely to benefit from passing trade, whereas a high street travel agency in a busy location should attract a constant stream of clients. For a leisure company looking for a suitable site for a new *visitor attraction*, the prime location is likely to be close to major centres of population. Location, therefore, is closely linked to accessibility, at the regional and local level.

planned maintenance: see *maintenance*

planning: a structured, dynamic process that seeks to provide the right *leisure* and *tourism* facilities, in the best location, at the right time and at the right price, to meet current and future *demand*. In the public sector, planning takes place at a number of levels: at national and regional levels, planning tries to ensure the best mix and geographical spread of facilities in a country or region. Locally, planning is about meeting the needs of communities within the limited resources available. Private sector enterprises also have to plan their future *strategies*, to ensure long-term viability in changing market conditions. It is also the function of planners to ensure that resources are not abused and to promote development that is sustainable in the long term.

planning permission is required for the construction and alteration of buildings above a certain size, and for change of use of existing buildings. In leisure and tourism, this would include major construction projects, such as the building of a *leisure centre* or an extension to a *hotel*. The conversion of a house into a hotel would also need planning approval, granted by the local district council, under the 'change of use' ruling. The need to apply for planning permission exists to protect the environment and local people from unsuitable development.

planning regulations are the rules and conditions that apply when an individual or organisation seeks *planning permission*. They are contained in Acts of Parliament but are enforced by local councils, sometimes leading to different interpretations in different parts of the country. Planning regulations are particularly strict in the *National Parks* and other protected areas, such as *Sites of Special Scientific Interest (SSSIs)* and *Areas of Outstanding Natural Beaury (AONBs)*.

play is an activity carried out in people's *leisure time*, designed to give them pleasure and satisfaction, as well as allowing a degree of self-expression. Play has no age barriers, although it is most usually associated with children's activities; a pre-school child may play in a sand pit, teenagers play musical instruments, middle-aged people play sports such as tennis and bowls, while retired couples play dominoes or cards. Play can be spontaneous, such as children throwing snowballs, or it may be more organised and formal, such as a football match or tennis tournament. Indeed many games have specific rules associated with them, often regulated by their *governing bodies*.

PLC: see *public limited company*

point-of-sale (POS): usually refers to promotional materials that are displayed at the point where a *customer* makes a sale, e.g. a counter in a travel agency, a box office in a theatre or a desk at an airport. In the case of a retail travel agency, typical point-of-sale materials would include posters, hanging cards and window displays.

policy: a statement of the overall *objectives* of an organisation and its *strategies* for achieving these objectives. Larger organisations produce policy documents, which set out clearly what they hope to achieve. (See also *mission statement*.)

politics is the term used to describe the affairs of government, at international, national and local level. Politics affects everybody's daily lives, from the rate of tax paid on earnings, the state of the roads, what happens in schools, the quality of housing and the defence of the country, to name but a few. To many people, politics equates to power and control of *resources*. We live in a democracy in the UK, so that our political representatives are elected to represent the views of the majority.

Governments can have a considerable effect on *leisure* and *tourism* in their countries, taking either a positive or negative attitude to the industries. Most countries view tourism positively, as a way of generating foreign exchange, creating jobs and promoting their countries to the outside world. Local politicians devise leisure and tourism policies that should reflect the needs of local communities.

poll tax: see *Community Charge*

pollution is an unfortunate consequence of much *leisure* and *tourism* activity, e.g. noise pollution from events, contamination of waterways by motor craft and pollution of the air from car exhausts. Increasing concern for environmental issues has forced organisations to take the impacts they have on the environment seriously. Many developers of leisure and tourism facilities are required to carry out *environmental impact assessments (EIAs)* as part of the *planning* process.

portfolio analysis: the process of examining the current range of products and services offered by an organisation, *forecasting* future needs and putting measures in place to make changes to what is offered to the *customer*. This is most commonly undertaken with the help of the *Ansoff's matrix* model, the *Boston Consulting Group matrix* or a *SWOT analysis*.

portion control is a method of *stock control* used extensively in all sectors of the catering trade to reduce waste, produce consistency and help cost control. Under a system of portion control, the ingredients needed for a complete meal or a particular dish are calculated and agreed in advance. Portions must be monitored constantly and adjusted as necessary, depending on *customer needs*.

POS: see *point-of-sale*

post-industrial society: the term used to describe the stage reached by many Western societies in the latter half of the twentieth century. It is characterised by a decline in traditional primary and secondary industries, such as coal mining, shipbuilding and engineering, in favour of the *service sector* of the economy. The growth of service industries such as banking, information technology, *leisure* and *tourism* is an important part of the post-industrial society, which is also a period of rapid social changes, e.g. more single parents, improved health care and an ageing population.

positive action: see *positive discrimination*

positive discrimination: the practice of giving preferential treatment to a section of the community that is currently under-represented. Sometimes referred to as positive action, an example in *leisure* and *tourism* would be providing extra facilities and events for *ethnic minority* groups in a community. Positive discrimination also occurs in recruitment, when it is considered desirable to appoint a person from a particular ethnic background because they are under-represented in the organisation's workforce.

post-modernism is a philosophy that looks beyond the mass consumption of the post-industrial society and at the underlying social, cultural and political factors that shape the late twentieth century Western society. *Tourism* and *leisure* are essential features of post-modernism.

postal survey: a type of *primary research* that involves mailing a *questionnaire* to a random sample of *repondents* and, once completed, having the questionnaires returned by post. Postal surveys are a relatively cheap method of data collection, since there is no need to recruit and train *interviewers*. It is not possible, however, to obtain the same depth of response as in a *face-to-face interview* or *focus group*. *Response rates* can also be relatively low, but may be improved by sending a reminder to the respondents to return their questionnaires.

potential demand consists of those people who are not currently using or buying a particular product or service, because of a problem on the *demand* side. Such people are likely to buy in the future when their circumstances change, i.e. potential demand will become *effective demand*. The circumstances in question may be that they have a low *disposable income*, no access to private transport or health problems.

pousada: a type of *serviced accommodation* found in Portugal, often made available in converted buildings of historic interest, such as castles, stately homes and abbeys. Pousadas are controlled by the Portugese Government Tourist Office and can be found all over Portugal, particularly in country districts 'off the beaten track'. *Tour operators* use pousadas as the basis for *fly-drive* and other touring packages. (See also *parador*.)

PPE: see *personal protective equipment*

PR: see *public relations*

PR agency: a firm that works with an organisation to handle some, or all, of its *public relations* work. Larger leisure and tourism organisations will use a PR agency regularly to handle all of their links with the *media*, while smaller enterprises may contract with an agency for a specific task or event, e.g. the launch of a new product or staging an event. While some PR agencies are free-standing, many have links with *advertising agencies*.

pre-feasibility study: a brief analysis of a potential project to ascertain whether an organisation should invest further *resources* in having a fully costed *feasibility study* carried out. A pre-feasibility study will concentrate on estimated *revenue* and expenditure, as well as the expected level of *demand*.

preference shares are certificates which give their owners (*shareholders*) the right to a proportion of the profits of a *company*. Preference shares pay a fixed *dividend*, unlike ordinary shares whose return will vary from year to year. In the event of a company going into liquidation, preference shareholders receive priority over ordinary shareholders in terms of dividend payments. (See also *debentures*.)

press conference: a type of *public relations* activity where representatives of the various news *media* are invited to attend a staged event, such as the launch of a major leisure company's annual report or the opening of a new *tourist attraction* by a celebrity, in the hope that the organiser will gain valuable exposure in the press or on television or radio.

press day: an invitation to the *media* to attend an event or facility before it is open to the public, e.g. the Nemesis ride at *Alton Towers*, or the trade, e.g. the *World Travel Market*. The expectation is that the journalists will include information on the event or facility in their articles and programmes, thereby gaining valuable publicity for the operators. (See also *familiarisation trip*.)

press release: a written document circulated by an organisation to newspapers, magazines, radio and TV stations to keep them informed of current events, with the hope of gaining publicity. The issuing of press releases, sometimes called news releases, is an important *public relations* activity, which can form part of an overall *promotional strategy*. The disadvantage of press releases is that the originator has no control over what an editor may choose to include or exclude, sometimes leading to a mixed message being given or a remark taken out of context. Advances in electronic communication mean that press releases are increasingly being sent via *electronic mail*.

pressure group: an organisation that uses the collective talents and beliefs of its members to *campaign* for a particular issue or against a specific proposal. Organisations such as the *Ramblers' Association* and the *Campaign for the Protection of Rural Wales* are actively involved in campaigning on countryside issues and *lobbying* central, local and European politicians to further their cause. Pressure groups sometimes form for a short period of time to fight specific developments, e.g. the extension of the M3 motorway at Twyford Down in Hampshire.

Prestel: a *viewdata* system developed by British Telecom and used in travel agencies to access *principals' computerised reservation systems (CRSs)* using a *VDU* plus a telephone line. The uptake of Prestel in travel agencies has not been as rapid as that of its major competitors, *Istel* and *Fastrak*. It does, however, offer access to over 300 000 pages of information, including data on weather, currency rates and travel news.

price is a crucial element in an organisation's *marketing mix*, which is influenced by many factors including *demand*, the state of the economy, competitor products and services, the *objectives* of the organisation and the costs of providing a product or service. In leisure and tourism, it is customary to charge different amounts for the same product at different times of the year and even different times of the day, reflecting changes in demand. A *package holiday* to Spain, for example, will cost more in August than in January, while a round of golf at a local municipal course may well cost more on a Sunday morning when compared with a Wednesday afternoon. (See also *pricing policy*.)

pricing policy: the practice of determining the price for a *product* or range of products, within on organisation's overall *objectives*. Setting a pricing policy is notoriously difficult with leisure and tourism products, given the volatility of the industry and its *customers*, the perishable nature of the products on offer, the influence of seasonality and high levels of competition. An organisation's pricing policy should be developed from its *marketing plan* and will reflect the market segment(s) being targeted and the image that it wants to portray. The most common pricing policies adopted by leisure and tourism organisations include *skimming, cost-plus pricing, penetration pricing* and *competitive pricing*.

price war occurs when one or more competitors decide to continually reduce their prices for a product or service in the hope of gaining extra market share. With the opening of the *Channel Tunnel*, there has been a price war between *le Shuttle* and the ferry operators on the Dover-Calais route. If a price war continues over a long period of time, it is likely that one of the competing companies will be forced out of business, since it will be unable to stand the losses.

primary data is *data* that is collected for the first time, usually as part of a *market research* study. Unlike *secondary data*, which refers to already-published information, primary data involves the use of *surveys, observation* and *focus groups* to collect new facts and figures. Although there is a good supply of statistical information relating to the leisure and tourism industries, it is highly likely that an organisation, at some stage in its development, will need to collect primary data that is specific to its own operations, e.g. a *leisure centre* carrying out a visitor survey or a *visitor attraction* observing and recording the flow of vehicles and people.

primary ratio: see *return on capital employed (ROCE)*

primary research is the process of collecting and analysing *primary data* from a range of different sources. It is sometimes known as *field research.*

primary sector: the part of a nation's economy concerned with the extraction of raw materials, e.g. farming, mining and fishing. (See also *service sector, secondary sector.*)

prime costs: see *direct costs*

Prince's Trust: an organisation, founded by the Prince of Wales in 1976, that helps young, disadvantaged people and organisations that work with them or on their behalf. It awards grants to young people between the ages of 14 and 25, who may be unemployed, homeless or lacking in confidence, and who would benefit from some financial help to accomplish something positive. Eligible projects include owning and playing a musical instrument, finding and holding down a job, becoming a sports' instructor or preventing erosion of a river bank. The Trust's sister organisation, The Prince's Youth Business Trust, helps young unemployed people to become self-employed through practical support, *loans* and bursaries to set up their own businesses.

principal is the name given to a company that a *travel agent* does business with and whose products and services it sells. For example, if a branch of *Thomas Cook* sells a *Thomson's* holiday, the agent in the deal is Thomas Cook and the principal is Thomson. The most common principals that a high street travel agency will deal with are tour operators, airlines, ferry companies, *British Rail*, car hire companies and hotel groups. For selling the principal's products, the agent receives a *commission.*

printed media: refers to newspapers, magazines and journals, aimed at either consumer or trade buyers.

private limited company: a firm whose owners benefit from *'limited liability'*, but which cannot advertise the sale of its shares nor obtain a listing on the Stock Exchange, as is the case with a *public limited company (PLC)*. Many commercial leisure and tourism enterprises in the UK are private limited companies, with examples as diverse as country house hotels, tourist attractions and leisure clubs. Although trading as a private limited company does have certain advantages over *sole traders* and *partnerships*, there are disadvantages, such as the need to publish annual accounts and complete complex administrative and legal requirements.

private sector leisure and tourism: the sector of the industries that is concerned principally with commercial activities and maximising profits. The majority of leisure and tourism organisations are private sector enterprises, e.g. *hotels*, airlines, travel agencies, *tour operators*, car hire firms, *tourist attractions* and transport operators. Private sector enterprises range in size from large *multinational corporations* and *public limited companies*, such as *Forte* and *British Airways* PLC, to small one-person operations providing support services to leisure and tourism, e.g. *couriers*, guides and sports instructors. (See also *public sector leisure and tourism.*)

privatisation: the transfer of former public sector bodies and services to private sector enterprises, e.g. British Telecom, *British Airways* and the *British Airports Authority* were all previously public corporations, but are now private sector organisations. Supporters of privatisation argue that the competitive nature of the private sector leads to better *products* and standards of service than was the case under state control.

Opponents suggest that private sector operators will only be concerned with profit maximisation, with no concern for wider *social objectives* and community benefits. Currently, *British Rail* is being privatised, with rail franchises being offered to commercial train-operating companies.

PRO: see *public relations officer*

product is one of the four key elements of an organisation's *marketing mix*, along with *place, price* and *promotion*. Leisure and tourism products are very different from many other everyday products we buy and use, since it is often not possible to see or touch the product, e.g. a package holiday or a 30-minute session in a swimming pool; this is known as *intangibility*. Leisure and tourism products also demonstrate *perishability* and are very often non-standardised, i.e. the experience that a person gets on the same holiday from one year to another could be very different. Some leisure and tourism products can also be unpredictable and fragile, since customers who feel unhappy with a product or standard of service may take their custom elsewhere.

product development: the techniques and processes that an organisation will undertake to make its *product portfolio* as appealing as possible to existing and potential customers. Product development is often founded on extensive market research and may be supported by techniques such as the *Boston Consulting Group (BCG) matrix* and *Ansoff's matrix*.

product endorsement is when a personality lends his or her name to a *product* or service in order to stimulate sales or build an image. The use of a personality gives an organisation, destination or product added credibility. In leisure and tourism, the star of Bergerac, John Nettles, has been used extensively to market Jersey as a holiday destination, while Paul Hogan has appeared frequently on British TV screens to raise the profile of Australia for holidays.

product knowledge is an essential requirement of a successful *sales process*. Staff working in leisure and tourism must have regular *training* to help them learn about the features and benefits of the *products* they are selling. Good product knowledge creates the impression of a professional organisation, since staff can suggest alternatives if a customer's first choice of product is not available, or provide in-depth information on the range of products available. In the leisure and tourism industries, product knowledge is sometimes gained by staff experiencing the products and services first-hand, e.g. *familiarisation trips* for travel agency staff.

product life cycle: a concept which suggests that all products and services follow the same pattern of growth during their lifespan. The five stages in the product life cycle are:

- launch – when a product or service is introduced, with heavy promotional effort
- growth – sales grow steadily with increasing profits
- maturity – sales begin to slow down, perhaps because competitors are offering products with greater benefits
- saturation – sales have reached a plateau
- decline – sales drop off quickly

The concept can be useful to an organisation in developing its *marketing strategy*, since it can show past peaks and troughs in sales performance, thereby giving

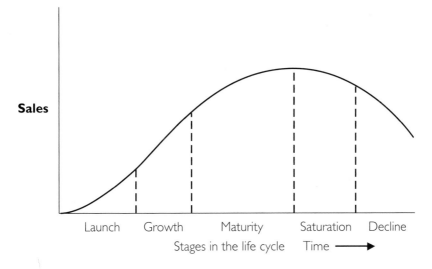

The product life cycle

pointers to possible new *product development* and promotional activity. Critics of the product life cycle concept argue, however, that it cannot be used to forecast future developments effectively since it is a retrospective model. (See also *destination life cycle.*)

product orientation: a business philosophy and *management style* that focuses on the details of *products* and services supplied rather than the needs of *customers* (*market* or *customer orientation*), e.g. a hotelier may invest in a new health and fitness suite only to find that his or her customers are more interested in drinking in the bar and watching television.

product portfolio is the mix of products or services offered by an organisation to its *customers*. If it wishes to survive in the longer term, it must monitor customer reactions constantly and make alterations to its portfolio on the basis of its findings. Large leisure and tourism organisations have extensive product ranges aimed at different segments of the market.

professional body: an organisation set up by, and representing the interests of, professional people in certain industry sectors. There are many professional bodies in leisure and tourism, including the *Tourism Society*, the *Institute of Leisure and Amenity Management (ILAM)* and the *Hotel and Catering Institutional Management Association (HCIMA)*. Professional bodies keep members up to date with what is happening in their particular sector by organising regular meetings, disseminating information and running training events. Most professional bodies control membership by applying certain criteria, such as the holding of particular qualifications or periods of employment in the industry.

profit is the status that arises when an organisation's total *turnover* exceeds its total *costs*. *Gross profit* is the difference between sales revenue and the cost of sales, while *net profit* is usually calculated by deducting payroll, *direct costs*, *indirect costs*, and financing costs from the gross profit figure, before tax. The profit after tax is the net profit attributable to *shareholders* after taxes have been paid. The different types of profit are shown in a company's *profit and loss account*.

profit and loss account: a financial statement that shows an organisation's income and expenditure over a given period of time, generally 12 months, resulting from its normal trading activities. A company's profit and loss account will show whether it is carrying forward a deficit or surplus into the next accounting period and is a useful tool for comparing *financial performance* over different time periods. It will also indicate, if read in conjunction with the *balance sheet*, the success or failure of *management* policies in deploying its resources to generate profits. An example of the structure of a profit and loss account is given below

Manor Country House Hotel
Profit and loss account for the year ending 31/3/96

	£000
SALES	
Rooms	140
Food and beverage	150
Other	20
TOTAL	310
Cost of sales	70
GROSS PROFIT	240
Expenses	160
OPERATING PROFIT	80
Interest	40
NET PROFIT	40

Profit and loss account

profit centre: a clearly identifiable aspect of an organisation's work that generates revenue, thereby contributing to overall *profitability*. Sometimes called revenue centres, the profit centres for a typical hotel, for example, are likely to include:

- rooms
- valet services
- food and beverage
- conference and banqueting
- telephone and business services
- special events

The managers of profit centres will be allocated specific *budgets* and performance criteria against which their performance will be measured. (See also *cost centres*.)

profit-sharing scheme: a type of remuneration where an employee receives an extra payment, in addition to his or her basic pay, which is directly related to the overall *profitability* of the organisation. For example, a 10 per cent increase in the profits of an international airline over a 12-month period may result in its employees receiving a bonus equivalent to 10 per cent of their annual salary. Such schemes are offered in many of the larger leisure, travel and tourism companies as an *incentive* for staff to work more efficiently and increase the organisation's profitability and their own pay levels.

profitability: a measure of the size of *profit* an organisation has earned compared with previous years or throughout the year, when comparing actual with budgeted results. It is measured in terms of total *assets* employed, long-term capital or number of employees.

programme evaluation and review technique (PERT) is a *management* technique used in major construction projects, such as *tourist attractions*, leisure complexes and hotel developments, to make sure that projects are completed at the least expense and in the shortest possible time.

programming: a way of making sure that a leisure or tourism facility is used to its full capacity at all times. Programming is most commonly associated with leisure and sports centres, but is equally applicable to theatres, local community centres, concert halls and a number of other facilities. In the public sector, programming aims to ensure that facilities are used by as wide a cross-section of the local community as possible, i.e. meeting the *social objectives* of the local authority. Programming must not only take account of the needs of customers but also the availability and expertise of staff, as well as the physical *resources* at the organisation's disposal.

prohibition notice: a written order, served by a health and safety inspector, when he or she discovers a contravention of the *Health and Safety at Work, etc. Act,* which could result in serious personal injury. The notice, which can be served on either the person undertaking the activity or the person in control of it, effectively stops the activity in question until such time as the specified action to render the situation safe has been completed to the satisfaction of the inspector.

project management: an important part of *operations management* that covers *planning*, scheduling, controlling, implementation and *evaluation.* The building or extension of facilities, or the staging of events, all require a degree of project management regardless of the scale of the project. Project managers sometimes use techniques such as *PERT* and *cost-benefit analysis (CBA)* to help their decision making.

promotion is one of the four key elements of an organisation's *marketing mix*, along with *place, price* and *product.* Promotion is used to:

- inform customers of product benefits
- make customers aware of particular products and services
- stimulate *demand*
- provide *incentives* to purchase
- remind customers of the existence of a product or service

Leisure, travel and tourism organisations use a variety of promotional techniques, referred to as the *promotional mix.* These include advertising, *direct marketing, public relations, personal selling* and *sales promotion* techniques.

promotional mix: the different promotional techniques that an organisation will use to raise awareness of its products and services and stimulate sales. These could include *advertising, direct marketing, sales promotion* and *public relations* activities.

promotional strategy is the way in which an organisation implements its *promotional mix* in order to achieve its *marketing objectives.* This could be through a strategy that concentrates solely on one type of promotional technique, e.g. *direct mail.*

Ponds Forge International Sports Centre: International Hall

Side 1 – seating   Side 2 – scoreboard

Session		1	2	3	4	5	6	7	8	9	10	Rotunda	Function Suite	
1	8.45-9.30am												A	B
2	9.30-10.15am		School bookings				Active lifestyle (Women's day)					Equipment set up		
3	10.15-11.00am													
4	11.00-11.45am													
5	11.45-12.30pm		Aero step									Educational gymnastics		
6	12.30-1.15pm						Public badminton							
7	1.15-2.00pm		Badminton											Business bookings
8	2.00-2.45pm		Sheffield University Students Union				Sheffield University Students Union					Educational gymnastics		
9	2.45-3.30pm													
10	3.30-4.15pm													
11	4.15-5.00pm													
12	5.00-5.45pm		Badminton				Badminton							
13	5.45-6.30pm		Advanced aerobics/circuit training									Karate		
14	6.30-7.15pm													
15	7.15-8.00pm						Corporate 5-a-side bookings							Self defence for women
16	8.00-8.45pm													
17	8.45-9.30pm		Public badminton									Fencing club		
18	9.30-10.15pm													

An example of a leisure centre programme (courtesy of Ponds Forge. Note that this programme excludes major sporting events)

Protestant work ethic: a movement that developed in Europe in the fifteenth and sixteenth centuries and which attacked the excesses and corruption of the pleasure-seeking nobility, leading to a sharp decline in the availability and respectability of *leisure* and *recreation*.

PRP: see *performance-related pay*

PSA: see *Passenger Shipping Association*

PSARA stands for Passenger Shipping Association Retail Agents' Scheme, a training initiative developed by the *Passenger Shipping Association (PSA)* as a way of increasing the knowledge and understanding of shipping and cruising among *travel agency* staff.

psychocentric: one of a number of types of tourist behaviour developed by Plog in 1977 as part of a research study for airline companies. Psychocentrics tended to be mainstream in their behaviour, rather unadventurous when it came to travelling, preferred familiar surroundings and had below average income levels. (See also *allocentric, mid-centric.*)

psychological carrying capacity: see *carrying capacity*

psychometric testing: a technique sometimes used by organisations when selecting and recruiting staff. It usually takes the form of a multiple choice test, designed to discover an applicant's personality type and to answer such questions as whether he or she would be a good team member, or would the applicant work well under pressure.

public address (PA): an amplification system used in a wide variety of situations in leisure and tourism, e.g. at *events*, concerts, in leisure centres and at sports matches. From a health and safety point of view, it is important to make sure that the PA system is audible to all, particularly in the event of an accident or other incident. An alternative system should be available as a back-up should there be a power failure.

public corporation: a state-owned organisation established to provide a service to the public. Many former public corporations in the UK have been *privatised* under the Conservative government, e.g. British Steel, British Telecom and *British Airways*, which are all now commercial concerns operating as *public limited companies (PLCs)*. *British Rail* is currently a public corporation, but is due to be privatised from the beginning of 1996.

public excursion fare (PEX): a special discounted fare offered by an airline to those booking and travelling on the same day on certain specified routes. (See also *standby, APEX.*)

Public Entertainments' Licence (PEL): a licence that will be needed by any leisure or entertainment facility that provides public dancing, music or other public entertainment of a like kind in any of its buildings. Application for a PEL is made to the local council, who may, in some areas, insist that a licence is issued for open-air entertainment. As is the case with the granting of most licences, the decision as to whether a PEL is successful or not will depend on a number of factors, including the nature of the event, the suitability of the premises, the impact of the event on the surrounding area and the character of the applicant.

public limited company (PLC): a large organisation with a minimum *share capital* of £50 000, which finances its expansion by offering shares to the public on the *Stock Exchange*. Some of the best-known leisure and tourism organisations in the UK are PLCs, including Airtours PLC, *British Airways* PLC, *Forte* PLC and the *Rank Organisation* PLC. Investors in public limited companies have the benefit of *'limited liability'*, limiting their liability in the event of failure to the amount they have invested in the company. PLCs often have a parent company acting as the head of a group with a number of subsidiary companies working beneath it, e.g. Harvester and Travelodge are subsidiaries of Forte PLC, the parent company.

public open space: an area of land to which the public has free access for enjoyment and *recreation*. Public open space includes parks, gardens, commons, sports grounds, bowling greens and public golf courses. Bodies such as the *National Playing Fields Association (NPFA)* campaign for tracts of public open space to remain accessible to all.

Public Order Act 1986: government *legislation* that seeks to protect the general public by providing legal restraints against private or public nuisance. Aggrieved neighbours, for example, may decide to pursue an action in the courts against the organisers of a rock concert or a noisy speedway event. For the action to have any chance of success, there must be continuity of nuisance, i.e. it must occur more than once over a reasonable period of time. In reality, individuals may get a faster result by complaining to their local environmental health department.

public relations (PR) is an important part of the *promotion* element of the *marketing mix* in leisure and tourism. It is defined by the Institute of Public Relations as 'the planned and sustained effort to establish and maintain goodwill and mutual understanding between an organisation and its publics'. The last word in the definition is used in the plural deliberately, since an organisation has to deal with a wide range of people while carrying out its business, including customers, suppliers, trade unions, the press, councillors (in the public sector), *shareholders* (in the private sector), tax inspectors, members, neighbours, voluntary helpers and many more. PR is most often associated with press or media relations, when an organisation builds a relationship with journalists, radio reporters and television stations, in order to gain publicity. This is most often achieved through issuing *press releases* and organising *familiarisation trips*. Good PR can also help when a tragedy strikes an organisation or unfavourable stories begin to circulate.

public relations officer (PRO): a person given the *responsibility* for carrying out an organisation's *public relations* function. He or she will handle all relationships with the press, including creating news stories and hosting press visits and familiarisation trips. The job of the PRO is to maintain the 'external face' of an organisation and they may occasionally be called upon to react quickly to a potential problem linked to the organisation. The PRO may write *press releases* or liaise with an *advertising agency* to handle this work.

public right of way: a route over which members of the public have freedom to travel, usually only on foot, but in certain circumstances also on horseback or bicycle. Some rights of way have been created under government *legislation*, while others have developed through continuous use over a long period of time. *Local authorities* are responsible for ensuring that rights of way are adequately maintained. (See also *bridleway*.)

public sector leisure and tourism is the sector of the industries concerned with providing a service to a local community or society in general, rather than having profit maximisation as a prime *objective*. This does not mean that public sector operators are not concerned with giving value-for-money in the facilities and services they provide. Increasing *competition* from the rival facilities in the private sector has forced public sector managers to adopt many commercial practices in order to survive and expand their operations. Leisure and tourism facilities provided by the public sector include:

- libraries and *museums*
- sports and *leisure centres*
- *visitor attractions*
- arts centres and galleries
- *tourist information centres*
- swimming pools
- parks and play areas
- community centres

Public sector provision operates at both local and national level. *Local authorities* play a vital role in providing *leisure* and *recreation* facilities for local communities, while organisations such as the *Sports Council* and *English Tourist Board* co-ordinate and sponsor national initiatives.

purchase ledger: a record of an organisation's purchases over a given period of time, listing *creditors* by name and also recording any payments made to them.

pyramid structure: see *hierarchical organisation*

Q

QA: see *quality assurance*

qualitative data is information, often gathered as part of a *market research* process, that is concerned with an organisation's standing in the marketplace, rather than an exact measurement of its performance. It may be data that reflects an individual's opinion or attitude, e.g. whether the holidaymakers on a *package holiday* were happy with their *accommodation* in the resort or the opinions of a family on the facilities on offer in a tourist attraction. Qualitative data can be collected in a number of ways, including *surveys* and *focus groups*.

quality is one of the 'buzzwords' in the leisure and tourism industries in the 1990s. A whole host of organisations, in the public, private and voluntary sectors, have pledged their commitment to improving the quality of the products, services and facilities they offer their customers. Quality is synonymous with satisfying customer *needs*, i.e. the introduction of any quality system or set of quality standards must place the customer as the focus of all activity. This is borne out by the *International Standards Organisation (ISO)*, which defines quality as 'the totality of features and characteristics of a product or service that bear on its ability to satisfy stated or implied needs'. Some leisure and tourism organisations have sought external recognition of their quality initiatives, either by gaining certification under *BS 5750* or the *Investors in People* scheme.

quality assurance (QA) is the process of attempting to make sure that the standards of product and service quality are right first time every time, to achieve total customer satisfaction. In a leisure or tourism organisation, QA will involve attention to such factors as the products on offer, levels of *customer service*, assessment of performance standards and *after-sales service*. (See also *quality control*.)

quality circle is a practice used in *operations management* to improve an organisation's *efficiency* and *effectiveness*. Found commonly in Japanese firms, quality circles involve regular meetings between employees and management/supervisory staff to discuss work methods, problems and solutions, with a view to deciding how best to achieve quality targets. Quality circles help reinforce the notion that quality is a shared responsibility and that everyone should strive to ensure quality in their individual efforts.

quality control: unlike *quality assurance*, which aims to make sure that quality standards are met from the outset, quality control is concerned with monitoring product and service quality by identifying and addressing quality problems, through checking and inspection.

quality press: generally considered to be newspapers, such as The Times, The Guardian, The Daily Telegraph and The Observer, that are non-tabloid in format and offer a balance of news, comment and *advertising*. Such 'quality' newspapers are generally, but not exclusively, read by people in the higher *socio-economic* groups.

quality standards are levels of performance and product quality which organisations seek to achieve in order to satisfy customer needs and thereby remain competitive. Some organisations seek external recognition of their work performance, e.g. by gaining a quality standard such as *BS EN ISO 9000* or by implementing *Investors in People*. Others operate very well without the need to formally register for recognition, based on the fact that management and staff have practised a customer-focused approach for many years.

quango stands for quasi-autonomous non-governmental organisation. Although usually linked to a government department and primarily funded from public money, quangos enjoy greater freedom than bodies under direct government control, with board members appointed rather than elected. Examples of quangos in leisure and tourism include the *Sports Council, British Tourist Authority* and the *Arts Council*. Opponents of quangos argue that the non-elected status of their members may lead to political bias, while those in favour say that the freedom from *'red tape'* means that quangos can work speedily in reaching their *objectives*.

quantitative data is factual information that can be measured, often gathered as part of a *market research* process, e.g. the number of visitors to a theme park, the stock of accommodation in a holiday resort or the country of origin of visitors to Britain. Such data is invaluable for *management* decision making and may influence, for example, an organisation's marketing strategy or range of available products. Quantitative data is available from a number of *secondary* and *primary research* sources, including *surveys, observation* and sales figures. (See also *qualitative data*.)

questionnaire: a document containing a series of questions designed to help an organisation gain valuable data to help with its forward *planning* and decision making. Specialists in the design of questionnaires suggest that there are a number of important steps to go through before finalising the questionnaire, including making a list of expected 'outcomes', formulating the questions that will achieve these, carrying out a pilot survey with the first draft of the questionnaire, amending as necessary, and lastly producing sufficient quantities of the final version for the main survey. Questionnaires are one of the most common methods used by leisure and tourism organisations to gain their *market research* information. (See also *questionnaire design*.)

questionnaire design is the process of developing a questionnaire so that it meets fully the *objectives* of the *survey* in which it is being used. Questionnaire design is a skilled and time-consuming procedure, often best left to professionals in *advertising agencies* and market research bureaux. There are many guidelines that should be followed when attempting to design an effective questionnaire, including:

- always put sensitive questions, e.g. concerning age, occupation, marital status, etc. at the end of the questionnaire
- avoid ambiguous questions
- avoid using jargon
- don't be tempted to include superfluous questions
- keep questions simple
- avoid *'leading questions'*
- use appropriate language

quorum refers to the minimum number of people at a meeting to allow the decisions made at the meeting to be valid. Under the constitution of a Leisure Services

Committee of 24 members, for example, it may have been decided that there must be a minimum of 12 people in attendance for a quorum to exist and for the Committee to be able to transact business. Any less than 12 members would make the Committee meeting 'inquorate'.

quota sample: the most common type of *sampling* used in research studies. When using a quota sampling method for a *market research* survey, *interviewers* are given instructions as to the number of respondents in certain categories that they must interview, e.g. defined by age, gender or social class. For example, if a golf club's records show that 75 per cent of its members are men, interviewers carrying out a survey would be instructed to recruit one woman for every three men, so as to make the sample representative of the total 'population'. (See also *random sample.*)

REVISION: There is a set of revision lists at the back of this book to help you prepare for GNVQ unit tests. See pages 246–250 for unit tests in GNVQ Advanced Leisure and Tourism.

R

RABs: see *Regional Arts Boards*

Race Relations Act 1976: government *legislation* making it unlawful to discriminate on the grounds of colour, race, nationality or ethnic origin. Under the terms of the Act, employers must not discriminate in matters relating to staff recruitment, training and promotion. The Act established the *Commission for Racial Equality (CRE)*, with powers to issue non-discrimination notices to employers and trade unions found to be infringing its requirements.

rack rate refers to the full, published price at which a hotel room is sold. Depending on levels of *demand*, it is likely that the rack rate will be discounted for particular *customers*, at specific times of the week or year, and for special events. Most hotels offer high discounts at weekends, when they are not being used by business travellers.

racking policy refers to the *tour operators' brochures* that a *travel agent* will have on display in the agency. Independent agents will carry a wide range of brochures from both specialist and mass market operators, whereas the multiple agents will have clearly defined policies as to which particular brochures they are allowed to stock. This will be determined by, among other things, levels of *commission* on offer and whether the agent has a trading link with the operator, e.g. *Thomson* owns Lunn Poly and Going Places is part of the Airtours Group.

RADAR: see *Royal Association for Disability and Rehabilitation*

Railtrack: see *British Rail*

rail travel is an element of the UK *transportation* scene, made up of a network of public services provided by *British Rail* and a small number of private rail operators catering for tourists from the UK and overseas, e.g. the North York Moors Railway and the Ffestiniog Railway.

Ramblers' Association: a registered charity working to defend the beauty and diversity of the British countryside for the benefit of walkers of all ages. Founded in 1935, the Association has been active in lobbying central and local governments on issues relating to access in the countryside. It campaigns to keep Britain's thousands of miles of rights of way open, to ensure that public woodlands remain accessible, to protect Britain's *National Parks* and to make the countryside available to the whole community. The Ramblers' Association currently has more than 100 000 members and nearly 400 local groups throughout England, Scotland and Wales.

random sample: when every member of a 'population' has an equal chance of being selected in a research study. For a survey based on a randon sample, which is considered to be the most accurate type of sample, individuals are normally preselected from a sampling frame, such as the electoral register. *Interviewers* are then asked to carry out interviews at the selected households chosen at random. Many government surveys operate in this way. (See also *sampling, quota sample.*)

Rank Organisation PLC was founded in 1937 and is now one of the world's leading *leisure* and entertainment companies, with a turnover of more than £2 billion in 1994. Rank became the dominant influence in the British film industry by the end of the Second World War and today is one of the largest 100 companies in the UK, employing some 40 000 people. It has interests in film and television, including ownership of Odeon Cinemas, in holidays and hotels, with *Butlin's* as the *brand leader* in the UK holiday market, and in recreation and leisure, with 150 amusement centres spread throughout the UK and a number of casinos operating under the Grosvenor banner. Rank is also the leading bingo and social club operator in the UK, owning some 160 outlets known by the 'Top Rank' and 'Mecca' brand names. It is also an equal partner in Universal Studios in Florida.

rate of exchange refers to the price at which one *currency* is exchanged for another. European currencies outside the *Exchange Rate Mechanism (ERM)* are allowed to fluctuate in line with demand and supply. Adverse changes in exchange rates can have serious consequences on the demand for holidays in a particular country.

rate of return: a measure of the *profits* of a business, expressed as a percentage of the total *capital* employed in the venture.

ratio analysis: the development of performance measures from financial and operational information and its use for management decision making. Ratios such as the *return on capital employed (ROCE)* and *occupancy rates* can be used to compare the internal performance of an organisation and how it compares with its competitors.

RCI stands for Resort Condominiums International, the world's leading *timeshare* exchange company. RCI operates a 'clearing house' for the owners of timeshare properties worldwide, who want to exchange their property for one in a different country or a different time of year. As an example, the owner of a week's timeshare in a lodge at Loch Rannoch in Scotland could deposit his or her time period into the RCI 'bank' and select, say, a week in a timeshare apartment in Florida. RCI was founded in 1974 and is now a global business, serving more than 2 700 resorts and 1.7 million member families from a network of 56 offices.

receiving country: see *tourist receiving country*

recreation: the activities that people carry out in their *leisure time*, which may be active or passive, and take place inside or outside the home. The term comes from the Latin word 'recreatio', meaning that which refreshes or restores. *Countryside recreation* and *community recreation* are particular elements of the total recreation sector, the former concentrating on pursuits such as rambling or mountain biking, while the latter is concerned with providing recreational facilities for all sectors of a community, irrespective of their social status, race or gender.

Recreation Managers Association of Great Britain (RMA): with some 800 members nationally, the RMA aims to promote the interests of individuals associated with the *management* of sports clubs, leisure centres, health clubs, ice rinks, bowling centres and hotel leisure centres. RMA's stated *objectives* include providing members with a forum for the exchange of ideas and information, preserving and enhancing the standards of recreation management in the UK and fostering an appreciation by both management and club members of the importance of the association's work.

recruitment agency: a firm specialising in finding suitable applicants for jobs. Leisure and tourism organisations will sometimes use the services of a recruitment agency for filling senior appointments, such as a Director of Marketing or a Head of Leisure Services. The agency will advertise the posts and select suitable applicants for interview. Agencies are also used in situations where posts are difficult to fill, e.g. some manual jobs in the hotel and catering sector. Agencies specialising in leisure, travel and tourism posts advertise their services in the relevant trade newspapers and journals.

recruitment and selection: a structured process that aims to identify and employ the most suitable person for a job vacancy. It has five clearly defined stages:

- job analysis – identification of what the job entails
- finding suitable applicants – by *advertising*, through agencies, internal candidates, etc.
- selection – drawing up a short list and interviewing candidates
- appointment – making a formal offer of employment
- induction – ensuring that the new member understands the working of the organisation

Recruitment and selection can be carried out 'in-house' or left to a recruitment consultancy to organise.

'red tape': the term given to unnecessary paperwork and procedures, most often associated with public bodies. The government has made a pledge to reduce red tape wherever possible, although many people would say that further moves to privatise services and facilities is likely to lead to more, not less, unnecessary paperwork.

redundancy: the *dismissal* of an employee on the grounds that their job has ceased to exist, rather than because of anything to do with their conduct or work performance. Redundancy may be voluntary or compulsory, with redundant staff being eligible for certain redundancy payments, depending on how long they were employed with the organisation and how many hours they worked per week.

redundant building grants: sums of money, administered by the *Rural Development Commission,* made available to the owners of derelict buildings in the countryside to return them to productive use. Eligible uses for the buildings would include tourist accommodation, craft workshops and *telecottages.*

Regional Arts Boards (RABs) are ten autonomous, strategic bodies that work in partnership with *local authorities* and a wide range of other public, private and voluntary sector bodies to promote the arts within their particular region of England. They are concerned with all arts and crafts, including visual, performing, media and published, and work at regional level as partners of the three national agencies which provide most of their funding, namely the *Arts Council, British Film Institute* and the *Crafts Council.*

Regional Tourist Board: an official organisation that works in tandem with a *National Tourist Board* on matters of interest in a particular region. In the case of England, there are 10 Regional Tourist Boards working under the auspices of the *English Tourist Board (ETB).* The English Regional Tourist Boards operate on a more commercial basis than the ETB, earning revenue from commercial membership subscriptions, advertising sales and other commercial ventures. A typical English Regional Tourist Board will have a diverse range of members, including:

- *local authorities*
- hoteliers
- regional airports

- *bed and breakfast* establishments
- caravan parks
- operators of *tourist attractions*

Regional Tourist Boards seek to co-ordinate tourism initiatives in their regions, particularly *marketing* and publicity, as well as providing a service to both members and the general public.

The Regional Tourist Boards in England (as at September 1996)

relaunch is the need to make a *product* or service available for a second or subsequent time, usually in a modified form. A leisure facility, for example, may install new *virtual reality (VR)* amusements or update its decor in order to retain its *customers* or appeal to a new *market*. *Tour operators* are sometimes forced to withdraw brochure stocks from travel agencies and relaunch their holiday products, often in response to price reductions by competitors.

remuneration is the tangible reward that employees receive in return for giving their time, commitment and expertise to an employer. The remuneration for the majority of staff working in leisure and tourism will consist of a weekly wage or monthly salary. To this may be added *commission* or *incentive* payments, based on sales achieved. Many workers in leisure and tourism will be offered a range of *'perks'*, such as free or discounted use of facilities or subsidised travel, as a form of remuneration. *Profit-sharing schemes* also operate in larger leisure and tourism companies.

repeat business is crucial to the success of any leisure, travel or tourism organisation, since existing *customers* generate a higher profit contribution than new clients and provide a much firmer base from which to develop new business. Indeed, research from the US Office of Consumer Affairs shows us that it takes five times as much effort, time and money to attract a new customer as it does to keep an existing customer. Companies use a number of techniques to encourage repeat business, and thereby promote *brand loyalty*, such as special offers and *incentives*, e.g. *frequent flyer programmes*.

report: a type of *written communication* used extensively in leisure and tourism for a variety of reasons, including:

- to present statistical information
- to investigate the feasibility of a new development
- to recommend changes to a *management* or staff structure
- to meet legal requirements
- to investigate a disciplinary matter involving members of staff

A report should follow a logical sequence and structure, beginning with its *terms of reference*, followed by procedure, findings, conclusions and recommendations. Depending on the type of report, it may also be useful to include a bibliography and a section detailing sources of information.

reservation systems: procedures and equipment that leisure and tourism organisations use to sell products such as *package holidays,* airline flights, hotel accommodation, car hire, theatre tickets and leisure facilities. They work on the basis that there is a known stock of product to be sold and an up-to-date count of what is still on offer is always easily obtainable. Reservation systems can be either manual or computer-based, the latter providing greater storage capacity, flexibility and speed of operation. The development of new technology, particularly in the travel sector, has led to the widespread use of *computerised reservation systems (CRSs)*, particularly in the airline and tour operating sectors.

resort: the name given to a holiday destination, which may be a town or city, e.g. Palma or Rome, or a purpose-built complex, such as Disneyland Paris. Resorts are the focus for many elements of the *leisure* and *tourism* industries, including *accommodation*, catering, *arts and entertainment, transportation* and leisure facilities. The popularity of resorts is changing constantly, as people's fashions, tastes and preferences change, as shown in the *destination life cycle* concept.

resort representative: see *courier*

resources: a general term used to identify the tools that a manager has at his or her disposal to be able to achieve an organisation's *objectives*. Resources may be financial, human, operational or physical. It is the job of a manager to marshall his or her resources, gaining the best possible outcomes. The term can also be used to denote the *natural attractions* of a tourist area, e.g. lakes, mountains, streams and beaches.

respondent: the name given to the person in an interview survey who answers the questions asked by an *interviewer*.

response rate is a measure of the number of replies to a survey as a proportion of the total number of *questionnaires* distributed or *respondents* questioned. In general, *self-completed questionnaire* surveys have a lower response rate than *face-to-face interviews*. If a response rate is too low, bias may be introduced into the survey and its subsequent analysis. Response rates can sometimes be improved by sending reminders to respondents.

responsibility: an obligation on a member of staff to carry out certain tasks or make particular decisions. An employee will be held responsible for his or her performance at work, measured against targets and *performance criteria*. Failure to achieve targets, or poor performance in the workplace, may result in a reprimand from a line manager. (See also *authority, accountability, delegation.*)

responsible tourism: see *'green' tourism*

retail price index (RPI) is the main method of measuring *inflation* in the UK economy. It is based on the weighted average of the prices of a standard range of household products, calculated on a monthly basis. The RPI is also used as a broad indicator of wage rises in the economy.

return on capital employed (ROCE) is the most widely used indicator of the *profitability* of an organisation, since it is meaningless to look at profitability without also analysing the *resources* used to generate the profits. Sometimes called the primary ratio, ROCE is calculated as follows:

$$\text{FORMULA: return on capital employed} = \frac{\text{net profit}}{\text{capital employed}}$$

The calculation of ROCE has many variations, which leads to inconsistency and sometimes distortion. The ratio can be used to compare the amount of profit made per £100 invested in an organisation, which will be useful to potential investors and business operators.

return on investment: a term which is sometimes used to mean *return on capital employed (ROCE)*.

revenue is another name for *turnover*. It is sometimes referred to as sales revenue.

revenue centre: see *profit centre*

RIDDOR stands for the Reporting of Injuries, Diseases and Dangerous Occurrences

Regulations 1985, which contain the laws relating to the reporting of accidents and incidents in the workplace. Under the Regulations, any employer has a duty to inform the relevant authorities of any fatal or serious injuries to employees or other people in an accident connected with any business. In the case of leisure and tourism organisations, the incidents should be reported to the local Environmental Health Department.

risk assessment: a systematic investigation of the potential risks to the health and safety of employees and anybody else who may be affected by an organisation's work activities, e.g. spectators, *visitors* and contractors. All employers with five or more employees must formally carry out risk assessments under the regulations of the *EU Directives on health and safety*.

RMA: see *Recreation Managers Association of Great Britain*

ROCE: see *return on capital employed*

roll-on/roll-off (RORO): a type of ferry onto which vehicles are loaded and unloaded by means of ramps. Recent tragedies, such as happened with the Estonia and Herald of Free Enterprise ferries, have led to calls for greater safety on RORO vessels.

room occupancy: see *occupancy rate*

RORO: see *roll-on/roll-off*

Royal Association for Disability and Rehabilitation (RADAR): a national voluntary organisation working with and for people with physical disabilities. RADAR acts as a *pressure group* to improve the environment for disabled people, in areas such as health, education, social services, employment, housing, mobility, *leisure* and *tourism*.

Royal Society for the Protection of Birds (RSPB) is Europe's largest wildlife *conservation* charity taking action for birds and their environment. It has more than 890 000 members in the UK, who enjoy free access to over 100 nature reserves and have access to a network of local members' groups. The RSPB leads action for bird conservation by promoting conservation of birds and their habitats, carrying out research, working with central and local government to find solutions to conservation problems, and buying and managing land as nature reserves. The RSPB has a junior section, known as the Young Ornithologists' Club, to encourage bird conservation from an early age.

RPI: see *retail price index*

RSPB: see *Royal Society for the Protection of Birds*

RTB: see *Regional Tourist Board*

Rural Development Commission: the government agency concerned with the well-being of the 10 million people who live and work in England's rural areas. It has a statutory duty to advise government on all matters relating to the economic and social development of rural England. During 1993/94 the Commission, sometimes referred to as simply the Development Commission, allocated £12.4 million towards the building of new premises, £1.7 million to economic projects such as training, tourism and environmental improvement, and nearly £2 million for social and community projects. It sees its priorities as stemming unemployment in rural areas, addressing the shortage of affordable housing and halting the decline in village services.

rural tourism: any type of tourist activity that takes place in the countryside, including *farm tourism*, countryside events, nature trails and rural attractions. Rural tourism is seen as a way of maintaining the social, cultural and economic viability of country areas, by creating employment, generating income and giving farmers the opportunity to diversify into diferent leisure and tourism enterprises. The growth in rural tourism in recent years has gone hand-in-hand with greater concern for the environment and countryside generally.

S

Sabre: a *computerised reservation system (CRS)* developed by American Airlines and made available to *travel agents* worldwide.

SAF: see *Sports Aid Foundation*

safety audit: a systematic investigation of a facility aimed at identifying potential safety risks and *hazards*, with a view to reducing the risk potential and minimising the likelihood of personal injury. A safety audit will include investigations of similar factors to those contained in a *risk assessment.*

safety officer: a member of staff given the responsibility within an organisation for implementing health and safety procedures and monitoring their effectiveness. Depending on the size of the organisation, the post of safety officer may be a full-time appointment or carried out on a part-time basis by an employee with other responsibilities.

Safety of Sports Grounds Act 1975: government *legislation* aimed at ensuring a safe environment at spectator sports' facilities, including rugby and football grounds. (See also *Taylor Report.*)

sale and leaseback is a way for an individual or organisation to raise *capital* by selling a *fixed asset,* such as land or a building, and immediately taking out a long-term lease with the new owner to carry on using the asset for business purposes. It is a technique often used by companies that are experiencing financial difficulties, e.g. a hotelier who has cash-flow problems may enter into a sale and leaseback agreement as a way of surviving in business.

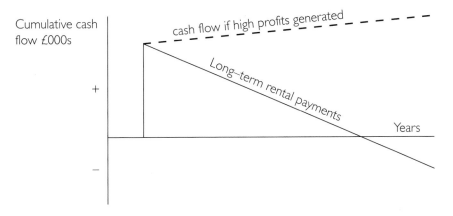

Impact on cash flow of sale and leaseback

Sale of Goods Act 1979 states that all goods sold or hired must be 'fit for the purpose' for which they were bought, of 'merchantable quality' and must match their description, whether verbal or written. Under the Act, *tour operators,* for example, should not be found liable if they have exercised due care when selecting the different elements of their packages. Under the *Package Travel Directive,* however, operators cannot disclaim responsibility for poor products and services supplied by third parties, e.g. hoteliers and airlines.

sales administration systems: procedures and techniques for recording sales data, issuing of tickets and other documentation, updating customer databases, processing orders and tracking sales progress. Such administrative systems are invariably computerised, with the benefits of speed, accuracy and large storage capacities.

sales budget: a chart that shows the predicted level of sales over a given time period. It is often the starting point of an organisation's financial planning process, since the *demand* for products and services is often the overriding factor in determining success or failure. In *forecasting* its likely sales, a company will take into account many factors, including past sales figures, existing and potential *competition*, the state of the market and the results of any market research work. Sales budgets are often constructed so as to allow actual figures achieved to be entered alongside the budgeted sales. (See also *expenditure budget.*)

sales invoice: see *invoice*

sales ledger: a chronological record of an organisation's *debtors* by company account, with details of sales made on *credit*, any sales returns and payments made to debtors.

sales process: a sequence of six key stages, which every sales person should undertake in order to achieve a successful sale of a product or service. The stages are:

- raising customer awareness
- establishing rapport with the customer
- investigating customer *needs*
- presenting the product or service
- *closing the sale*
- providing an *after-sales service*

Identifying and following these six stages indicates that selling is a structured activity that can be learned and is not just for those who are 'born sales people'.

sales promotion: one of the key aspects of *promotion* within a leisure and tourism organisation, along with *advertising, direct marketing, public relations* and *personal selling.* Some of the most common sales promotion techniques are competitions, discount vouchers, free demonstrations, *brochures, extra product*, 'giveaways' and exhibitions. The main features of sales promotion techniques are that they are temporary and aim to stimulate demand in the short term. The dynamic nature of the leisure and tourism industries means that organisations are having to respond constantly to fluctuations in demand. Sales promotion offers the flexibility needed to be able to respond to these changes.

sales revenue: see *revenue*

sales staff are people involved in all aspects of an organisation's *sales process*, from establishing rapport with a customer, to *closing a sale* and providing an *after-sales service.* Sales staff need a wide range of skills and qualities, including personality, good *communication* skills, a determination to succeed, consistency, enthusiasm, product knowledge and self-motivation. Most sales staff will be involved in far more than actual selling activity, either face-to-face or over the telephone. A sales person's job may also entail liaison with other work colleagues, travelling, entertaining, networking with external organisations and individuals, gaining *product knowledge* and servicing distribution channels.

sales turnover: see *turnover*

sampling is the practice of selecting the proportion of a total 'population' to be included in a research study, as opposed to a *census*, when the whole 'population' is surveyed. If the selection of the sample is fair, accurate and based on proven statistical methods, the responses of the people surveyed should mirror those of the total 'population', within known limits of accuracy. (See also *random sample, quota sample.*)

SASH: see *Standardised Approach to Sports Halls*

scheduled air services: flights that operate to a published timetable on specific routes. Unlike *charter flights*, scheduled services are committed to operate even if the *load factor* is very low. Scheduled services are particularly appropriate for business travel, although some package holidays do use scheduled services (known as *inclusive tours by excursion*).

Scottish Tourist Board (STB) is the official *tourist board* responsible for tourism *promotion* and development in Scotland. Established under the *1969 Development of Tourism Act*, the STB is funded primarily by *grant-in-aid* from the Scottish Office. The aims of the STB are to encourage UK residents and *overseas visitors* to visit the country, by providing advice to tourism businesses, funding tourism projects, co-ordinating the *tourist information centre* network in Scotland, running *marketing* campaigns and advising central and local governments. The STB has been particularly active in pressing for changes in *accommodation grading schemes*, particularly the *Crown Classification Scheme*.

Scottish Vocational Qualifications (SVQs): see *National Vocational Qualifications*

sea travel is the category of *transportation* that includes ferries, cruise liners, hovercraft and hydrofoils.

seasonality: variations in the *demand* for *products* and services at different times of the year. The demand for package holidays, for example, is very seasonal, with periods of high demand corresponding to school holidays in the UK. Many holiday regions in Britain also experience seasonal fluctuations, with high demand in peak periods followed by troughs in the winter, when the facilities in many resorts close altogether. Public agencies and private companies try to extend the season whenever possible, by targeting people who can take holidays outside of the main peaks and offering discounted rates at these times. Extending the season makes economic sense, since it allows hoteliers and other tourist businesses to offer year-round employment.

Seaside Award: a scheme introduced in 1992 to provide information about a wide range of beaches in the UK. Co-ordinated by the *Tidy Britain Group*, Seaside Awards are given to beaches which are clean, well managed and display information about current and previous water quality. There are two categories of beaches, resort and rural, which are assessed for a variety of criteria, including safety, *management*, cleanliness and information. A Seaside Award resort beach is one which actively encourages visitors and has developed its facilities to provide varied recreational opportunities. A rural beach is one which has limited facilities and is visited and enjoyed for its less developed, more natural characteristics.

seaside resorts have experienced a hard time in recent years in terms of numbers of *visitors*. Although there are examples of UK resorts that have prospered, many have seen their tourist numbers drop since the mid-1980s, due in part to the availability and low prices of overseas *package holidays*, but also to the fact that the seaside product no longer meets the needs of a more discerning public. Many of the resorts were developed to cater for the needs of a type of tourist who has all but disappeared; one who travelled by train, stayed in a boarding house and was content to walk along the promenade, play in the sand and spend money on the amusements. The need to improve the image of British seaside resorts was recognised with the introduction of the English Tourist Board's Seaside Campaign in 1992, when 35 resorts throughout England and the Isle of Man joined forces to encourage *customers* to return.

seat-only sales: the name given to purchases of flight tickets without any *accommodation*. These sales are an important part of the *travel industry*, with tourists prepared to find their own accommodation, or use the facility to fly to their *second home* or *timeshare* accommodation abroad. Business travellers on a budget also make use of seat-only sales from time to time.

second home: a property bought especially for use as a holiday home at certain times of the year and sometimes let to friends and other holidaymakers on an infrequent basis. Too many second homes in a single location can sometimes force up the prices of property and cause problems for local people, who may not be able to afford to buy. Second homes can also change the social fabric of certain rural areas, especially when their owners retire and come to live on a permanent basis.

secondary data is information available from existing sources, usually in written form, but increasingly now available from electronic sources such as *CD-ROMS* and the *Internet*. Secondary data is available from both internal sources, such as an organisation's address lists, sales figures and results of visitor *surveys*, as well as from external sources, including company reports, government data, *professional bodies* and independent consultants.

secondary research: sometimes referred to as *field research*, this is the process of collecting and analysing *secondary data*, from a range of different sources, internal and external to an organisation.

secondary sector: the part of a nation's economy concerned with producing manufactured items from raw materials, e.g. engineering, construction and electronics. (See also *service sector, primary sector.*)

secondary spend is the money spent by *customers* over and above the cost of the primary reason for their visit to a leisure or tourism facility, e.g. money spent in the café at a *visitor attraction*, drinks bought from a vending machine at a *leisure centre* or money spent on *duty-free* goods on a cross-Channel ferry. Many organisations devote a great deal of attention to providing secondary spend opportunities, which may yield a higher profit margin than their primary activities.

secret ballot: a vote, held in secret so as not to pressurise individuals into voting in a particular way. Under the *Trade Union Act 1984*, the government has made it a requirement that trade unions hold secret ballots of their members before authorising strike action. A vote held in secret, as opposed to a show of hands, is likely to give a better indication of an individual's true feelings.

section 4 grants were made available to *tourism* businesses under the *1969 Development of Tourism Act* to encourage new tourism projects. Although initially available in England, Scotland and Wales, the *English Tourist Board* no longer has powers to distribute section 4 grants, although they remain available through the *Wales* and *Scottish Tourist Boards*. The grants have been used mainly for improvements to hotel accommodation, but areas such as marina developments, tourist attractions and *farm tourism* have also benefitted.

security has two meanings in leisure and tourism. The first is to do with *loans*, where some form of security is often required by the lender in case the borrower should default on repayments. Security in this case could include the deeds to property or an insurance policy. The other meaning of security is more general and relates to the security of people, property, staff and information, relating to leisure and tourism facilities. Staff must be trained in safe and secure procedures in the workplace, and to be on their guard for suspicious characters and circumstances.

security hazards: a variety of existing and potential problems that a leisure and tourism organisation may need to be aware of and possibly insure against, e.g. violence to staff, theft of information, valuables, cash and other property, fraud, sabotage and accidental damage.

SEETB: see *South East England Tourist Board*

segmentation: see *market segmentation*

selection: see *recruitment and selection process*

self-appraisal: see *self-evaluation*

self-catering accommodation is regarded as any type of *accommodation* where guests take care of themselves and where, unlike *serviced accommodation*, there are no, or very few, services provided for them during their stay. It can take many forms, including:

- chalets in holiday camps
- cottages and apartments
- converted farm buildings
- forest lodges
- villas
- *timeshare*
- camping and caravanning

Holidaymakers like the freedom and value-for-money that all forms of self-catering accommodation offer, particularly families with young children. Self-catering units may be part of an accommodation complex which provides a range of central services, such as restaurants, swimming pools and games facilities.

self-completed survey: a survey that requires the person answering the questions (the *respondent*) to fill in a *questionnaire* themselves, rather than giving answers to an interviewer, as is the case with a *face-to-face interview*. Self-completed surveys have the advantage of being cheaper than interview surveys, since there is no need to recruit and train interviewers. They do, however, have their drawbacks, such as lower response rates, which can be improved by sending a reminder to the respondent. Also, if a respondent does not fully understand a question, there is no interviewer to ask for clarification.

self-evaluation is the term used when a person reviews his or her progress in a given situation against pre-determined *objectives* and *performance criteria*. Sometimes called self-appraisal, it takes place most commonly in work situations, particularly for individual members of a team. Self-evaluation can produce useful *feedback* both for the individual member of staff and his or her line manager. Such an appraisal can be fed into any wider staff development review that the organisation may undertake.

self-guided trail: a route used by walkers, cyclists or car drivers, who follow a series of signs and/or a route map, to learn about places and people featured on the trail. Most self-guided trails are provided for walkers and are found in woodland and other country areas, marked with numbered or colour-coded signs, which are cross-referenced to an explanatory leaflet. Self-guided trails are a common type of *interpretation*, aiming to enhance a person's experience of the place they are visiting.

selling is a structured activity involving *communication* between a buyer and a seller, which is designed to inform the *customer* and persuade him or her to purchase the products or services on offer. Although the obvious objective of any selling activity is to ultimately achieve a sale, it should be seen as a continuous process that can help cement customer relationships, build customer loyalty and provide lasting benefits in an enhanced level of *customer service*.

All staff in leisure and tourism are likely to be involved in some form of 'selling' in the course of their work. Selling in private sector organisations will be geared towards meeting commercial objectives, while public and voluntary sector bodies will be using selling to help achieve wider social and community aims. (See also *sales process*.)

selling skills: techniques that enable staff to be able to make a successful sale, by identifying *customer needs*, presenting products in the correct manner, *closing the sale* and offering an *after-sales service*. Effective selling demands a high level of *interpersonal* and *communication* skills on the part of the sales person.

semi-variable costs: expenditure that is made up of a fixed element, that remains the same irrespective of an organisation's level of business activity, and an element that fluctuates in line with its output. Examples of semi-variable costs in leisure and tourism include telephone, *fax* and *telex* charges, all of which have a constant rental element plus added charges related to the level of use.

sensitivity analysis: a technique used in *forecasting* to measure the overall effect on a *business plan* of any changes in the elements that go to make up the plan. A theme park, for example, may base its financial projections on an annual attendance figure of 150 000; with the aid of a computer spreadsheet, the effect of, say, a ten per cent reduction or increase in visitor numbers on the overall financial position can be calculated quickly.

service charge: an additional amount, usually expressed as a percentage, added to the selling price of a meal to cover service. Some menus indicate that service is included in the cost of the meal, indicating that no extra gratuity is expected; in this case, the French term 'service compris' is sometimes used.

service sector: the part of a nation's economy that is made up of *tertiary industries*, i.e. those concerned with providing a service rather than extracting raw materials (*primary sector*) or producing manufactured goods (*secondary sector*). The service sector includes retailing, banking, insurance, financial services, information technology, shipping, leisure, travel and tourism. Like many industrialised societies, the UK is moving away from an economy based on primary and secondary industries towards one that is becoming dominated by the service sector. It is estimated that more than half of the country's *gross national product (GNP)* presently comes from service sector industries and that by the turn of the century three out of every four jobs in Britain will be in service industries. The service sector makes an important contribution to Britian's *balance of payments.*

serviced accommodation refers to *hotels,* guesthouses and any other type of *accommodation* where guests are offered a range of different services during their stay, such as food, portering, valet services and possibly entertainment. *BTA* statistics show that there are in the region of 27 000 hotels in the UK, to which can be added an estimated 20 000 *bed and breakfast* establishments, guesthouses and providers of farmhouse accommodation.

Set-Aside: a voluntary scheme for farmers aimed at reducing the surpluses of certain crops in the *European Union.* Under the scheme, implemented by the *Ministry of Agriculture, Fisheries and Food,* farmers agree to take areas of land out of production in return for an annual payment. Such land is able to be developed for alternative uses, which could include sporting and *leisure* facilities, or tourist amenities.

Seven Wonders of the World: works of art and architecture regarded by Ancient Greek and Roman observers as worthy of exceptional note. The Seven Wonders were:

- The Pyramids of Egypt
- The Hanging Gardens of Babylon
- The Statue of Zeus at Olympia, Greece
- The Temple of Artemis at Ephesus, Greece
- The Mausoleum of Halicarnassus
- The Colossus of Rhodes
- The Pharos of Alexandria

Sex Discrimination Act 1975: *legislation* introduced to outlaw discrimination on the grounds of gender. The Act states that employers must not treat people of a particular gender any less favourably when it comes to recruitment, *training* and promotion. There are certain circumstances when the employment of staff of a particular sex is allowable, e.g. an advertisement for an attendant to work in the female changing rooms at a sports centre could legally ask for female candidates only to apply.

sex tourism: the practice of attracting tourists with the offer of sexual encounters. Countries such as Thailand and the Philippines specialise in sex tourism, which is increasingly being condemned by many Western states and religious leaders.

SGITs is an acronym for special group inclusive tour rates, which are discounted *scheduled airline* fares offered to *tour operators* who sell *inclusive tours by excursion (ITX).*

share capital: that part of a company's *capital* made available from *shareholders.*

shareholder: an individual or institution that holds *shares* in a *company* or number of companies. The shareholder will buy shares as an investment and will hope that, in the long term, the return on investment (known as the *dividend*) will be greater than that available from other sources. Depending on the type of shares held, the shareholder will enjoy a number of other rights, including the right to attend the *annual general meeting (AGM)* and vote on the election of new directors.

shares are certificates giving their holders part ownership of a *company* and the right to receive a proportion of its profits by way of a *dividend*. There are different types of shares, such as *ordinary shares*, *debentures* and *preference shares*, each giving different shareholder rights. Companies issue shares as a way of raising *capital* for business expansion.

shell leaflet: a promotional leaflet which contains colour pictures and images, but no written text. Organisations add their own text, thereby generating a colour *brochure* at a reduced cost.

shift work: a work pattern which is implemented when employees are needed for longer than a standard eight-hour day. A *leisure centre*, for example, that is open from 7 am to 11 pm is likely to have two eight-hour shifts, one from 7 am until 3 pm and a second from 3 pm until 11 pm. Staff will be rotated, sometimes working the early shift and sometimes the late shift. In certain circumstances staff will be paid extra for working unsocial hours.

shopping: see *leisure shopping*

short break: a short-duration trip in the UK or abroad as a main holiday or second, additional vacation. Although the traditional British two-week holiday is in something of a decline, short breaks have been a resounding success story since the early 1980s. Their popularity lies in the changing leisure habits of much of the population, linked to changes in working practices, making the two-week break unpopular with a large section of the travelling public, many of whom have sufficient *disposable income* to be able to enjoy more than one holiday each year. Developments in *transportation*, such as the opening of the *Channel Tunnel*, and cheaper ferry and airline fares, have boosted the market for short breaks to the Continent, with city breaks alone accounting for some 600 000 travellers per year.

short haul: name given to *destinations* on the near Continent, Holland, France, Belgium, parts of Germany and the Scandinavian countries (See also *long haul.*)

short take-off and landing (STOL): a type of aircraft technology that allows an aeroplane to operate on a reduced length runway. STOL aircraft, such as the Dash 7 and British Aerospace 146, have influenced airport developments, particularly serving the needs of business travellers, by allowing development close to the heart of cities and business districts. London City Airport in Docklands was developed on the basis of accepting aircraft with STOL technology.

shoulder period refers to the times either side of *peak season*. In the case of overseas *package holidays*, shoulder periods would be, for example, either side of July and August, and the time just before and just after Easter. The term 'shoulder' comes from the shape of the demand graph for the holidays, which resembles the shoulders on a body.

Since there is less demand in the shoulder periods, prices for leisure and tourism products and services will generally be lower than for *peak season*.

shuttle service: a type of frequent *transportation* that carries passengers on popular routes with a minimum of check-in procedures, e.g. airline shuttle services between London and Manchester, and Glasgow and Aberdeen.

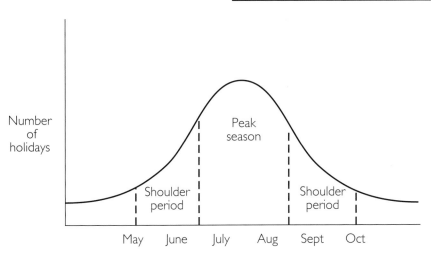

Example of shoulder periods

SIBH: see *Society for the Interpretation of Britain's Heritage*

SIC: see *Standard Industrial Classification*

single currency: the final stage of *Economic and Monetary Union (EMU)* for the member states of the *European Union (EU)*, when there would be a single currency operating across all countries. There is much debate within Europe as to whether this will eventually happen and be agreed upon by all countries.

Single Market: the agreement that was to allow, by the end of 1992, the free movement of goods, services, people and capital between the member states of the *European Community* (now *European Union*). The aims of the creation of the Single Market were to reduce *'red tape'* by removing trade barriers, create more competition between companies, make travel between member countries easier and create more jobs. Despite the optimism of the early 1990s, much still has to be done to complete the process, although some measures are in place, e.g. reduction in frontier controls.

single supplement: an extra payment for *accommodation* or other travel services paid by a person travelling alone. A hotel, for example, may feel justified in making an additional charge for single occupancy of a double room, since it is losing revenue. Single supplements for hotel accommodation are often resented by tourists and are now not universally levied.

Site of Special Scientific Interest (SSSI) is an area designated by *English Nature* because it has special examples of mammals, birds, insects, plants or geological features. Most SSSIs are in private ownership, with around 40 per cent owned or managed by public bodies such as the Ministry of Defence or the *Forestry Commission*. English Nature provides advice to the owners of SSSIs on protecting the nature conservation value of their land. Designation of a piece of land as a Site of Special Scientific Interest may mean that its owners are barred from undertaking certain activities, e.g. ploughing.

situation analysis: see *SWOT analysis*

Skal Clubs are international groups of senior *travel trade* employees who meet regularly to socialise and promote mutual understanding. There are more then 500 Skal Clubs throughout the world, which arrange luncheons and dinners for members and guests. Membership is restricted to those who have held a position of responsibility in the *travel and tourism industry* for at least five years.

skimming is when a high *price* is charged initially for a new *product* or service that is unique and that attracts *customers* who are willing to pay a high price for status reasons. Creating an artificially high price for a product can help to give it an up-market image. Examples of skimming in leisure and tourism include flights on Concorde, trips on the Venice-Simplon Orient Express and *virtual reality* products. Adopting a skimming policy may lead to problems in the long run when competitors enter the market with similar products offered at lower prices.

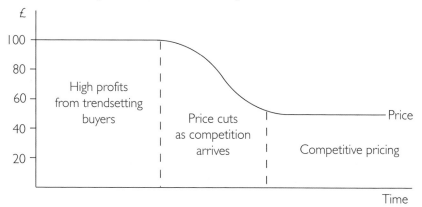

Skimming the market

sleeping partner: an individual who enters into a *partnership* agreement and contributes finance, but takes no part in the day-to-day running of the business. This may be for purely investment purposes or for tax reasons. It is important to remember that the decisions of a sleeping partner are binding on all other partners.

smart card: a further development of a *credit* or *debit card* that stores an individual's personal and financial information on a microchip within a plastic card. Some people believe that smart cards will soon become commonplace in society, while others point to the possible loss of liberty if the information contained on the card is misused.

social class: see *socio-economic classification*

social costs: unlike economic costs, which are relatively easy to quantify, social costs are the social, environmental and operational effects of a particular project or decision, which are borne by a local community or by society in general. An analysis of the social costs of a project are an essential part of a *cost-benefit analysis (CBA)*, i.e. the widening of a road may result in the loss of trees and amenity land, extra pollution, more noise, loss of housing and may lead to more vehicle accidents. All of these social costs, sometimes called external costs, need to be quantified and considered against the economic costs of the proposal. It is often left to *pressure groups* and public sector bodies to make developers aware of the social costs of their actions.

social objectives: whereas private sector organisations will set themselves commercial objectives, such as increasing *market share* or maximising revenue, non-commercial organisations will have wider social objectives, which could include:

- increasing participation in leisure activities in an inner city area
- providing facilities for disabled visitors at a theme park
- running courses for disadvantaged children at an outdoor activity centre
- gaining support for an environmental cause
- protecting country areas from further *development*

Although social objectives are not always easy to measure, the introduction of *compulsory competitive tendering (CCT)* and other efficiency initiatives has forced local authorities to put a value on them, so that social aims can be measured along with the more conventional financial and operational objectives.

social tourism is the name given to the development and encouragement of tourist facilities and services for disadvantaged members of society, e.g. those on low incomes, disabled people, single-parent families, the elderly and other deprived minorities. This can be achieved through voluntary measures, such as fund-raising by charities for holidays and day trips, or by local and central government initiatives such as grants and low-interest loans. The tourism policy of the *European Union* includes the encouragement of social tourism as one of its priority areas. In the UK, the work of the *Holiday Care Service* has helped many individuals find suitable *accommodation* for their needs.

Social Trends is a government publication that provides national data about a wide range of topics, including many allied to the leisure and tourism industries. Social Trends, which is published by the *Office of Population Censuses and Surveys (OPCS)*, contains data about, for example, how people use their leisure time, how many are members of particular societies, how many attend football matches and what proportion of the population owns or has access to a car. Much of the data is taken from other OPCS sources, including the *General Household Survey (GHS)*, as well as surveys sponsored by the tourist boards, e.g. the *International Passenger Survey (IPS)*.

Society of London Theatre (SOLT) is a trade association which represents theatre managers, owners and producers of the 50 major commercial and grant-aided theatres in central London. The Society plays a major role in *industrial relations* with the main unions serving the needs of employees in music and the arts. Members of SOLT benefit from a range of services, including legal advice, promotional work and *lobbying* on matters of concern.

Society for the Interpretation of Britain's Heritage (SIBH) is an independent membership organisation that aims to stimulate awareness of the *interpretation* of Britain's *heritage*. It promotes the highest standards of interpretation to ensure sensitive conservation of the national heritage for public enjoyment, appreciation and education.

socio-cultural impacts of leisure and tourism include both positive and negative outcomes. Socio-cultural problems include:

- overcrowding
- loss of traditional industries and crafts

- distortion of local customs
- alteration of religious practices
- loss of languages
- loss of authenticity

On the positive side, leisure and tourism can contribute to the revitalisation of neglected regions and customs, the rebirth of local arts and crafts, and greater understanding between different cultures. Many people consider that the negative socio-cultural impacts of leisure and tourism are far more harmful than harmful *environmental impacts*, since they may take generations to eradicate.

socio-economic classification: an attempt to classify individuals into one of six 'social class' groups on the basis of their occupation. Developed originally by JICNARS (Joint Industry Committee for National Readership Surveys), the classification has been used by marketers to develop products and market them to specific groups, based on the notion that all people in a particular social class grouping will have similar patterns of buyer behaviour. The classification has been criticised by marketing professionals for being too general. Today, classifications based on *life style* and *life cycle* are favoured by marketers.

Social grade	Social class	Typical occupations
A	Upper Middle	Higher managerial, admin. and professional (e.g. judges, surgeons)
B	Middle	Intermediate managerial and admin. (e.g. lawyers, teachers, doctors)
C1	Lower Middle	Supervisory, clerical, junior management (e.g. bank clerk, estate agent)
C2	Skilled working	Skilled manual workers (e.g. joiner, welder)
D	Working	Semi- and unskilled manual workers (e.g. driver, postman, porter)
E	Those at lowest level of subsistence	Pensioners, widows, casual workers, students, unemployed people

Socio-economic classification

soft tourism: see *'green' tourism*

software: the programs and other applications that operate on computer *hardware*. *Personal computers (PCs)* can be loaded with a wide range of software packages for business, domestic and leisure uses. Some of the most common packages used by businesses are *databases, spreadsheets, desktop publishing (DTP)* and *word processing* software. Software programs are either pre-installed on a computer's internal memory or downloaded from floppy disks or CDs (if a *CD-ROM* drive is installed). Today, most software runs on 'Windows'-based systems, developed by the Microsoft Corporation.

sole trader: the simplest form of business unit in which an individual has full ownership and control of an enterprise, with the advantage of swift decision making and lack of bureaucracy. Many leisure and tourism businesses start as sole traders, perhaps converting to *partnerships* or *limited companies* as they expand their operations. Disadvantages of operating as a sole trader include the fact that the owner is personally liable for all the debts of the business, there may be limited capital available for expansion and, often overlooked in leisure and tourism, the long hours the sole trader often has to work to make a success of his or her venture.

SOLT: see *Society of London Theatre*

solvency: see *liquidity*

South East England Tourist Board is the official *Regional Tourist Board* covering the counties of Kent, Surrey, East Sussex and West Sussex.

Southern Tourist Board is the official *Regional Tourist Board* covering the counties of Oxfordshire, Buckinghamshire, Berkshire, Hampshire, the Isle of Wight and part of Dorset.

spa: a natural attraction that many towns have exploited for *tourism* purposes. Spa towns in the UK, such as Cheltenham, Buxton and Llandrindod Wells, have used the healing powers of spa waters as a way of attracting tourists since the early seventeenth century. In recent years, there has been something of a revival in the promotion of UK spa towns, under the direction of the *British Spas Federation (BSF)*.

special needs: the general term given to those people who have extra requirements or who demand special care and attention. In leisure and tourism, these may be children, older people or those with physical disabilities.

spectator safety has become an important issue since the tragic fire at Bradford City Football Club in 1985 when 56 people died and the Hillsborough Stadium disaster in 1989 when 96 football fans were killed. Early legislation to improve matters included the *Safety of Sports Grounds Act 1975*, which gave the operators of grounds certain responsibilities in relation to health and safety. The Hillsborough disaster led to the publication of the *Taylor Report* into safety at football stadia.

spectator sports: see *sports spectating*

sponsorship is an important, if uncertain, source of extra income for certain sectors of the UK leisure and tourism industries, particularly *spectator sports* and the arts. It varies enormously in scale, from the Endsleigh Insurance Company's sponsorship of soccer's First Division to a local builder providing the cost of the kit for a local junior hockey team. Either way, the principle is the same, with both the builder and Endsleigh expecting a return on their investment, in the form of wider publicity in the *media* leading to increased levels of business.

Sponsorship for the arts at local, regional and national levels is encouraged by the *Association for Business Sponsorship of the Arts (ABSA)*, while a group of commercial and public sector bodies known as the Institute of Sports Sponsorship (ISS) meets regularly to promote sports sponsorship. The *CCPR* estimates that sponsors contributed around £250 million in 1991 in support of sporting events and projects. It operates its own sports sponsorship advisory service.

sport is a major component of the UK *leisure and recreation industry*, with some 36 million people taking part in sport or physical recreation at least once a month (*sports participation*). Millions more watch or follow sport on a regular basis (*sports spectating*). Sport brings with it a number of economic and social benefits, including:

- a contribution to better health and a sense of personal well-being
- a vital role in children's education
- generating nearly £10 billion of financial expenditure for the economy
- providing around 470 000 jobs
- promotion and enhancement of Britain on the international scene

Public sector sport is administered by the *Sports Council*, which is funded directly from the *Department of National Heritage*. Local authorities in England and Wales spend approximately £1.5 billion on sports and leisure facilities and services, contributing to the quality of life and prosperity of their areas.

Sport and Recreation Information Group (SPRIG) is a non-profit making organisation made up of individuals and organisations working in a number of *sport* and *leisure* information fields, with representatives from the various sports councils, ILAM, local authorities, colleges and various other interested bodies. SPRIG aims to encourage collaboration throughout the information profession, with a view to raising the profile of sport and recreation documentation. It publishes a twice-yearly bulletin, which includes articles on information services, notification of meetings, book reviews and conference reports.

Sport for All is the name given to the broad *policy* objective of the *Sports Council*, emphasising their aim of increasing *participation* in sporting activities among individuals and groups across all sections of the community, regardless of race, creed, colour, ability, social status, mobility, income, age, location and gender. Studies conducted from the 1970s onwards into the use of leisure and recreation facilities in the UK have invariably concluded that the majority of users of such facilities were white, male, car-borne and middle class. The Sports Council sees *sports equity* as one of its major priorities for the 1990s.

Sports Aid Foundation (SAF) was established in 1976 to raise funds to help British sports people compete in major international events. Grants are awarded to individual competitors to assist with preparation and training expenses, travel and subsistence while away from home, special diets and equipment. The SAF is an independent body funded by joint promotions with commercial sponsors, national and regional events and individual donations. The SAF Charitable Trust offers grants to young people to develop their talents and to sports people with disabilities.

Sports Council: an independent body, established in 1972 by Royal Charter, and financed largely through funds from the *Department of National Heritage*. It has a remit covering British sport as a whole, although there are separate Councils for Scotland, Wales and Northern Ireland. It consists of members appointed by the Secretary of State and around 550 permanent employees. The Sports Council has four main aims:

- to increase *participation in sport* and physical recreation – by providing grants to sports organisations, running general campaigns to increase participation and funding staff to help *governing bodies* to increase participation in their particular sport

- to increase the quality and quantity of sports facilities – by providing advice and financial assistance for developing sports facilities, identifying examples of good practice in design and management, and funding research into local and national sport facility requirements
- to raise standards of performance – by financing the *National Coaching Foundation*, encouraging sponsorship of sport, running the campaign against drug abuse in sport and managing six centres of excellence, including three National Sports Centres at Crystal Palace, Bisham Abbey and Lilleshall, the National Water Sports Centre at Holme Pierrepont, the National Centre for Mountain Activities at Plas y Brenin and the National Cycling Centre in Manchester
- to provide information for and about sport – the Council is the country's main central source of information and data about sport, with a national information centre in London and nine regional centres housed in its regional offices

At the time of writing, plans are being developed for a major restructuring of the administration and focus of government support for sport. A new *United Kingdom Sports Council (UKSC)* and *English Sports Council* will be established in place of the Sports Council from 1 April 1996. (See also *Lottery Sports Fund* and *National Lottery.*)

sports development is an educational process championed by the *Sports Council* and put into practice by Sports Development Officers (SDOs) throughout the UK. It is about making sure that adequate structures are in place to allow people, regardless of their starting point, the opportunity to learn basic skills in the sport of their choice. It represents an awareness that the notion of '*Sport for All'* requires an investment in people as well as facilities. There are more than 1 000 SDOs in the UK working with community groups, coaches and local authority officials to help improve sports performance. (See also *Champion Coaching*).

sports equity seeks to ensure fairness at all levels of *sport*, to recognise that there are inequalities in the ways in which sports are organised, and taking steps to eradicate the unfairness for the mutual benefit of all sports people. The *Sports Council* regards the promotion of sports equity as one of its major objectives for the 1990s. (See also *sports development.*)

sports participation is an important aspect of the nation's use of its *leisure time*, with Sports Council figures showing that nearly two-thirds of the adult population of Britain take part in sport and physical recreation at least once a month. The *General Household Survey (GHS)* shows us that, after walking, swimming is the most popular sporting actvity, with 42 per cent of all adults participating in the 12 months prior to interview. Other sports activities, in descending order of popularity, are snooker, keep-fit, cycling, darts, golf, ten-pin bowling, running and soccer.

Although there has been a gradual increase in sports participation in recent years, there is some concern about the low participation rates in some sections of society, notably women, people from ethnic minorities and those on low incomes. These concerns have led organisations such as the Sports Council to introduce schemes such as *Sport for All* to address this problem of *sports equity.*

sports spectating is an important *leisure time* activity in the UK, with association football being the most popular spectator sport, although attendances have fallen in the 1980s and 1990s. Spectator sports, including hockey, cricket, bowls, darts and tennis, operate under the auspices of their relevant *governing body*, which sets the rules and determines policies. Commercial involvement, however, is never far away, although its scale varies from one spectator sport to another. *Sponsorship* is big business in some sports and large football clubs, including Manchester United and Tottenham Hotspur, are *public limited companies (PLCs)*.

spreadsheet: a powerful *computer* application that can be used to perform a range of numerical and financial calculations, so as to aid *management* decision making. Spreadsheet packages are used extensively in both large and small leisure and tourism organisations for providing financial information such as cash-flow forecasts, budget predictions and tax returns.

In its simplest form, a spreadsheet is little more than a grid consisting of horizontal rows and vertical columns, into which data is written. Spreadsheets are particularly useful for a process known as *sensitivity analysis*, when the outcome of alterations to one or more elements of a speadsheet will automatically be calculated by the program.

SPRIG: see *Sport and Recreation Information Group*

SSSI: see *Site of Special Scientific Interest*

Stabiliser is the name given to a type of 'closed shop' arrangement operated legally by *ABTA* up until the end of 1993. Under a process known as Operation Stabiliser, ABTA *travel agents* could only sell package holidays from tour operators who were themselves members of ABTA, and the holidays of ABTA tour operators could only be sold through ABTA travel agents. The Stabiliser was introduced in the mid-1960s to safeguard the public interest, and that of ABTA members, against unscrupulous agents and operators. The arrangement was dismantled in 1993, since it was considered to be against the public interest and also because the introduction of the *EU Package Travel Directive* rendered the Stabiliser obsolete.

staff appraisal: a formal system for reviewing an employee's performance at work and agreeing targets and support for the future. The appraisal, sometimes called a staff development review, normally takes the form of an interview between a member of staff and his or her line manager, at which each party will look back on past achievements and identify areas for further development. The outcome of the appraisal, which may be part of a wider remuneration exercise linking pay to performance, should be a written staff development plan agreed by the member of staff and the person carrying out the appraisal, listing personal development objectives and the activities needed to achieve them.

staff development review: see *staff appraisal*

'staff' functions are carried out by specialists within an organisation in support of *line managers*, who are given the *responsibility* for achieving specific business objectives. Typical 'staff' functions include personnel, accounting and finance, research and development, *marketing* and administration. Many large leisure and tourism organisations will operate a *matrix organisation*, combining both 'line' and 'staff' functions.

staff motivation is concerned with encouraging, enabling and empowering employees to enjoy their work and contribute effectively to an organisation's activities.

Motivation is closely related to *job satisfaction*, a complex issue that depends on many interlinking factors, such as the quality of the working environment, the attitude of senior management, co-operation with colleagues, pay and reward systems, terms of employment, status and recognition of achievements. Motivated staff will bring benefits to an organisation, such as reduced absenteeism, better standards of customer service and greater productivity. (See also *Herzberg*.)

staff records are held by *leisure* and *tourism* organisations, with details of past employees and current staff. The records will contain a range of information, including personal details, job title and grade, accident and sickness records, absenteeism, *payroll* information, references and records of any *staff appraisal* interviews. The records may be held on a manual or computerised system.

staff training: any learning activity that enables members of staff to gain knowledge, learn new skills or update existing skills relating to their work situation. Staff training is sometimes divided into those activities that take place at work (*on-the-job training*) and activities carried out away from work (*off-the-job training*). A structured programme of staff training can increase staff morale, increase productivity, improve levels of *customer service*, reduce costs, increase flexibility and trigger new ideas.

stakeholder is a term used to describe all those who have an interest in the affairs of an organisation and who have an influence on its *management*. In private sector organisations, stakeholders will include owners, *managers, shareholders*, staff, *customers*, banks and statutory agencies, e.g. Inland Revenue, *Health and Safety Executive*, etc. Stakeholders in public sector organisations will include local councillors, council officials, local communities and society in general. Stakeholders have an important role to play in helping determine *objectives* and in setting *policy*.

Standardised Approach to Sports Halls (SASH): an initiative promoted by the *Sports Council* in the 1980s to stimulate the provision of a greater number of local sports halls by offering a building of standard design that could be constructed in any region. The original design incorporated four badminton courts with ancillary services. The adoption of a standard design would reduce both capital and operating costs, thereby offering local communities a value-for-money solution to widening community involvement in *sport* and *recreation*.

Standard Industrial Classification (SIC): a system that places jobs in various employment categories in order to analyse movements in particular occupations and provide indicators of trends in employment generally. Co-ordinated by the *Department for Education and Employment*, the SIC includes a number of categories of interest to leisure and tourism, including jobs in hotels, restaurants, transport services and libraries. There is not, however, a single category for either 'tourism' or 'leisure', making estimates of employment in these industries an inexact science. Figures for employment in various industry sectors are published regularly in the Employment Gazette.

standby: the name given to a discounted fare offered by airlines and other travel companies to travellers who are prepared to turn up without booking in advance, in the hope of securing a seat.

'stars': see *Boston Consulting Group matrix*

stately homes are an important part of the *UK tourism* scene, enjoyed by both *overseas visitors* and British people alike. Many stately homes are in the ownership of the *National Trust*, while others are privately owned. The high costs of maintaining stately homes has led many owners to open their doors to the public, e.g. Beaulieu, Longleat and Chatsworth, to name but a few. The income from day visitors, overnight guests, special events and *corporate hospitality* has been ploughed back into the running of the houses and their grounds for the benefit of generations to come.

Statistical Office of the European Communities: see *Eurostat*

Stats MR is a commercial organisation that provides *market research* services to major *travel and tourism* companies on a subscription basis. Mass market tour operators, such as *Thomson*, Airtours and First Choice Holidays, use the data supplied by Stats MR to forecast future market trends and refine their *product portfolios* and *marketing strategies* accordingly.

statutory refers to any regulation which has the backing of government *legislation*, e.g. an Act of Parliament such as the *Development of Tourism Act 1969*.

STB: see *Scottish Tourist Board*

steamships were introduced in Britain soon after the development of the railways in 1830. The Peninsular and Oriental Steam Navigation Company (P&O) was one of the first companies to harness the power of steam for passenger travel, running the first regular long-distance services to India and the Far East in 1838. The Cunard Steamship Company started services between Europe and North America in 1840. The development of jet aircraft during and after the Second World War led to the introduction of trans-Atlantic passenger aircraft travel, which was to have a devastating effect on the *demand* for passenger shipping.

'steep' pyramid: a type of *hierarchical* structure in which there is a very narrow span of control, i.e. power and responsibility within the organisation rest with a small number of senior managers, below which there are many tiers of *management*. 'Steep' pyramid structures, sometimes called tall hierarchies, tend to be very centralised and bureaucratic, with decisions having to pass through many channels for confirmation. (See also *'flat' pyramid*.)

steering group: a group of people given the task of overseeing or implementing a new initiative or project through to its completion. (See also *committee*.)

STEP analysis: see *PEST analysis*

stock control is the practice of *managing* stocks of goods to ensure a continuous supply. It is a broad term covering the storage of stock, recording of stock levels, stocktaking and withdrawing items from stock. The development of automated systems such as *EPOS* have greatly simplified and speeded up an organisation's stock control function. In leisure and tourism, stock control will be necessary for items such as drinks, food, souvenirs, equipment and clothing.

Stock Exchange: the place where stocks and *shares* are bought and sold. Britain's principal Stock Exchange is located in the heart of the City of London, although there are exchanges at a number of regional centres, including Birmingham and Glasgow. The London Stock Exchange is one of the busiest in the world, along with the New York and Tokyo Exchanges.

The 'steep' pyramid structure

STOL: see *short take-off and landing*

storming refers to the stage of team development immediately following *forming*, when team members have got to know each other and are more willing to challenge others' views and opinions, thereby leading to a group with a clarified purpose. (See also *norming, performing.*)

strap line is a term used in *advertising* to denote a phrase or saying that is used regularly to accompany a promotional campaign. Examples of strap lines used in leisure and tourism are 'the world's favourite airline' (*British Airways*), 'we try harder' (Avis) and 'we're getting there' (*British Rail*). Strap lines are a type of *branding* that is used to create an *image* and ultimately generate extra business.

strategy: the techniques, practices and methods that an organisation will use to help achieve its aims and *objectives*. (See also *strategic planning.*)

strategic alliance: the linking of one organisation with another, falling short of a full merger or takeover, for their mutual benefit. An example in the travel industry is the alliance between *Thomas Cook* retail travel agencies and First Choice Holidays, to compete with the likes of Lunn Poly (owned by *Thomson*) and Going Places (owned by Airtours). Both parties will hope to benefit from a strategic alliance; in the case of the Thomas Cook/First Choice alliance, both will expect to increase their *sales revenue.*

strategic marketing: the medium- to long-term process of determining how best an organisation can achieve its *marketing objectives*. A tour operator, for example, may have set itself a *marketing objective* of capturing 50 per cent of the total market for *package tours* from the UK to Greece. Its strategic *marketing plan* will indicate how it intends to achieve this, giving details on levels of *advertising* and other promotional work, costs of the marketing activities, the timescale within which it is operating, its range of products, etc. Within its overall marketing strategy the company will develop specific *marketing plans*, giving greater detail and costings.

strategic planning is the process of determining the methods that an organisation will implement in order to meet its *objectives*. It tries to answer the following questions:

- what do we want to achieve?
- where are we now?
- where do we want to be in *x* years' time?
- what do we have to do to get there?
- how do we know when we've arrived?

In seeking to answer these questions, the organisation will need to adopt a strategic *planning* process that will include the following stages:

1 clarification of the organisation's aims and objectives
2 analysis of its current financial and market position
3 the development of action plans to achieve the desired aims
4 implementation of the action plans
5 monitoring and evaluation of the plans

Given that the strategic planning process aims to achieve the best use of an organisation's *resources*, it is equally applicable to public, private and voluntary sector leisure and tourism organisations.

strengths: see *SWOT analysis*

Structure Plan: a document, produced by a local planning authority under the 1968 Town and Country Planning Act, setting out the future strategy for the area. Structure Plans include detailed plans relating to a number of *local authority* responsibilities, such as housing, transportation, social services, education and *leisure* and *tourism*. Structure Plans are a useful starting point for an organisation wishing to establish or expand its operation, since it will give broad indications of what the authority will look favourably upon and what it is trying to discourage, e.g. in terms of tourism, they may welcome new businesses that focus on activity centres but discourage more caravan sites on environmental grounds. Structure Plans are generally prepared by *county councils*, with *district councils* producing their own *Local Plans*.

suggestion scheme: a device that encourages staff to make suggestions for improvements to the product or service they are supplying, the environment in which they are working, ways of reducing costs or the *management style* within the organisation. The suggestion scheme is often linked to a series of incentives for staff, such as cash bonuses or gifts.

surface travel is the term used to denote *transportation* by road and rail, including private cars, hire cars, coaches, motorbikes, bicycles, private railways and public railways.

superstructure is generally accepted to mean any construction that takes place above ground and which uses a pre-existing *infrastructure*. In the case of leisure and tourism, superstructure projects would include *hotels*, *attractions* and *transportation*. The majority of superstructure developments in leisure and tourism are financed from private sector sources.

supervisor: an employee who is given *responsibility* for the well-being and work performance of other members of staff in an organisation, e.g. a travel supervisor overseeing the work of three travel clerks in a travel agency. Supervisors are sometimes given the task of convening groups of staff to discuss work methods and productivity (*quality circles*).

supplement: an extra payment, sometimes called a surcharge, levied for the provision of a particular benefit, e.g. an additional payment for occupying a *hotel* room with a sea view, an extra payment for travelling from a regional airport or an extra charge for travelling in business class rather than economy class on an airline.

suppliers are individuals and organisations that provide goods and services in support of an enterprise. The range of suppliers to leisure, travel and tourism organisations is vast, including equipment suppliers, food companies, vehicle suppliers and clothing manufacturers. In terms of *customer service*, it is essential for organisations to make suppliers aware that their (the suppliers') contribution to a firm's business activities is just as important as their own.

suppressed demand consists of those people who are not currently using or buying a particular *product* or service, because of a problem on either the *demand* side (*potential demand*) or the supply side (*deferred demand*).

summary accounts: the term used to describe financial statements that summarise a series of transactions over a given period of time, e.g. a company's *profit and loss account* and *balance sheet.*

surcharge: see *supplement*

surveys are by far the most common method used by leisure and tourism organisations to collect *primary data*. A survey involves the collection of data from a proportion of a total 'population', which researchers refer to as the sample; in this context, 'population' means the total number of people who could be interviewed. For example, the owner of a *tourist attraction* may decide to interview a 10 per cent sample of visitors on a particular day. If the total number of visitors is 2 000 (the 'population'), 200 interviews (the sample) will need to be carried out. The most common surveys used by leisure and tourism organisations are *face-to-face interviews*, *self-completed surveys* and *telephone surveys.*

sustainable tourism: an emerging concept that seeks to address the long-term environmental and socio-cultural issues surrounding uncontrolled tourist development worldwide. An extension of *'green' tourism*, it is part of a much wider global debate on sustainable development, highlighted by the *Brundtland Report* in 1987 and the *Earth Summit* in Rio in 1992. Various bodies concerned with travel and tourism have issued policy statements and guidelines for sustainable tourism, including the *Association of Independent Tour Operators (AITO)*, *World Tourism Organisation (WTO)*, *World Travel and Tourism Council (WTTC)*, *Tourism Concern* and the *English Tourist Board (ETB)*. The challenge facing the industry, especially the mass market operators, is to implement these guidelines for the benefit of present and future *host communities.*

sustainability: see *Brundtland Report*

Sustrans is a registered charity which designs and builds routes for cyclists, walkers and those in wheelchairs. It aims to encourage sustainable transport *policies*, so as to lessen dependence on the motor car. Sustrans employs practical engineers and designers, aiming to create at least one traffic-free route into every urban area in Britain, and to link these to form a *National Cycle Network*. Sustrans was one of the first beneficiaries of *National Lottery* funds, receiving £42.5 million to further its work.

SVQs: see *Scottish Vocational Qualifications*

SWOT analysis: one of the most common techniques that an organisation can undertake to try and establish where it stands in the marketplace and what it needs to do to maintain or improve its competitive position. SWOT stands for strengths, weaknesses, opportunities and threats, which for a local authority *leisure centre* could include:

Strengths	**Weaknesses**
● Commitment and enthusiasm from staff ● Excellent pool facility with high usage ● Established balanced pool programme ● Lack of immediate competition	● Staffing problems/turnover/commitment to customer care ● Ageing dryside environment ● Unco-ordinated and restrictive marketing ● Limited market research
Opportunities	**Threats**
● Growing market ● Press attention and interest ● Corporate business market ● Re-launch of facilities potential	● New competition ● Decrease in disposable incomes ● Local management of schools ● Changing demographic patterns

Example of a SWOT analysis for a local authority leisure centre

A SWOT analysis, sometimes called a situation analysis, will form the basis for a re-assessment of *products* and *marketing strategies*, leading to improved organisational performance.

synergy: a term used to describe the positive relationship between individuals, products or organisations which results in 'the whole being better than the sum of its parts'. By way of example, two organisations that decide to merge would expect the sum of their individual turnovers of £2 million and £3 million respectively to be greater than £5 million.

synthetic surface: artificial playing surface that allows sports to take place in adverse weather conditions. They are found in sports stadia, athletics grounds and *leisure centres*, sometimes referred to as 'Astroturf' after the *brand name* of one of the leading manufacturers.

T

table d'hôte refers to a menu with a fixed price for a specified combination of courses. A table d'hôte menu is sometimes known as a 'fixed menu' or may be given a particular name such as 'chef's special'.

tactical marketing is short-term *marketing* activity carried out in response to unforeseen or unplanned occurrences in the marketplace, e.g. the introduction by a nearby competitor hotel of a series of themed events may lead a hotelier to reduce his or her prices or increase publicity. Tactical marketing is quite different to *strategic marketing*, which is planned and costed well in advance.

tactical pricing: the practice of constantly altering the prices of products and services, often in response to competitors' price changes, with the aim of maintaining *market share*. Tactical pricing is a short-term activity within an organisation's overall *pricing policy* and is often carried out in the highly competitive tour operations and airline sectors of the *travel industry*.

tactics: short-term measures that an organisation carries out in response to a *threat* or business *opportunity*. Tactics are temporary measures that tend to be over and above its overall business *strategy*.

takeover: the *acquisition* of one company by another, through purchasing more than 50 per cent of its *share capital* and thereby gaining full management control.

TALC: see *tourist area life cycle*

tall hierarchy: see *'steep pyramid'*

tally counter: a device used to count the number of people or vehicles using, for example, a *tourist information centre*, leisure centre, an event or *theme park*. Some tally counters are operated manually, while automatic counters operate electronically.

Target Group Index (TGI) is a national survey of consumers and their purchasing habits funded by the British Market Research Bureau. TGI is an annual survey covering nearly 5 000 brands bought regularly from shops in the UK. It includes some questions on people's use of their *leisure time*, which is of a rather general nature.

target market: the *customers* that an organisation considers will be the most likely to buy its products and services, and to whom all marketing activity will be targeted. The target market for a newly opened theme park, for example, may be families living within a 20-mile radius of the attraction. With the help of computer-based systems such as *ACORN*, it is possible to estimate the size of the total market for a product or service and undertake an effective *target marketing* exercise.

target marketing is the practice of selecting particular groups or individuals (known as the *target market*), and using the different components of the *marketing mix* to encourage them to buy or use products or services. In order to be able to carry out effective target marketing, an organisation will need detailed *market research* data and have undertaken a *market segmentation* exercise.

taxation: payments to local and central governments for the provision of a range of local and national services, including leisure and tourism facilities. Taxes are levied on individuals and organisations, and may take the form of *direct* or *indirect taxation*. Local taxes include the *Council Tax* and *Uniform Business Rates*. The Conservative government has pledged to reduce the levels of income tax paid by individuals.

Taylor Report: a written report into the safety of football grounds, undertaken by the Right Honourable Lord Justice Taylor in reponse to the Hillsborough disaster of 1989, which led to the deaths of 96 football supporters. The Taylor Report, published in January 1990, made 76 recommendations, the most significant of which were:

- the formation of a Stadia Advisory Design Council
- the establishment of the *Football Licensing Authority*
- the elimination of standing accommodation at grounds by August 1994 for the top two divisions in England and Wales, and the top division in Scotland

In addition, the recommendations of the Taylor Report have resulted in perimeter fences being taken down, better trained stewards, the employment of safety officers by clubs and improved internal and external ground *communication* systems.

TCA: see *Traffic Conference Area*

TDA: see *Timeshare Developers' Association*

TDAPs: see *Tourism Development Action Programmes*

team: a group of people working collectively towards a clearly defined goal. In order to be totally effective, a team must be given the necessary *authority* and *resources* to carry out its task, should be made up of individuals committed to the task and operate in an 'open' fashion, with team members sharing their concerns and ideas. Teams may develop formally or informally. Teams created in a work environment often operate on a formal basis, with a leader, clear channels of *communication* and defined lines of authority and responsibility. Informal teams tend to develop organically rather than through an organisational structure and may form for social or work-related reasons. (See also *teamwork*.)

team building is the process of creating and developing a group of people so that they operate in an effective and efficient fashion, thereby achieving their goals. Building an effective team follows six main stages:

- giving the team clear *objectives*
- selecting appropriate team members
- providing the team with other necessary resources
- developing a team approach to operations
- encouraging the development of individual team members
- evaluating the performance of the team and its individual members

Team building should focus on the improvement of *interpersonal skills*, decision making and communication.

team evaluation: the process when the members of a team take time to reflect on their individual and collective performances and achievements. This usually takes place soon after the finish of an event, when details are fresh in their minds, and will include consideration of both formal and informal feedback from a variety of sources, including:

- customer *surveys*
- attendance figures

- sales returns
- views of observers

The overall aim of the process is to evaluate whether the event was successful in meeting its objectives.

team leader: an individual who takes on the *responsibility* for guiding the development and operation of a group of people, to help achieve the team's *objectives*. In leisure and tourism, the team leader must be more than just a figurehead, but an effective *manager* as well. Whenever possible, a team leader should be involved at the team building stage when team members are being selected. The leader will act as a facilitator when the real teamwork is underway, helping to support team members and letting them know exactly what is expected of them. To be totally effective, a team leader needs a mixture of essential characteristics, including:

- enthusiasm
- an effective communicator
- good *planning* skills
- an excellent negotiator
- a supportive manner
- an action-orientated approach

It is important for *management* to realise that a team leader must be given the *resources* and authority to enable the team to achieve its objectives.

team objectives: the targets that a *team leader* and team members are expected to achieve. Team objectives may be set by the team itself, by management or by an external agency, and must be realistic, achievable, measurable and set within a timescale. The objectives will help determine the team's working methods and assist in *planning* tasks, and are an essential guide when team performance is being evaluated.

team rationale: an important first stage in building an effective team, concerned with informing all those concerned with the operation of the team exactly why it has been set up and what it is expected to achieve.

team structure: the precise arrangement of staff in a team situation, so as to use team members as effectively as possible and best achieve the team's aims and *objectives*. The structure may be formal, with clearly defined lines of authority and responsibility, or informal, with growth occurring organically. Informal teams develop for social and work-related reasons, giving people the chance to have their say in a less confrontational setting than that offered by a formal team set-up.

team training refers to any formal or informal activities that team members undertake to improve their knowledge and skill levels, thereby helping the team to achieve its objectives. This could include training in *interpersonal skills*, administrative procedures, technical skills, such as using computer *software*, or *management* skills. All team members, whether full-time, part-time or volunteers, should be included in any team training programmes.

teamwork: individuals working together in a cohesive manner to achieve a common goal. Teamwork is an essential part of the *leisure* and *tourism* industries, and is common in all sectors, including conference organisation, hotel management, retail travel and *leisure centre* operation. Teamwork brings benefit to both individuals and

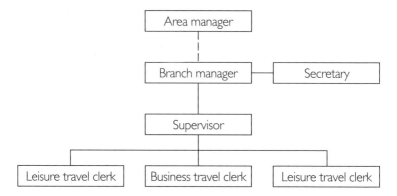

A formal team structure in a travel agency

the organisations they work for; individuals may enjoy greater *job satisfaction,* an enhanced sense of their worth to their employer, the chance to be innovative and creative, and gain increased rewards for their efforts. Organisations are likely to benefit from increased efficiency, a higher level of sales, reduced staff conflict and a happier workforce. Above all, management is keen to see that by developing teamwork within an organisation, it is getting more than just 'the sum of the parts'.

TECs: see *Training and Enterprise Councils*

technology: equipment and systems that facilitate *communication,* decison making, marketing and management, within and between organisations. Leisure, travel and tourism are industries that have always made extensive use of new technology equipment and systems. *Computerised reservation systems (CRS),* the use of computers in leisure centres and sophisticated *database marketing* systems, are all examples of this trend. Increasing competition within the industries will force organisations to use new technology to the full, e.g. in the fields of *transportation,* global communications and *home-based leisure.*

teleconferencing: a technique that allows a number of people to hold a round-table meeting over the telephone, where each person can hear, and be heard by, the other members of the group. Teleconferencing reduces the need for people to travel long distances merely to attend meetings. Unlike *video conferencing,* however, people taking part in a teleconference cannot see each other.

telecottage: an establishment in a rural area that provides a range of *computers* and communications equipment for use by *teleworkers* in the local area. Telecottages are often subsidised by local councils, enterprise agencies or *Training and Enterprise Councils (TECs)* as a way of contributing to the creation of jobs and economic development in country districts.

telemarketing is a type of direct selling over the telephone, when a representative of a *company* contacts a member of the public or an organisation with the intention of making a sale. This kind of selling, sometimes known as telephone marketing, is common in the USA, but its use in UK leisure and tourism is limited to business-to-business sales and selling products such as *timeshare* and membership of certain clubs.

telephone marketing: see *telemarketing*

telephone survey: a technique used to gain both *qualitative* and *quantitative data* to help with an organisation's decision making. Telephone surveys are gaining in popularity in leisure and tourism, as a way of getting a quick response to an event, facility or service. They are used widely in the USA, but are largely restricted in UK leisure and tourism to business-to-business activities, such as following up enquiries after trade shows and selling business services. Companies specialising in selling *timeshare* also use telephone surveys to target potential customers.

telephone technique is the style and tone that a person adopts when making a telephone call. Many leisure, travel and tourism organisations spend time and money developing the telephone technique of key members of staff, such as sales teams and *customer service* staff. An efficient and friendly manner on the telephone can create a good impression of an organisation and is part of a wider *public relations* strategy. Many trainers suggest that staff should always smile when talking on the telephone, since this automatically makes the speaker sound more pleasant.

teletext: an electronic broadcast system capable of receiving and displaying pages of information on adapted television sets. BBC TV's Ceefax and ITV's Teletext are the two systems currently operating in the UK. Teletext is becoming an inceasingly popular way of getting information on *holidays,* flights and other travel products, since it is regularly updated by the service providers.

telex: communications equipment which links machines via telephone lines and allows messages to be sent and received instantaneously. A message is typed on machine A and sent to machine B, which automatically prints it out. Telexes are used in travel and tourism to confirm arrangements and send passenger *manifests*. The introduction of low- cost *fax* machines has reduced considerably the use of telex machines in recent years.

television: one of the most powerful *media* in society today, with the ability to influence people's life styles, their purchasing habits and fashion trends. Watching television is also an important leisure activity in its own right, with 99 per cent of households owning a television set and viewing figures approaching 20 million for the most popular programmes. With the development of satellite technology, world-wide audiences of hundreds of millions are easily achievable.

teleworking is the practice of working from home but maintaining a link with an organisation, with the use of *computers* and communications equipment, such as *fax* machines and *electronic mail (E-mail)*. Teleworking is a growing trend in the UK, since it offers workers more flexibility and reduces an organisation's *overheads*. (See also *telecottage*.)

tender: a document outlining a bid for the provision of a product or service, with the lowest bid usually being given the contract. The privatising of many *local authority* services, including leisure facilities, has meant that many councils now put jobs out to tender, whereas formerly the tasks would have been given to staff on the payroll. (See also *compulsory competitive tendering*.)

terminal has two meanings in leisure, travel and tourism. The first is a building at an airport or ferry port which houses all the facilities for departing and arriving passengers, including check-in, immigration and catering facilities. The second is the name given to a *computer* that is part of a network, operating either within an organisation or linked to the outside world.

terms of reference: the first part of a written *report* giving the reason why the report has been written, for whom it has been undertaken, what it hopes to achieve and the date by which it is to be completed.

tertiary industry: an industry located within the *service sector* of the economy, e.g. banking, insurance, leisure, travel and tourism.

test market: the practice of testing a new product or service in a tightly controlled area, so as to measure sales activity, prior to a full nationwide launch. The test market area might be as small as a town or as large as a region, e.g. the south-west of England. Test marketing is a cost-effective way of ensuring that all the *advertising* and promotional work associated with a new *product* or service has not been wasted.

TGI: see *Target Group Index*

TGV stands for 'train à grande vitesse', the name given to the high speed rail network operated by SNCF, the French railway organisation. France has adopted a policy of publicly funded rail transport that has resulted in one of the most comprehensive and efficient operations in Europe.

Thatcher years: the period between 1979 and 1990 when Margaret Thatcher was Prime Minister. It was a time when policies were put in place to advance *privatisation*, reduce the influence of trade unions and promote free market operations, in the hope of creating a more efficient economy for Britain. Many regard the Thatcher years as a time when the gap between rich and poor widened. The terms *'yuppie'* and *'dinky'* were coined, denoting individuals who were driven by money and status symbols and who took part in high-risk activities in their *leisure time.*

theatres are an important component of the UK *arts and entertainment* sector. There are approximately 130 professional theatres in Britain, half operated by private sector companies, with the majority of the theatres being in the West End of London. According to data in Social Trends, total attendances at West End theatres remained constant between 1987 and 1992 at 11 million per year, although the popularity of traditional musicals, comedy shows and shows for children fell, at the expense of a rise in the popularity of modern musicals such as Grease and Starlight Express. (See also *Society of London Theatre.*)

Theatrical Management Association (TMA) is a trade association representing theatre owners, grant-aided theatres, local authority-controlled venues, commercial producers, opera and ballet companies, children's theatre companies and community theatres in England, Scotland, Wales and Northern Ireland. Founded by Sir Henry Irving in 1894, the TMA now has some 400 members, who have access to a range of services, including negotiation expertise, industrial relations advice, campaigning, *training* and legal advice.

theme park: a purpose-built attraction offering a wide range of facilities, including *white knuckle rides*, live entertainment, events, catering, shops and amusements. The bigger British theme parks have been modelled on North American examples, particularly the popular *Disney* complexes in Florida and California. Theme parks are aimed particularly at families and young people, who pay an all-inclusive entrance charge which permits an unlimited number of rides. Examples of the most success-ful theme parks in the UK are *Alton Towers* in Staffordshire, Chessington World of Adventures and the American Adventure near Derby.

Theory X: see *McGregor*

Theory Y: see *McGregor*

Third World countries: see *developing countries*

Thomas Cook: an *entrepreneur* who was destined to have a far-reaching impact on the early development and future of travel. He organised his first excursion by rail in 1841 from Leicester to Loughborough for his local Temperance Association. Within 15 years, spurred on by the success of his first trip, Cook was running a fully com-mercial travel company which, along with *American Express*, has survived to become one of the founding companies of today's *travel trade*. Today, the Thomas Cook Group has sales of over £17 billion per year, employs over 12 000 people who serve some 20 million customers a year and operates through a network of some 1 300 wholly owned and representative locations in over 100 countries. It is a *vertically inte-grated* organisation, having interests in both retail travel agencies and tour operations. In 1993, Thomas Cook was taken over by the German travel company LTU, itself owned by Westdeutsche Landesbank.

Thomson On-line Program (TOP) was the first attempt by a *tour operator* to allow *travel agents* to directly access its main reservation's computer, to check availability of holidays and make bookings, without the need to talk to Thomson sales staff on the telephone. First developed in 1986, the TOP system has become the 'industry stan-dard', imitated by all major mass market tour operators. Today all Thomson holiday bookings by agents must be made through TOP. Access is via the agent's *viewdata* ter-minal or *VDU* and a suitable *gateway* facility.

Thomson Tour Operations is the number one UK outbound *tour operator* in terms of package holidays sold. It is part of the multinational Thomson Corporation, with its headquarters in Canada. Thomson is an example of a *vertically-integrated* organisa-tion, owning both the Lunn Poly travel agency chain and Britannia Airways. Thomson offers a full range of holiday products, sold under a variety of *brand names*, including Thomson Cities and Thomson Small and Friendly. Thomson was a pioneer in terms of *viewdata* systems, introducing its *TOP* system in 1986.

threats: see *SWOT analysis*

TIC: see *tourist information centre*

Tidy Britain Group: a national litter abatement agency that works closely with local communities, central and local government for improved local environments. It co-ordinates a number of environmental improvement schemes in the UK, including *Britain in Bloom*, the *Seaside Award* and the *Blue Flag Campaign*. The Group also con-ducts research into the types and disposal of litter found in Britain.

time series charter: a *charter flight* arrangement where a *tour operator* contracts with an airline for the use of an aircraft for a specific period of time, normally the dura-tion of the season or a whole year. (See also *flight series charter*.)

time zones are artificial divisions of the world's surface into 24 time bands. All time zones are based on the *Greenwich Meridian*, which is 0° longitude. Travelling west from the Greenwich Meridian gives us time zones that are behind *Greenwich Mean Time (GMT)*, while time zones east of Greenwich are ahead of GMT, e.g. New York time is five hours behind GMT whereas that of South Africa is two hours ahead of GMT. It is important to remember that many countries in the world, including the UK, operate some form of daylight saving time, with clocks altered to make maximum use of daylight.

timeshare: the practice of buying a period of time (usually in blocks of weeks) in an *accommodation* facility, rather than owning the accommodation outright. The advantage to the customer is that he or she does not have to worry about the maintenance and security of the property for most of the year, although an annual maintenance charge is usually levied. The disadvantage is that the owner has the same property for the same period of time each year. This can be overcome by letting the property independently or through a timeshare exchange company such as *RCI,* giving people the chance to stay in a range of properties around the world.

Timeshare is most commonly associated with self-catering apartments and villas, although it is possible to find timeshares in hotels and even on yachts! The selling of timeshare apartments in Europe has something of an image problem, with a small number of companies using questionable sales techniques.

Timeshare Developers' Association (TDA): an independent trade association representing UK *timeshare* operators. Membership of TDA is confined to companies that follow a strict *code of conduct,* concerning selling methods, promotion techniques and property specifications. The TDA hopes that by promoting a professional image of the industry among its members and the public in general, 'cowboy' operators will be driven out of business.

TLC: see *Tourism and Leisure Consortium*

TMA: see *Theatrical Management Association*

TNA: see *training needs analysis*

toll: a charge levied on travellers for using a road or a canal, crossing a bridge or going through a tunnel. A proportion of the tolls collected is used for maintenance and repair, or to pay off interest charges incurred as a result of construction costs.

TOP: see *Thomson On-line Program*

Top Clubs: see *Youth Sport Trust*

Top Play: see *Youth Sport Trust*

Top Sport: see *Youth Sport Trust*

topography: the variety of natural features that go to make up a landscape, such as mountain ranges, valleys and hilltops. The varied landscapes found in Britain today are the result of human activities over thousands of years, coupled with the effects of climate and the underlying geological formations. The topography of an area will determine which *leisure* pursuits can be carried out, e.g. orienteering in woodlands, rock climbing in mountain areas and fishing in rivers.

TOSG: see *Federation of Tour Operators*

total quality management (TQM) is a *management* philosophy which recognises that customer needs and organisational objectives are inseparable. Rather than merely a well-documented set of procedures, as is the case with *BS EN ISO 9000*, TQM is an all-embracing concept, taking *quality assurance* a stage further, and is designed to permeate throughout an organisation, from the top to the bottom. Creating a TQM culture in an organisation should be seen as a long-term aim, based on encouraging staff enthusiasm and ownership of services, with a view to meeting or exceeding the expectations of customers.

tour operator: an individual or organisation that organises *inclusive tours (ITs)* to a variety of domestic and international destinations. In the *travel industry* they take on the role of a wholesaler, since they buy their 'raw materials' in bulk, e.g. aircraft seats and hotel bedspaces, and break the bulk into manageable products, i.e. the package holidays themselves. These are then sold to customers by travel agents, the retail outlets. Some operators, known as *direct sell*, do not make their products available through travel agents, but prefer to sell direct to the public. The main types of tour operators found in the UK are:

- mass market operators, e.g. *Thomson*, First Choice, Airtours, etc.
- specialist operators, e.g. Vacances Franco-Britannique (VFB), Himalayan Kingdoms
- domestic operators – companies that specialise in tours in Britain, e.g. Rainbow Holidays, YHA, etc.
- *incoming tour operators* – companies that specialise in tours of Britain for overseas visitors, e.g. Evan Evans, British Heritage Tours, etc.

Many UK tour operators are members of trade associations, including the *Association of British Travel Agents (ABTA), Association of Independent Tour Operators (AITO)* or the *British Incoming Tour Operators' Association (BITOA)*.

Tour Operators' Code of Conduct is one of the codes of conduct operated by *ABTA* and drawn up in conjunction with the *Office of Fair Trading*. It lays down the minimum standards of tour operators' brochures, requiring that they contain clear, comprehensive and accurate descriptions of facilities and services offered. The Code details rules which govern booking conditions in brochures as they relate, for example, to the cancellation or alteration of tours, holidays or other travel arrangements by the tour operator. The Code also contains strict rules concerning the prompt handling of complaints and regulations relating to the conduct between travel agents and tour operators (See also *Package Travel Directive.*)

Tour Operators' Study Group: see *Federation of Tour Operators*

tourism is destined to become the world's biggest industry by the beginning of the next millenium, forecast to double its output between 1990 and 2005, according to the *World Travel and Tourism Council (WTTC)*. It is defined by the *World Tourism Organisation (WTO)* as '...the activities of persons travelling to and staying in places outside their usual environment for not more than one consecutive year for leisure, business and other purposes'. Another definition from the *Tourism Society* is that tourism is '...the temporary, short-term movement of people to destinations outside the places where they normally live and work, and their activities during the stay at these destinations...'. Both definitions reinforce a number of key points about tourism, namely that it is concerned with people who are:

- away from their normal place of residence
- on a visit that is temporary and short term
- engaged in activities that would normally be associated with leisure and tourism
- not necessarily staying away from home overnight
- not always away from home for holiday purposes, but may be on business

When it comes to the location of tourist activity, there are three principal strands within the industry:

1 domestic tourism – people taking holidays and trips in their own country
2 inbound tourism – people entering a country other than their own for holidays and trips
3 outbound tourism – people leaving their own country to take a holiday or trip abroad

Tourism has considerable *economic* and *socio-cultural impacts* on destinations, some negative and some positive. The negative environmental and socio-cultural impacts of tourism have become the subject of considerable debate since the mid-1980s, leading to calls for types of tourism that are less environmentally and culturally damaging. Terms such as *'green' tourism*, responsible tourism and *sustainable tourism* are now common within the study of tourism. (See also *UK tourism.*)

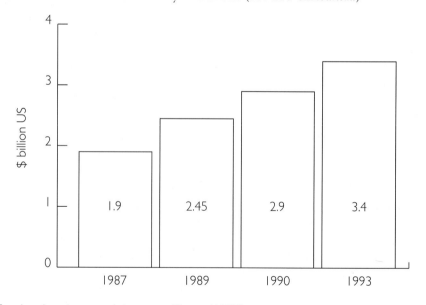

Travel and tourism growth in output (Source: WTTC)

Tourism and Leisure Consortium (TLC): a group of organisations with an interest in leisure and tourism, who have come together to help ensure a co-ordinated approach to the development of *occupational standards* and *National Vocational Qualifications* across all sectors of the industry. Membership includes a number of Industry Lead Bodies, *NCVQ* and government departments.

tourism balance: see *travel balance*

Tourism Concern is a membership organisation set up in 1989 to bring together British people with an active concern for tourism's impact on community and environment, both in the UK and worldwide. Tourism Concern advocates tourism that is just, participatory and *sustainable,* and aims to look past the cosmetic 'green issues', such as recycling and energy conservation, to the way that tourism affects the people living in destination areas. Tourism Concern seeks to achieve its aims by campaigning, networking, informing, educating and developing a resource base.

Tourism Development Action Programmes (TDAPs): a series of initiatives co-ordinated and part-funded by the *English Tourist Board* in the late 1980s. TDAPs were partnerships between the public and private sector, typically involving district councils, county councils, attraction operators, hoteliers and other accommodation providers, aimed at developing a planned approach to tourism development in a particular region of England. The first TDAPs covered 20 areas including Bristol, Torbay, North Pennines, Shropshire, Cornwall and Bradford. TDAPs have more recently come to be known as Local Area Initiatives (LAIs).

Tourism Intelligence Quarterly is an information service provided by the *BTA/ETB* which collates and interprets current statistical information relating to international tourism, as well as tourism into, within and out of Britain.

tourism planning: a dynamic process that aims to make the best use of available resources to provide the correct range of tourism facilities in an area, without causing long-term negative effects to local people, their culture or environment. Tourism planning is normally co-ordinated by public sector agencies, such as *National Tourism Organisations (NTOs)* and *local authority* tourism and planning departments, working in partnership with commercial companies. The tourism planning process includes an element of regulation, in order to conserve natural and built resources for future generations and control undesirable developments.

Tourism (Sleeping Price Display Order) 1977 was introduced in Britain in February 1978 and requires *hotels, motels,* guesthouses, inns and *self-catering* establishments with four or more letting bedrooms to display in their entrance halls the maximum and minimum prices charged for each category of room.

Tourism Society is the *professional body* representing the interests of individuals making a career in the tourism industry. Founded in 1977, the Society is managed by a council elected by the membership, and is funded by subscriptions, *sponsorship* and other income-generating activities. Within the Society there are two specialist groups, the *Association of Teachers and Trainers in Tourism* and the Consultants' Group. The Society's objectives include improving industry-wide recognition of members' professionalism, linking the mutual interests of individuals in the many sectors of tourism and communicating information and knowledge through meetings, seminars and publications.

tourist: defined by the *World Tourism Organisation (WTO)* as 'a visitor whose visit is for at least one night and whose main purpose of visit may be classified under one of the following three groups: (a) leisure and holidays; (b) business and professional; (c) other tourism purposes'. Tourists may be divided into those who travel in their own country (domestic tourists) and those who travel between countries (international tourists).

tourist area life cycle (TALC): see *destination life cycle*

tourist attraction: see *attractions*

tourist board: a general term to describe an official body that has certain responsibilities for tourism at international, national, regional or local level. The structure of tourist boards in the UK is as follows:

- *British Tourist Authority* (the *National Tourism Organisation*) – responsible for promoting the whole of Britain abroad
- National Tourist Boards of the four home countries (Wales, England, Scotland and Northern Ireland) responsible for tourism planning, development and marketing in their own countries
- *Regional Tourist Boards* – responsible for co-ordination of development and promotion in their own regions
- Local tourist boards/tourism associations – members of the industry working in partnership to promote their facilities to tourists

Tourist boards obtain their funding from a number of sources, including *grant-in-aid* from central government, *local authority* funding, *sponsorship*, commercial membership subscriptions, commercial activities and European funding.

tourist enclave: an enclosed area within which *tourists* are isolated from the residents of a destination (the *host community*) often for security reasons. Tourist police are sometimes deployed in the zoned area to give further protection to tourists. Enclaves occur particularly in developing nations, where the gap between rich visitors and the poor residents is most marked.

tourist generating country is the country of origin of a traveller, as opposed to the *tourist receiving country,* which is the destination country that travellers arrive at. Current figures from the *World Tourism Organisation (WTO)* show that the USA is the number one generating country for international travel in terms of expenditure.

tourist information centre (TIC): a purpose-built facility offering information on a range of local, and sometimes national, *tourist attractions, events, transportation* and accommodation. In Britain, the National Tourist Boards co-ordinate a network of over 800 TICs, although the great majority are funded by their *district* or *county councils*. TICs play a vital role in marketing their local areas, providing up-to-date information and a warm welcome. Some larger centres offer a selection of extra services, such as an accommodation booking facility, a *book-a-bed-ahead* service, local guides or computerised information. With reductions in funding from local and national sources, TICs are looking to become more commercial in their operations, by charging for their services and selling a range of *products.*

tourist receiving country is the *destination* country that travellers arrive at, as opposed to a *tourist generating country,* which is where they come from. Current figures from the *World Tourism Organisation (WTO)* show that France is the most popular tourist receiving country for international travel in terms of number of arrivals.

tourist tax: a levy imposed on tourists and collected by either central or local government. It may take the form of a hotel levy, visitor tax, airport tax or charge for other tourist services. Tourist taxes are an important source of revenue for countries whose economies rely heavily on tourism, particularly the developing countries of the world.

trade directory: an information source compiled exclusively for the use of organisations in a particular industry sector, rather than being generally available to the public. The Travel Trade Directory and UK Leisure Centre Directory are examples in the leisure and tourism industries. Trade directories are often updated annually and include contact points for a range of *suppliers* and public sector organisations.

trade discount: a reduction in the price of goods and services offered by one business to another and not normally available to the general public.

trade exhibition: an event, open exclusively to industry representatives, which gives the buyers of *products* and services the opportunity to meet with *suppliers*, to conduct business deals and discuss new business opportunities. Some of the best-known trade exhibitions, also known as trade fairs, in the leisure and tourism industries are the *World Travel Market* and RecMan.

trade fair: see *trade exhibition*

trade journals: see *trade press*

trade press: magazines, newspapers and journals that are aimed specifically at industry and business people, rather than consumers. In leisure and tourism, this would include publications such as Caterer and Hotelkeeper, Travel News and Leisure Manager. The trade press seeks to keep people working in industry up to date with developments in their sector and will include relevant articles and paid *advertising*.

trade union: an association formed to protect the interests of working people. Since the Trade Union Act of 1871, the trade union movement has used its influence and collective power, latterly through the work of the *Trades Union Congress (TUC)*, to grow into an important industrial and political force, that has influenced government policy and provided support for workers. Trade unions negotiate with management on behalf of their members on such matters as pay, working conditions, *pension* rights and *contracts of employment*. Recent legislation, including the *Trade Union Act 1984* and the *Trade Union Reform and Employment Rights Act 1993*, have sought to regulate the workings of trade unions and improve competitiveness.

Trade Union Act 1984: government legislation which obliged *trade unions* to hold a *secret ballot* of members before authorising a strike and to ensure that executive committee members are elected by the union's membership and offer themselves for re-election every five years.

Trade Union Reform and Employment Rights Act 1993: *legislation* which critics say was enacted to weaken the power of *trade unions*, while those in favour considered it to be a further step towards making trade unions more accountable to their membership. The Act included provisions to abolish the remaining wages councils, required unions to give employers at least seven days' notice of industrial action and to oblige union members to give periodic written agreement to the deduction of union subscriptions from their pay.

Trades Description Act 1968 is a key piece of *consumer protection* legislation that aims to protect customers against false descriptions, either verbally or in writing, by those who are providing services. Any description of, for example, a hotel or leisure club must be truthful at the time it was written (if circumstances subsequently change, then the operator must inform the customer of the nature of the changes). The Act places a duty on the owners and managers of leisure and tourism facilities to produce *brochures* and other promotional materials that are not intended to deceive the customer.

Trades Union Congress (TUC) is the national organisation representing British *trade unions*. Formed in 1868, the TUC aims to promote the interests of the trade union movement as a whole, act as a voice for organised labour at national level, settle inter-union disputes and promote international labour solidarity, particularly within Europe.

Trading Standards Officer (TSO): an official employed by a local authority with the general task of 'policing' traders to ensure that consumers are being given a fair deal and that *consumer protection* legislation is being implemented in their locality. It is common for TSOs to advise on problems relating to holidays where, for example, the product sold was below standard or did not match descriptions given in promotional materials. In this regard the TSOs will apply the conditions contained in the *Package Travel Directive.*

Traffic Conference Area (TCA): a zonal classification of the world's major airline routes into three areas:

- TCA1 comprises North and South America
- TCA2 includes Europe and Africa
- TCA3 is Asia

The TCAs were devised by *IATA* and are used as the basis for the settlement of air fares and timetabling.

training: see *staff training*

Training and Enterprise Councils (TECs) are government-funded *quangos* established in 1990 to provide Britain with a skilled workforce, through the local and regional co-ordination of *training* and vocational education. Managed primarily by local business people, the TECs do not themselves provide training, but contract training providers to deliver schemes in their area. The aim is to match the training provided to the needs of local employers. TECs are also responsible for promoting the *Investors in People (IIP)* initiative.

training needs analysis (TNA) is an auditing process that aims to identify the current level of technical and *management* skills within an organisation, the required level of skills needed to be wholly effective and highlight any shortfall or surplus in skill levels. If a shortfall is identified, which is often the case in the leisure and tourism industries, the TNA should make recommendations on the action necessary to bridge the training gap, which may be by a mixture of *off-the-job* and *on-the-job training.*

transnational corporation: see *multinational corporation*

transportation is one of the three key elements of the *travel and tourism industry*, along with *accommodation* and *attractions*/entertainment. The *British Tourist Authority (BTA)* estimates that in 1992, £2 564 million was spent on transportation within the UK, accounting for 14 per cent of all spending by domestic and overseas visitors.

Transportation can be sub-divided into surface, *sea* and *air travel*, each with its own distinct characteristics, products and markets. The rapid rise in transport networks and demand for new services and facilities, have led to severe pressures on many aspects of the UK transportation scene since the early 1960s, leading to a number of important issues and considerations, including:

- congestion and overcrowding in urban areas
- the impact of the *Channel Tunnel*
- privatisation of the rail network
- airport expansion and congestion
- loss of land for new developments

The move towards *deregulation* of travel has led to increased competition between operators and, in some cases, cheaper fares for the travelling public.

travel account: a statement of a country's earnings from *inbound tourism* and the expenditure by its residents on overseas travel. The travel account shows a country's *travel* (or tourism) *balance.*

travel agent: a company or individual that sells a range of holidays and other travel products to the general public and may offer business travel services as well. Travel agents are acting on behalf of two parties when they undertake their work. They act for the *customer,* referred to as the client, on whose behalf they are making the travel arrangements. They are also agents for the company that is supplying the product; this is sometimes referred to as the *principal* and may include a tour operator, airline, car hire company, ferry operator, *British Rail,* cruise line, theatre, hotel, etc.

Travel agents earn commission from the principals whose products they sell. As well as selling package holidays, travel agents, who may be part of a multiple chain or independent, also offer a variety of other products and services, including UK *short breaks,* travel *insurance,* foreign exchange, rail tickets, care hire and ferry bookings. Travel agents may be members of ABTA, the *Associtaion of British Travel Agents,* or NAITA, the *National Association of Independent Travel Agents.*

Travel Agents' Code of Conduct is one of the *codes of conduct* operated by *ABTA* and drawn up in conjunction with the *Office of Fair Trading.* The Code regulates all aspects of travel agents' relationships with their customers, covering their responsibility with regard to the standard of service they provide and the information they give to clients. It also lays down rules governing travel agents' trading relationships with *tour operators.*

travel and tourism industry: an all-embracing term used to describe the many private, public and voluntary sector organisations that provide services for the travelling public and work together to promote the economic and social benefits of the industry worldwide. It includes the commercial *travel industry,* e.g. *travel agents* and *tour operators,* plus public agencies, such as the *tourist boards* and *National Tourism Organisations (NTOs),* and the many companies and individuals that provide *accommodation, transportation* and *attractions/*entertainment services to customers. Travel and tourism is set to become the world's biggest industry in the next millenium. (See also *tourism.*)

Travel and Tourism Programme (TTP) is an industry/education initiative working in partnership to improve the knowledge and appreciation of the *tourism* industry and the service sector in general. The principal sponsors of the Programme are *American Express, Forte, British Tourist Authority (BTA), English Tourist Board (ETB)* and *Thomas Cook.*

travel balance: sometimes called the tourism balance, this is the difference between the value of a country's earnings from *inbound tourism* and the expenditure by its residents on overseas tourism. In Britain, the travel balance was in a surplus (positive) position until the beginning of the 1980s, i.e. the revenue from overseas tourism was greater than the expenditure on overseas tourism by British people. Since that time, however, the travel balance has been in deficit, due mainly to increased demand for overseas *package holidays.*

travel industry: considered to be a specialist sector within *tourism,* existing to serve people's holiday and business travel requirements. It ranges from high street *travel agencies,* which sell a variety of leisure travel products and services, to the tour operators who assemble the various components of *package holidays.* It also encompasses business travel, sometimes through specialist business house agencies. Specifically, the UK travel industry comprises:

- leisure travel services
- business travel services
- tour operators
- ground arrangements
- escorting tours
- tour management
- guiding services

The travel industry employs around 100 000 people in the UK in a wide variety of jobs, such as travel consultants, *couriers,* business travel clerks and tour managers.

travel motivators: see *motivators*

travel propensity refers to the proportion of a population who are actively involved in travel, whether for business or leisure purposes. Travel propensity is higher in Western developed countries than in the developing nations of the world.

travel trade: the term used to describe all commercial sectors within the *travel and tourism industry,* including *travel agents, tour operators,* coach operators, car hire firms, airlines, ferry companies and providers of specialist support services.

Travel Training Company (TTC) is a subsidiary of the *Association of British Travel Agents (ABTA).* Formerly known as ABTA National Training Board, the TTC offers a range of in-house training courses for travel industry staff, as well as the *ABTAC* qualification and air travel courses. It also acts as an agent to the travel services *Industry Lead Body* to help educate the industry about *national vocational qualifications (NVQs)* and to administer aspects of the scheme.

traveller's cheque: a *cheque* issued in one country that can be exchanged for cash in the local *currency* of another country, e.g. a £10 traveller's cheque could be exchanged for, say, French francs or Spanish pesetas. Traveller's cheques are a convenient way of carrying money and offer travellers the security of knowing that if they are stolen, the issuing company will normally replace them immediately, free of charge.

Travicom: an early type of airline *computerised reservation system (CRS)* introduced in the UK in 1977. Travicom became part of the *Galileo* network in 1987.

TSO: see *Trading Standards Officer*

TTC: see *Travel Training Company*

TTP: see *Travel and Tourism Programme*

TQM: see *total quality management*

TUC: see *Trades Union Congress*

turnover is the total sales of an organisation for a given time period. Sometimes called sales revenue, revenue or sales turnover, it is calculated by multiplying the quantity of goods and services sold by the price of the goods and services, e.g. the turnover of a coach company may be made up as follows:

total coach tours sold (150) × price of each tour (£125) = turnover of £18 750

It is important to remember that turnover is not the same as *profit,* which is what remains when all *costs* have been deducted from the turnover.

two-way communication involves the sending of information and a response from the person receiving the message. It is generally preferable to *one-way communication,* where information passes in one direction only, since it enables a discussion to take place and any misunderstandings between the parties to be cleared up. Examples of two-way communication methods used in leisure, travel and tourism include telephone conversations, face-to-face conversations, meetings and *video conferencing.* Although initially more time-consuming than one-way communication, two-way communication has many advantages and should be used whenever possible.

U

UBR: see *Uniform Business Rate*

UDCs: see *Urban Development Corporations*

UK: see *United Kingdom*

UK tourism is an expanding industry that makes a significant contribution to the national economy. The total value of *tourism* to the UK in 1992 was nearly £30 billion, equivalent to 5 per cent of *gross domestic product (GDP)*. Since 1985 the number of people employed in UK tourism has risen by 31 per cent to a total of approximately 1.5 million. More than 20 million *overseas visitors* came to Britain in 1994, while the fine summer weather of 1995 is sure to set new records for domestic tourism. The structure of the UK tourism industry is complex, covering a range of sectors including the travel industry, accommodation, catering, transportation and visitor attractions. Public sector involvement comes at national level in the form of the *National Tourist Boards* of the four home nations, plus the *British Tourist Authority (BTA)*. Local authorities also play a vital role in providing facilities for tourists.

UKSC: see *United Kingdom Sports Council*

UKTS: see *United Kingdom Tourism Survey*

UN: see *United Nations*

undifferentiated marketing is a type of *marketing strategy* where the same marketing approach is offered to all those who go to make up a total market.

unfair dismissal: a claim by an employee that he or she has been unfairly treated in having their employment terminated. An *industrial tribunal* would regard any cause other than *gross misconduct*, inability to carry out a job properly, absenteeism, *redundancy*, ill health or a legal restriction on a person's employment as possible grounds for a claim of unfair dismissal. Any such claim must be made to the tribunal within three months of the employment termination date.

Uniform Business Rate (UBR): a tax levied by a *local authority* on businesses in their area. UBR is payable for the provision of services such as street lighting and refuse collection and is the business equivalent of the *Council Tax*. It is levied on both manufacturing and service sector companies, including hotels, restaurants and cafés. The level of UBR varies in different parts of the country and reflects local property values.

unique selling proposition (USP) is the particular benefit that one *product* or service is said by its promoters to have over another product or service, i.e. the reason why customers will choose that item instead of all other competitors. The USP may be truly 'unique', e.g. a flight on Concorde, but is more likely to be a product feature that an organisation will promote to attract attention, e.g. a car hire company using the latest models of cars.

unitary authority: a *local authority* body that provides a mix of services previously supplied by both *district* and *county councils*. The government established the Local Government Commission under the 1992 Local Government Act to advise on changes to local government responsibilities. It is likely that there will be a rationalisation of service provision between a number of county and district authorities in England and Wales, including *leisure* services and *tourism*.

United Kingdom: refers to *Great Britain* and Northern Ireland.

United Kingdom Sports Council (UKSC): one of the new bodies set to replace the *Sports Council* on 1 April 1996. The UKSC will concentrate on helping to bring major international sporting events to the UK and to increase greatly the influence of the UK in international *sport*.

United Kingdom Tourism Survey (UKTS) is a monthly survey undertaken on behalf of the *English, Wales, Scottish* and *Northern Ireland Tourist Boards*. Formerly known as the British Home Tourism Survey (BHTS), the UKTS provides information on the volume and value of tourism by UK residents and details of the trips they take. The survey involves *face-to-face interviews* with a random sample of around 80 000 people per year in their homes. The sponsoring tourist boards receive monthly results of the survey and detailed statistical volumes of data on an annual basis.

United Nations (UN) was first established by charter in 1945 with the aim of promoting good international relations and maintaining world peace. Most countries of the world are members of the UN, which has its headquarters in New York. It has many operating divisions, including the UN Security Council, the International Monetary Fund and the United Nations International Children's Emergency Fund (UNICEF). The *World Tourism Organisation (WTO)* has links with the UN and encourages developing countries to seek assistance for tourism projects through UN specialist departments, including the the United Nations Development Organisation and the UN Environment Programme (UNEP).

upgrade is the movement of a passenger to a higher standard of *product* than he or she has paid for, e.g. allocating an economy class passenger to a business class seat on an airline, or a car hire company offering a customer a car in the next class up. It makes good business and *PR* sense to upgrade a customer if the situation allows and the company will not lose out financially.

Urban Development Corporations (UDCs) were established under the 1980 Local Government, Planning and Land Act to promote *urban regeneration* in areas of England and Wales which were suffering from the effects of the loss of their traditional industries. UDCs were set up in London Docklands, Merseyside, the Black Country, Teesside, Trafford Park (Manchester), Tyne and Wear, Bristol, Central Manchester, Leeds, Sheffield and Cardiff. UDCs have wide-ranging powers to acquire land and buildings, stimulate investment and develop infrastructure, in order to improve their immediate environments, create employment and promote regional prosperity. Many of the UDCs have seen the potential for *leisure* and *tourism* developments in their regeneration programmes, e.g. Albert Dock at Liverpool and the Black Country Museum.

urban regeneration: the process of revitalising derelict areas of towns and cities, often involving *partnership* arrangements between *public* and *private sector* organisations. Leisure and tourism often plays a significant part in urban regeneration projects, helping to create employment and add to an enhanced quality of life for residents and better facilities for tourists. Notable examples of urban regeneration schemes in the UK include the *Castlefields* area of Manchester, Bradford, Glasgow and London Docklands.

urban tourism: tourist facilities and services that are provided in towns and cities, for local residents, domestic visitors and overseas tourists. Tourist facilities in urban areas often contribute to *urban regeneration* and job creation.

USP: see *unique selling proposition*

REVISION: There is a set of revision lists at the back of this book to help you prepare for GNVQ unit tests. See pages 246–250 for unit tests in GNVQ Advanced Leisure and Tourism.

vacation: another name for *holiday*

validation: the process of making a travel ticket usable by stamping it with an official company imprint.

value added tax (VAT) was introduced in the UK in 1973 to replace purchase tax. It is an *indirect tax* levied on a range of goods, including household items and cars, and services, such as hotel accommodation and car hire. The current rate of VAT in Britain is 17.5 per cent, although there are moves to harmonise the rates of VAT in all member states of the *European Union*, as part of the move towards economic and monetary union. In Britain, certain products such as books, children's clothing, food, transport and newspapers are currently exempt from VAT, although economic pressures at home or in Europe may force this position to change in the future.

variable costs: expenditure that fluctuates in line with the level of an organisation's business activity, rather than remaining stable as with *fixed costs*. Variable costs in leisure and tourism include casual labour, telephone charges, publicity costs, postage, stationery and fuel for vehicles. (See also *semi-variable costs*.)

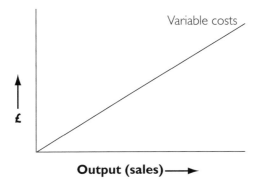

variance: the term used in budgetary control to signify the difference between actual and budgeted figures. Variances may arise in any items of revenue or expenditure, including labour costs, *sales revenue* and energy costs. The investigation of any differences between actual and budgeted figures is known as *variance analysis*.

variance analysis is the process by which an organisation investigates any variances in its budgets and takes corrective action. In the case of an *expenditure budget*, the term 'unfavourable' or 'adverse' is used when actual costs are greater than budgeted costs. Where actual costs are below budget, the variance is said to be 'favourable'. The opposite is true of revenue variances, where favourable variances occur when actual sales are above budget. The aim of variance analysis is to highlight areas needing immediate attention. Minor variances are common and are unlikely to require detailed analysis, but when a variance is large, either in monetary or percentage terms, the situation will need attention. Variance analysis can be carried out manually, but is more often undertaken with the help of a computer *spreadsheet* package.

VAT: see *value added tax*

VDU: see *visual display unit*

venture capital is a source of finance available to leisure and tourism businesses to increase their *equity*. It is most appropriate for growing businesses that are not yet ready to raise funds on the stock market. Venture capitalists are prepared to invest in high-risk businesses, including many in leisure and tourism, in return for a say in the management of the operation and a high rate of return on their investment. Leisure and tourism companies sometimes turn to venture capitalists when traditional financing institutions consider their plans too risky.

verbal communication is the transfer of information using the spoken word. Learning to communicate effectively is an essential feature of the leisure and tourism industries, given that staff come into regular contact with *customers, suppliers, professional bodies*, regulatory authorities and a host of other external bodies. Examples of verbal communication are meetings, telephone conversations, sales calls and advising customers face-to-face. (See also *written communication, electronic communication*.)

verbal warning: normally the first stage in a *disciplinary procedure* against an employee in the workplace, whose conduct, behaviour or performance does not reach suitable and acceptable standards. Should the problem persist, the member of staff is likely to receive a formal *written warning*.

vertical integration describes a process whereby companies at different levels of the distribution chain are linked in some way to give *competitive advantage*. For example, *Thomson*, the UK's number one *tour operator*, owns the Lunn Poly travel agency chain; Going Places travel agencies are owned by tour operator number two Airtours; while First Choice Holidays has an alliance with *Thomas Cook* agencies. By working together, the companies hope to secure increased sales, thereby improving their market share. Thomson is a good example of a company that has taken the process a stage further, since it also owns its own airline, Britannia Airways, and direct-sell operator Portland Holidays. Vertical integration can sometimes work against the public interest, by reducing choice in the marketplace. (See also *horizontal integration*.)

VFR: see *visiting friends and relatives*

video conferencing: an *electronic communication* technique which allows a group of individuals to hold a round-table conversation by using telephone and video technology. Video conferencing allows the members of the group to see each other and communicate on a face-to-face basis at any distance, even from one country to another. Developments in video conferencing equipment are beginning to make an impact on the need for executives to travel to different parts of the world purely to attend meetings. (See also *teleconferencing*.)

videotext: another name for *viewdata*

viewdata: a computer-based interactive system used by travel agents to display information on *VDUs* and to access the *computerised reservation systems (CRSs)* of *principals*, mainly airlines and tour operators, via a telephone line. *Istel, Fastrak* and *Prestel* are the best-known viewdata services used by travel agents.

virtual reality is a technology that allows a user to enter and interact with images generated by a computer. Special graphics, video images and stereo sound make the pretend world seem real. The concept came into being in the 1930s when scientists created the first flight simulator for pilot training. Today, virtual reality has many uses in industry as well as in *leisure* and *recreation*. Many arcade games now use virtual reality, giving people the chance to experience the sensation of driving in a racing car or flying in outer space.

visa: a stamp in a *passport*, or other official document, giving a traveller the right of entry to a particular country. Countries use visas as a way of discouraging travel, either for political, economic or socio-cultural reasons. The former Eastern Bloc countries are beginning to relax their requirements for all visitors to hold a visa, resulting in a growth in tourism to such countries as Slovakia, Lithuania and Latvia.

'visibles' are manufactured items and goods whose value is shown on a country's *balance of payments*, i.e. those that can be seen or touched, e.g. cars, food, electrical components and raw materials. Such items brought into a country are known as imports, while those sent abroad are exports. (See also *'invisibles'*.)

visiting friends and relatives (VFR) is an important, if often overlooked, aspect of a nation's tourism industry. According to statistics from the *British National Travel Survey (BNTS)*, staying in the homes of friends and relatives accounted for 21 per cent of all holidays taken by UK residents in Britain in 1994. This figure was only 1 per cent below the most popular accommodation used (caravans) and 1 per cent more than holidays taken in hotels. It is sometimes difficult to understand just why VFR is important to tourism; how is it that a person who stays for free with friends or relatives can be contributing to the local tourism economy? The answer is that the visitor, although enjoying free accommodation, will spend money on other goods and services in the locality, such as leisure facilities and restaurants.

visitor: a person who travels, for less than twelve months, to a place other than that of his or her usual environment, and the main purpose of whose visit is other than the exercise of an activity remunerated from within the place visited. Visitors can be divided into those who travel between countries (international visitors) and those who travel within a country (domestic visitors). A distinction can also be made between those who stay overnight (*tourists*) and those who do not (*excursionists*.)

visitor attraction: see *attractions*

visitor centre: a custom-built facility which offers a range of services, the most important of which is an opportunity to learn more about its surroundings through a number of *interpretation* facilities, such as information displays, an audio-visual programme or a series of guided walks. Visitor centres are found in both town and country, e.g. the Wedgewood Visitor Centre in Stoke-on-Trent and the Brockhole National Park Centre in the Lake District *National Park*.

Visitor Welcome Initiative (VWI) is a *customer care* programme co-ordinated by the *Countryside Commission*, designed to help the managers of sites in the countryside make sure that their visitors find a welcoming environment. The VWI provides a checklist of measures that sites should attempt to provide, from safe, off-road parking for the most basic sites, to a *visitor centre* and a children's play area at the largest. The Commission hopes that the Initiative will play an important part in making any visit to the countryside a welcoming experience for all.

visual display unit (VDU): a screen, usually linked to a *computer*, giving access to information from remote *databases* and other computers on a linked *network*. VDUs are commonplace in leisure and tourism, e.g. in travel agencies, at airports, in hotels and at tourist attractions. VDUs are associated with a number of *front office* functions, such as making reservations and selling tickets, as well as *back office* routines, including accounting and marketing. The rise in the incidence of stress-related illnesses associated with the use of VDUs in the workplace led to the introduction of the Health and Safety (*Display Screen Equipment*) Regulations in 1993.

vocational qualifications are different to academic qualfications since they are directly related to the world of work. The government sees the introduction and development of *National Vocational Qualifications (NVQs)* in a wide range of industry sectors as a major step forward in bridging the skills gap in the UK. Vocational qualifications are being offered increasingly in schools and colleges, in areas such as business, health and social care, and leisure and tourism, with the introduction of *General National Vocational Qualifications (GNVQs)*.

voluntary sector in leisure and tourism: non-profit making sector that supplements both the private and public sectors, and is made up of organisations concerned with, for example:

- *heritage*
- minority groups
- youth organisations
- *conservation* of the environment
- community schemes
- clubs and societies

Voluntary sector organisations vary greatly in their size and aims. At one extreme, a small group of like-minded people may decide to form a cycling club in their area, to improve their fitness and explore the countryside. At the other end of the spectrum, large organisations such as the *National Trust, Youth Hostels Association (YHA)* and *Royal Society for the Protection of Birds (RSPB)* all fall within voluntary sector leisure and tourism, each having its own distinct objectives and structures. Voluntary organisations at both national and local level often receive advice and *grant aid* from the private and public sectors, sometimes in the form of *sponsorship*, the arts being a good example of this arrangement.

VWI: see *Visitor Welcome Initiative*

W

Wales Tourist Board (WTB) was set up under the 1969 *Development of Tourism Act.* It is an independent statutory body, financed mainly by direct *grant-in-aid* from the Welsh Office. The Act requires the WTB to encourage people to visit Wales and people living in Wales to take their holidays there. It is also charged with encouraging the provision and improvement of tourist amenities and facilities in Wales. In order to fulfil these objectives, the WTB undertakes a wide-ranging programme of work, including:

- *promotion* and publicity in the UK and overseas
- providing advisory and information services
- providing financial assistance to any significant tourism project it believes will provide or improve tourist facilities and amenities
- promoting or undertaking research and giving advice on policy matters relating to tourism

The 1969 Act debarred WTB from marketing Wales overseas; that was the responsibility of the *BTA*. However, under the 1992 Tourism (Overseas Promotion Wales) Act, the WTB is now able to undertake overseas marketing activity to supplement the work of the BTA. In line with government policy, the Board has contracted certain activities to a number of companies, including its three regional offices, which are now companies limited by guarantee. Another company, Tourism Quality Services, provides inspection and grading services to the WTB, while Holiday Wales Ltd., based in Swansea, has taken over the central reservations service previously operated by the WTB.

Warsaw Convention: an international agreement, signed in 1929, which established minimum levels of *compensation* available to airline passengers in the event of death or personal injury resulting from their flight, or loss of personal possessions. The Warsaw Convention still applies today, although many countries have introduced their own higher compensation levels, e.g. the USA.

WCTB: see *West Country Tourist Board*

weaknesses: see *SWOT analysis*

Welcome Host is a *customer care* training programme first carried out in Britain by the *Wales Tourist Board*, from an original idea developed in Canada. The scheme has since been taken up by both the *Scottish* and *English Tourist Boards*, in conjunction with a number of *Training and Enterprise Councils* (TECs). The programme aims to raise the standard of service and hospitality offered to visitors by training staff from a wide range of organisations, including hotels and guesthouses, restaurants, petrol stations, shops, *tourist information centres*, leisure facilities and tourist attractions.

The key objectives of Welcome Host are professionalism and pride. The training concentrates on raising the level of communication when dealing with visitors, and focuses on the tourism attractions of the local area. During the first 16 months of the programme in Wales, over 11 000 people attended Welcome Host training sessions, a number that far exceeded the Wales Tourist Board's target of 4 000 for the first year of operation.

West Country Tourist Board (WCTB) is the official *Regional Tourist Board* covering the counties of Cornwall, Devon, Somerset, the Isles of Scilly, Avon, Wiltshire and part of Dorset.

Which? magazine: the official publication of the *Consumers' Association*. (See also *Holiday Which?*)

white knuckle ride is a term use to describe an exhilarating ride at a *theme park*, such as *Alton Towers* or the American Adventure. The name derives from the fact that passengers on these rides grip the safety bars so tightly that their knuckles turn white from the pressure. Many white knuckle rides in UK theme parks are based on examples found in the USA.

Wolfenden Report: a report published in 1960 with the full title 'Sport and the Community', which stressed the need for a greater range and distribution of better facilities for *sport* and indoor recreation for all people in their local communities.

word processing: the creation, storage, alteration and printing of textual information, including letters, reports, memoranda and other types of written communication, using a *computer software* package. Computers loaded with word processing software, such as Microsoft Word or WordPerfect, have all but replaced typewriters in the production of high quality documents in leisure and tourism organisations. A word processing package allows text to be moved or enhanced, grammar and spelling to be checked, charts and diagrams to be added, and personalised documents created using a *mail merge* facility.

work equipment safety: the Provision and Use of Work Equipment Regulations 1992 were developed as a direct result of the *EU Directives on health and safety*, to pull together and tidy up the laws concerning equipment used at work. The regulations place general duties on employers and list minimum requirements for work equipment to deal with selected hazards, whatever the industry. Employers must ensure that the equipment they provide is suitable for its intended use and is adequately maintained. 'Work equipment' includes everything from a hand tool, machines of all kinds, to a complete plant such as a *leisure centre* or indoor arena.

working capital is the balance of *current assets* over *current liabilities* in an organisation. Often called the 'life blood' of a business, working capital is the amount available on a day-to-day basis to meet the normal financial requirements of running a business, e.g. buying stock, funding credit offered to customers and meeting overhead costs. Working capital is also known as net current assets.

workplace conditions: the Workplace (Health, Safety and Welfare) Regulations 1992 were developed as a direct result of the *EU Directives on health and safety*, replacing a total of 38 pieces of old law and helping to make safety in the workplace a much easier topic to understand. The regulations cover four broad areas:

- the working environment – temperature, ventilation, lighting, etc.
- safety – use of materials in doors and partitions, opening of windows, etc.
- facilities – toilets, washing facilities, eating areas, drinking water, etc.
- housekeeping – cleanliness, maintenance, removal of waste, etc.

Employers must ensure that their premises meet the requirements of the regulations by 1996 at the latest.

workplace rules exist to regulate staff behaviour and ensure the safety and welfare of all employees, their employers and the *customers* they are serving. Although workplace rules will vary between organisations, it is likely that they will include regulations concerning:

- health, safety and security
- hygiene
- punctuality and attendance
- sickness and absence procedures
- dress and personal appearance
- behaviour
- conduct and language in the workplace
- attitude to colleagues and customers

All new members of staff should be introduced to the rules in their *induction* training and be issued with amendments as and when they arise.

workplace standards: see *occupational standards*

World Bank provides aid and technical assistance to *developing countries* to help with capital projects, particularly *infrastructure* developments such as road building and airport construction.

World Commission on Environment and Development: see *Brundtland Report*

World Heritage Site: a place designated by UNESCO as being of exceptional cultural, geological or historical interest. World Heritage Sites found in the UK include the City of Bath, Hadrian's Wall and Ironbridge Gorge in Shropshire.

Worldspan: a US *computerised reservation system (CRS)* introduced in 1990 by a number of major US airlines, including TWA, North-West and Delta. As well as its booking facility for airlines, hotels and car hire, Worldspan offers other features such as satellite ticket printing and a local area network (LAN) facility.

World Tourism Organisation (WTO) is the established inter-governmental agency for *tourism* policies worldwide, representing public sector tourism bodies from the majority of countries in the world. Linked to the *United Nations,* WTO exists to promote and support tourism *development* on a global basis in all sectors of the tourism industry. It is a major source of authoritative data on tourism developments and movements worldwide and is a major player in the move towards environmentally sound practices in the global tourism industry. It commissions research on all matters relating to world tourism, sponsors regional workshops and supports education and *training* initiatives in travel and tourism.

World Travel and Tourism Council (WTTC) is an industry-sponsored *pressure group* representing the interests of the world's leading airline and tourist organisations. Formed in 1990, WTTC aims to marshall the resources of Chief Executive Officers of transnational, commercial companies from all sectors of the *travel and tourism industry*, to lobby governments as to the economic, social and cultural importance of tourism to the world economy. Through the *WTTERC*, WTTC also promotes environmentally sustainable management in the tourism industry.

World Travel and Tourism Environment Research Centre (WTTERC) was established in Oxford in 1991 with a mandate to create a worldwide database and information network to further environmentally compatible growth in the *travel and tourism industry*. Its founding sponsors were four members of the World Travel and Tourism Council (WTTC), namely *British Airways, American Express, Thomas Cook* and Steigenberger Hotels, together with the *British Tourist Authority (BTA)*. Having developed its research database, WTTERC seeks to identify problem areas in respect of the environmental impacts of tourism and to promote good practice to further promote sound environmental management in the industry.

World Travel Market (WTM) is a major international trade exhibition for all sectors of the *travel and tourism industry*. Held every year in London in November, WTM brings together public and private sector tourism organisations to develop new relationships and create new business opportunities. Linked to the exhibition are a number of training seminars to help keep industry representatives up to date with new developments and initiatives.

World Wide Fund for Nature (WWF) is an international organisation, founded in 1961, which is concerned with all aspects of man's relationship with the environment. It has affiliated offices in 28 countries and more than four million supporters across the globe. As well as campaigning on issues of global concern, WWF is also committed to helping individuals and groups in the active resolution of environmental problems at local level. Since 1980, WWF has been involved in a range of broadly based environmental education programmes.

World Wide Web (WWW) is a hypertext-based series of pages of information available on *personal computers (PCs)*. WWW is currently the most popular system for navigating the *Internet*, giving access to global information on a vast range of topics, from electronic magazines to financial data.

written communication: a system of communicating that has the advantage of providing a permanent record of something that has taken place. Written communication methods are often more effective than, for example, verbal and electronic systems, since they enable complex information to be sent, e.g. statistical data; the quality of presentation can be altered to appeal to different audiences, and they provide evidence of confirmation of a previous arrangement, e.g. the list of passengers on an aircraft. Common written communication systems used in leisure and tourism include letters, *brochures*, memoranda, press advertisements, *annual reports* and *press releases*. (See also *verbal communication, electronic communication*.)

written warning: the stage of a *disciplinary procedure* against an employee who has continued with an unacceptable standard of behaviour or conduct, or poor performance, after receiving a *verbal warning*.

WTB: see *Wales Tourist Board*

WTM: see *World Travel Market*

WTO: see *World Tourism Organisation*

WTTC: see *World Travel and Tourism Council*

WTTERC: see *World Travel and Tourism Environment Research Centre*

WWF: see *World Wide Fund for Nature*

WWW: see *World Wide Web*

Y

YHA: see *Youth Hostels Association*

YHTB: see *Yorkshire and Humberside Tourist Board*

Yorkshire and Humberside Tourist Board is the official *Regional Tourist Board* covering the counties of Humberside, South Yorkshire, West Yorkshire and North Yorkshire.

Youth Hostels Association (YHA) is a registered charity founded in 1930. Its aim is 'to help all, especially young people of limited means, to a greater knowledge, love and care of the countryside, particularly by providing hostels or other simple means of *accommodation* for them in their travels, and thus promote their health, rest and education'. The YHA currently has 240 places to stay in England and Wales, many in coastal and countryside locations, others in city destinations, ranging from seventeenth century yeoman residences in the Peak District of Derbyshire, remote hillside cottages in Wales to state-of-the-art modern architecture in London's Docklands. With more than 25 000 members, the YHA makes an important contribution to the nation's tourism enterprise, as well as helping the economy of rural communities.

Youth Sport Trust: a registered charity established to assist with the development of sport in local communities. It helps implement a number of youth programmes, including:

- Top Play – consisting of core skills and fun sport for 4–9 year olds
- Top Sport – introducing games and sport to the 7–11 year age group
- *Champion Coaching* – improving the sporting performance of 11–14 year olds
- Top Clubs – helping clubs build a future in sport for children of all ages

'yuppie': stands for 'young urban professional', a term first used in Britain in the *Thatcher years* of the 1980s. 'Yuppies' were people who benefitted from the expansion of private enterprise, particularly the rise of the financial services sector of the economy. They were characterised as individuals working in banking who speculated on foreign exchange markets, drank in wine bars and enjoyed 'the good things in life'. In their leisure time, they took part in adventurous and glamorous pursuits such as hang gliding, motor sports and taking exotic holidays in far-off destinations. (See also *'dinky'*.)

Z

zero-base budgeting: a financial technique that attempts to curb excessive annual *budget* increases by setting the coming year's budget at zero and asking managers to fully justify every element of their budget requests. It is a useful tool for identifying areas of activity whose budgets could be trimmed.

zoning has two meanings in leisure and tourism. The first is a *management* technique used to separate conflicting, or potentially conflicting, recreational activities, e.g. fishing, sailing and power boat racing on a reservoir. In this instance, the zoning can be physical, i.e. erecting physical barriers to prevent conflicts, or temporal, i.e. allowing each competing use a period of time when its activity has priority over all others. The other meaning is a *planning* technique used to allocate different uses of land and facilities in a new *leisure* or *tourism* project.

REVISION: There is a set of revision lists at the back of this book to help you prepare for GNVQ unit tests. See pages 246–250 for unit tests in GNVQ Advanced Leisure and Tourism.

LEISURE AND TOURISM REVISION LISTS

The following pages provide revision lists for advanced GNVQ tests. This is to help readers use their *A–Z* as effectively as possible.

ADVANCED GNVQ LEISURE AND TOURISM
REVISION LISTS FOR UNIT TESTS

The author has analysed the NCVQ documents on the content and focus of the Mandatory Units, to identify the key terms for revision. For example, the 60 top revision terms for the Unit 1 test on investigating the leisure and tourism industries have been identified.

For the end of unit tests, look up the following terms, making sure that you understand the text and can memorise the definition.

Unit 1: Investigating the leisure and tourism industries

Unit 2: Human resources in the leisure and tourism industries

Unit 3: Marketing in leisure and tourism

Unit 4: Finance in the leisure and tourism industries

Unit 5: Business systems in the leisure and tourism industries

Unit 6: Developing customer service in leisure and tourism

Unit 7: Health, safety and security in leisure and tourism

Unit 1 : Investigating the leisure and tourism industries – top 60 revision terms

Accommodation
Air travel
Arts and entertainment
Balance of payments
Bank Holidays
Business house agency
Business tourism
Catering
Co-operative
Compulsory competitive tendering (CCT)
Conservation
Countryside recreation
Currency
Destinations
Development of Tourism Act
Disposable income
Domestic tourism
Economic impacts of leisure and tourism
Employment in leisure and tourism
Environmental impacts of leisure and tourism
Funding of leisure and tourism
General Household Survey
Heritage
Incoming tourism
Industrial Revolution
Joint use
Leisure
Leisure and recreation industry
Leisure centre

Leisure time
Leisure tourism
National Tourist Office (NTO)
Outbound tourism
Outdoor activities
Package holiday
Partnership
Physical recreation
Play
Policy
Principal
Private sector leisure and tourism
Public sector leisure and tourism
Rail travel
Regional Tourist Board
Sea travel
Seaside resorts
Socio-cultural impacts of leisure and tourism
Sport
Sports Council
Sports participation
Sports spectating
Tour operator
Tourism
Tourist attraction
Tourist information centre (TIC)
Transportation
Travel agent
Travel and tourism industry
Visiting friends and relatives (VFR)
Voluntary sector, leisure and tourism

Unit 2 : Human resources in the leisure and tourism industries – top 50 revision terms

Accountability
Ad-hoc team
Advisory Conciliation and Arbitration Service (ACAS)
Appraisal
Authority
Autocratic leadership

Body language
Business objectives
Centralised structures
Communication
Competition
Consumer protection
Contract of employment
Curriculum vitae (CV)

Customer care
Customer charter
Decentralisation
Demographics
Disciplinary procedures
Equal opportunities
Ethics
Executive director
Flat hierarchy
Functional structures
Grievance procedures
Group dynamics
Hierarchical organisation
Induction booklet
Interviewing
Job description
Job role
Management style
Manager

Non-executive director
NVQs
Objectives
Occupational standards
Organisational structures
Performance standards
Person specification
Recruitment and selection
Resources
Responsibility
Team objectives
Team structure
Trade union
Training
Training and Enterprise Councils
(TECs)
Training needs analysis
Vocational qualifications

Unit 3 : Marketing in leisure and tourism – top 40 revision terms

Advertising
Ansoff's matrix
Boston Consulting Group matrix
Brand loyalty
Closed question
Customer service
Database
Direct marketing
Economies of scale
Market segmentation
Market share
Marketing environment
Marketing mix
Marketing principles
Marketing research
Needs
Observation
Occupancy rate
Open question
Personal selling

PEST analysis
Place
Point-of-sale (POS)
Price
Primary research
Product
Product development
Product life cycle
Promotion
Public relations
Qualitative data
Quantitative data
Questionnaire design
Sales promotion
Sampling
Seasonality
Secondary research
Surveys
SWOT analysis
Trade journals

Unit 4 : Finance in the leisure and tourism industries – top 30 revision terms

Annual report
Balance sheet
Budget
Cash-flow
Cash-flow forecast
Credit
Current assets
Current liabilities
Director
Dividends funding
Financial accounting
Financial performance
Fixed assets
Fixed costs
Forecasting
Gross profit
Manager
Net profit
Profit and loss account
Profitability
Seasonality
Sensitivity analysis
Shareholders
Solvency
Stakeholders
Stock control
Taxation
Turnover
Variable costs
Variance
VAT

Unit 5 : Business systems in the leisure and tourism industries – top 30 revision terms

Administrative systems
BS 7750
BS EN ISO 9000
Communication systems
Computerised reservation systems (CRS)
Customer service
Data Protection Act
Electronic communication
Electronic mail
Environmental management
External communication
Face-to-face communication
Fax
Information processing
Information technology
Internal communication
Internet
Interpretation
Investors in People
Management information system (MIS)
Modem
Network
One-way communication
Quality assurance
Quality control
Quality standards
Two-way communication
Value for money
Video conferencing
Written communication

GNVQ revision lists

Unit 6 : Developing customer service in leisure and tourism – top 20 revision terms

After-sales service
Back of house
Closing a sale
Communication
Competitive advantage
Complaints
Customer
Customer needs
Customer service
External customer

Face-to-face communication
Feedback
Front of house
Image
Internal customer
Non-verbal communication
Point-of-sale (POS)
Sales administration systems
Training
Verbal communication

Unit 7: Health, safety and security in leisure and tourism – top 20 revision terms

Code of practice
Contingency plan
COSHH
Data Protection Act
Environmental management
EU Directives on health and safety
First aid
Hazards
Health and Safety at Work, etc. Act 1974

Health and Safety Executive (HSE)
Induction booklet
Legislation
Local authority
Professional body
Public relations
RIDDOR
Safety officer
Security
Security hazards
Training

NORTH LEAMINGTON SCHOOL